Essential Histories

The Plains Wars
1757–1900

Essential Histories

The Plains Wars
1757–1900

Charles M Robinson III

Routledge
Taylor & Francis Group
NEW YORK AND LONDON

This hardback edition is published by Routledge, an imprint
of the Taylor & Francis Group, by arrangement with
Osprey Publishing Ltd., Oxford, England.

For information, please address the publisher:
Routledge (USA)
29 West 35th Street, New York, NY 10001
www.routledge-ny.com

Routledge (UK)
11 New Fetter Lane, London EC4P 4EE
www.routledge.co.uk

First published 2003 under the title Essential Histories 59:
The Plains Wars 1757–1900 by Osprey Publishing Ltd.,
Elms Court, Chapel Way, Botley, Oxford OX2 9LP
© 2003 Osprey Publishing Ltd.

ISBN 0-415-96912-3

Printed and bound in China on acid-free paper

03 04 05 06 07   10 9 8 7 6 5 4 3 2 1

Library of Congress Cataloging-in-Publication Data

Robinson, Charles M., 1949-
  The Plains wars, 1757-1900 / Charles M. Robinson III.
     p. cm. -- (Essential Histories)
Originally published: Oxford : Osprey Pub., 2002.
Includes bibliographical references and index.
  ISBN 0-415-96912-3 (hardback : alk. paper)
1. Indians of North America--Great Plains--Wars. 2. Indians of
North America--Wars--1750-1815. 3. Indians of North
America--Wars--1815-1875.4. Red River War, 1874-1875. 5.
Dakota Indians--Wars, 1876. I.Title.II. Series.
  E78.G73R63 2003
  978.004'97--dc21

2003013965

Contents

Introduction 7

Chronology 11

Background to war
North and South 13

Warring sides
The soldier and the warrior 20

Outbreak
Wars handed down through generations 28

The fighting
Battle on the Plains 33

Portrait of a soldier
Survivors 70

The world around war
The slow move toward Indian rights 74

Portrait of a civilian
Women and children 79

Conclusion and consequences
An unresolved legacy 83

Principal Indian Characters 88

Further reading 90

Index 94

Introduction

The Plains Wars between the United States and the various Indian tribes and nations were not wars in the conventional sense. They were a series of ongoing clashes, culminating in two large-scale military actions: the Red River War of 1874–75 in the Southern Plains, and the Great Sioux War of 1876–77 in the Northern Plains. Although they are generally lumped together under the heading of "Indian Wars," the conflicts in the Northern and Southern Plains began in different eras, and often involved different peoples and motives. In some ways, these wars by region were oddly similar to the Second World War, in which one conflict raged in Europe and North Africa, while an entirely separate war was being fought in the Pacific and Far East. The wars between the

Texas

INDIAN TERRITORY

Darlington

Anadarko

NEW MEXICO

Kiowa-Comanche Agency ▲ ■ Fort Sill

Red River

Salt Fork

Warren Waggon Train Massacre
Fort Belknap ✗ Jacksboro
■ Fort Richardson

Fort Griffin ■ Lost Valley Fight
Clear Fork Fort Worth Dallas

Brazos

TEXAS

Waco

San Saba Mission
Presidio San Saba ○ San Saba ■ Parker's Fort
Fort McKavett ■

Colorado

Austin

Guadalupe San Marcos
San Antonio ○ Plum Creek
Presidio La Bahia

Linnville

N

MEXICO

The Hunkpapa chief Sitting Bull led the resistance against the Fort Laramie Treaty, and together with Crazy Horse, has become a modern symbol Indian determination. There are no authenticated photos of Crazy Horse, although it is known that he was pale and freckled, with red hair, unusual traits that Indians believe endow a person with a special spirituality. (Author's collection)

federal government and the Southern Plains tribes were essentially inherited, having their origins a century earlier when much of the region belonged to Spain. The Northern Plains wars were uniquely American, rising from the expansion of the whites into the territory west of the Mississippi River.

Plains Indians were warriors. Long before the coming of the white man, they warred with each other, just as people do throughout the world. The Cheyenne and the Pawnee had no more love for each other than the Frenchman may have had for the German in Europe, and acted accordingly. Death in close combat with an enemy, with one's deeds of valor told and retold by the campfires, was preferable to growing too old to hunt or fight, and sitting in the lodge, cold, toothless, and feeble. Cheyenne warriors dressed especially well for battle or in other times of danger, so that if they died, they would look their best upon entering the next world (Grinnell, *1956*, 12; Marquis, 83). The fighting tradition has been carried into modern times, with service in Vietnam, Desert Storm, and Afghanistan giving young men a chance to prove themselves as warriors. Some of the old warrior societies, such as the Kiowa Black Leggings, have been resurrected as veterans' organizations.

Some Indians allied themselves with the whites, as an opportunity to settle ancient grievances against other Indians. In a council with Brigadier General George Crook in June 1876, a Crow chief gave a lengthy indictment of the Lakotas and Cheyennes. The Crows, Arikaras, Shoshones, and others offered themselves as scouts for the army as a chance of gaining revenge for past abuses (Bourke, Diary, 5:388–91). Such was often the case when the government enlisted Indian auxiliaries. The scouts themselves had few illusions about white ambitions; they had

simply weighed up the odds, and considered the government as the lesser of two evils.

Whites, likewise, pitted Indians against other whites. In the Southern Plains, French influence was evident in Indian conflicts with Spain, because both countries had territorial ambitions in the region. In the North, commercial rivalries over the fur trade prompted American and Canadian interests to vie against each other for influence over the local tribes. The Indians themselves, recognizing these animosities, played one white faction against another for their own advantage.

Until 1849, management of Indian affairs was the responsibility of the War Department. That year, however, jurisdiction was transferred to the newly created Department of the Interior. The result was that while the Indians theoretically were under civilian administration, the military continued to be responsible for suppressing outbreaks. Because these outbreaks were so frequent and political corruption visibly rampant, the soldiers were convinced that the Interior Department was incapable of handling the situation. Thus Indian affairs became mired in interdepartmental rivalries, divided responsibilities, and lack of coordination or cooperation, and would remain so until the end of the Indian Wars. Many soldiers disliked Indian fighting. General Crook viewed both Indians and soldiers as victims, forced to fight each other to vindicate failed policies (Priest, Chapter 2; Robinson, *2001*, 220).

Besides the rivalries, Indian affairs were complicated by inconsistent government policies. On the one hand, the government tried to buy peace by issuing goods to the more warlike tribes. Indians quickly learned that if they stayed on their reservations and minded their own business, they would be neglected, but if they committed depredations, they would be rewarded (United States Department of the Interior). Too many depredations, however, brought a military response, but very often a campaign was hindered on the brink of success, by yet another government policy of negotiation.

When General U.S. Grant was inaugurated as president in 1869, he hoped to solve the problem of corruption by replacing civilian agency appointees with officers demobilized under the Army Reduction Act. General W.T. Sherman, who replaced Grant as general-in-chief of the army, believed it would have been "a change for the better, but most distasteful to members of Congress who looked to these appointments as part of their proper patronage." To prevent the appointments, congress approved a bill canceling the commission of any army officer who served in a civilian position.

Refusing to be defeated, Grant then turned the management of Indian affairs over to the various religious denominations. Agents appointed by the churches, he believed, would be above reproach, and would inspire the Indians by enlightened example. The Board of Indian Commissioners was created as a quasi-official agency to oversee distribution of the Indian appropriation. Indians on the reservations would be under the exclusive control of the agents, unless an agent specifically requested military intervention. Officially, this was known as the Peace Policy. Rather than solve the problem, however, the new approach only prolonged the agony, because, in common with less developed warrior societies throughout the world, Indians took inconsistency, indecision, and forbearance as signs of weakness, and behaved accordingly. (Tatum, 133; Sherman, 926–27; Leckie, 134–35)

A contemporary drawing shows the nation's four most famous Indian fighters: (clockwise from top) Brigadier General George Crook, Lieutenant Colonel George Armstrong Custer; Colonel Ranald S. Mackenzie, and Colonel Nelson A. Miles. (Author's collection)

Ultimately altruism failed. Two major wars finished the Indians as independent people, but in the year 2003, the issues raised by those wars remain unresolved.

Chronology

Early Chronology

1731–48 Clashes between Spaniards and Plains Apaches

1758 16 March Massacre of San Sabá Mission, Texas

1767 Rubi's inspection realigns Texas defenses; isolated presidios abandoned

1781–90 Ugalde's punitive expeditions against Plains Apaches

1821 Americans begin settling Texas

1820s–70s Fighting between Texas settlers and Plains tribes

1823 Arikara War on the Missouri River

1836 19 May Raid on Parker's Fort, Texas

1840 Comanche War in Texas

1840s–50s Settlers moving through Platte Valley disrupt Indian life

1846 Formal entry of Republic of Texas into the Union makes federal government responsible for defense

1849 Management of Indians transferred from War Department to Interior Department

1849–79 Gold and silver rushes in California, Nevada, Colorado, Montana, and South Dakota bring miners and prospectors into the plains

1851 First Fort Laramie Treaty attempts to pacify Northern Plains Indians; government begins acquisition of Santee Sioux lands in Minnesota

1853 Fort Atkinson Treaty tries to obtain peace with Southern Plains Indians

1854 19 August Grattan Massacre, near Fort Laramie, Wyoming, initiates Sioux Wars

1855–56 Harney expedition on the Northern Plains

1861–65 Civil War. Majority of federal troops withdrawn from frontier

1862 18 August–26 September Santee uprising in Minnesota

1863–68 Increased raids on western frontier

1864 Summer Sibley and Sully expeditions on the Northern Plains

13 October Elm Creek Raid, Young County, Texas

25 November First fight at Adobe Walls, Texas

29 November Sand Creek Massacre of Cheyennes by Colorado troops

1865 Sully and Connor expeditions on the Northern Plains

1869 President Grant implements Peace Policy

Southern Plains chronology

1865 Little Arkansas Treaty

1867 Spring and Summer Hancock's War

1868 Medicine Lodge Treaty

1868–69 Cheyenne War, Kansas and Oklahoma

1868 17 September Beecher's Island fight

27 November Custer attacks Indian villages on the Washita

1870–78 Slaughter of the buffalo

1871 18 May Warren Wagon Train Massacre, Texas; Kiowa Chiefs Satanta and Big Tree subsequently imprisoned

1874–75 Red River War on Southern Plains

Northern Plains chronology

1866–68 Red Cloud War, Wyoming and Montana

1868 Fort Laramie Treaty

1876–77 Great Sioux War

Subsequent events

1878–79 Cheyenne Outbreak

1879 Suit by Ponca chief Standing Bear

determines that Indians have legal
standing in court
Indian Rights movement gains impetus
White River Ute uprising

1887 Dawes Act divides reservations into
individual land holdings

1889 Break-up of Great Sioux Reservation

1889–90 Rise of the Ghost Dance Religion

1890 29 December Wounded Knee
Massacre of Lakotas by federal troops

1924 American Indian Nationality Act gives
Indians full citizenship

1934 Indian Reorganization Act allows
limited self-government and cultural
freedom

1944 National Congress of American
Indians organizes

1960s–70s Rise of American Indian
Movement

1969 Indians occupy Alcatraz

1972 Indians seize Bureau of
Indian Affairs Building in
Washington

1973 Outbreak at Wounded Knee

North and South

The Southern Plains

The first serious clashes between Plains Indians and whites occurred during the 18th century on the Southern Plains. As defined by William H. Leckie in his classic work *The Military Conquest of the Southern Plains*, the region occupies an area from the Platte river in the north to the Rio Grande in the south, and from the Rocky Mountains in the west to about the 98th meridian in the east.

The first Europeans to enter the plains were the Spaniards. Although the Coronado expedition explored the territory in the 1530s, it was almost two centuries before they made any serious attempt to settle. To them, the plains meant the west central part of modern Texas. The reasons for ignoring Texas for so long were economic – it did not appear to offer mineral wealth to exploit, or large congregations of Indian souls to save. The reasons for ultimately settling the province were strategic. It formed a barrier that protected the rich mining regions to the south and west. The primary threat was the French, who already occupied Canada and were rapidly colonizing the Mississippi valley. Thus the Plains Wars in Texas assumed the shape of a contest of empires, which became intertwined with existing rivalries between native tribes.

The first hint of trouble came when word reached the Spanish settlements that a French colony had been established on the Texas coast. This was the ill-fated expedition of René Robert Cavelier, Sieur de la Salle, and though it failed, its mere presence was enough to throw Spain into a panic. An initial attempt to establish a Spanish presence in the province in the 1690s failed, but the permanent French colonization of the Lower Mississippi at the beginning of the 18th century made further efforts imperative. By 1720, a string of missions stretched through eastern Texas, anchored at the edge of the plains by a mission, a presidio (frontier defense fort), and a town that ultimately became San Antonio (Fontana, 75–77, 122).

The Spanish occupation of Texas came in the wake of the introduction of the horse to the Great Plains tribes. This revolutionized Indian life, giving them unprecedented mobility, and allowing the various tribes to expand their range. The result was ruthless intertribal wars over hunting grounds, and territorial domain. The most powerful were the Comanches and Wichitas, who pushed the weaker Plains Apaches southward, into the areas of Spanish settlement. The Apaches, in turn, raided the settlements, stealing horses, plundering and murdering. By 1731, they had become so aggressive that they were able to attack the horse corral of the Presidio of San Antonio, and beat back a relief detail sent from the fort. In response, Governor Juan Antonio Bustillo of Coahuila, whose jurisdiction included Texas, organized a punitive expedition composed of veteran Indian fighters. In 1732, Bustillo's troops attacked an Apache encampment, killing about 200, capturing 30 women and children, and recovering 700 stolen horses. The Apaches, however, fought with a ferocity that the soldiers had never before experienced. Additionally, they realized this was not the main band. Aware that the Indians could attack, and possibly even destroy, the presidio, town, and missions virtually at will, the soldiers petitioned the government to negotiate a peace. They were supported by the commandant of the presidio, Juan Antonio Perez de Almazon, and the president of the San Antonio Mission, Fray Gabriel de Vergara, the latter of whom feared a general uprising and massacre similar to what had happened in

The South Plains

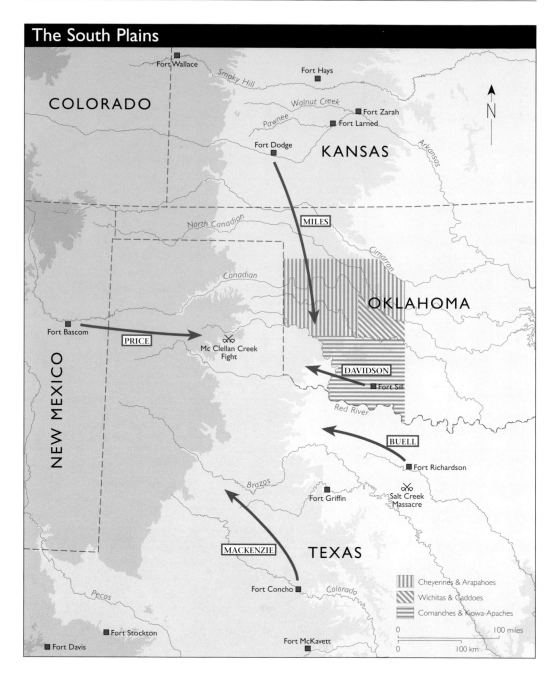

New Mexico in 1680. Despite these fears, little could be done, and Bustillo's punitive expedition was the first of three that would be undertaken against the Apaches between 1732 and 1748 (Simpson, xvi–xviii).

The Apache response was to play two enemies – Spaniards and Comanches – against each other. In late 1755, they began drifting in to a newly established mission and presidio near the present city of San Marcos, until more than a thousand had congregated. Their piety was lukewarm, just enough to make the priests hopeful. Their real motive appears to have been to seek Spanish protection from the Comanches, but they kept enough of a front so that the priests were encouraged. Because the local environment would not support such a large

Ruins of the San Sabá Presido at Menard, Texas. The Stone fortress was built after the massacre of 1758 to replace the existing stockade, and was partially reconstructed for the Texas Centennial in 1936. (Author's collection)

population, the priests petitioned the government to permanently relocate the mission and presidio to the San Sabá river, near the present city of Menard. San Sabá, it was hoped, would be the first of a chain of missions extending from San Antonio to Santa Fe, in New Mexico (Weddle, 35–37).

The San Sabá project was doomed from the start. The mood of the Apaches was questionable, at least to Colonel Diego Ortiz Parilla, a seasoned Indian fighter who was to command the presidio. When a delegation of Lipan Apaches arrived in San Antonio to discuss the project, the watchful Parilla suspected treachery. He was also uneasy about the coequal authority between himself and the president of the proposed mission, the strong-willed Fray Alonso Giraldo de Terreros, which he believed would create contradiction and confusion in a crisis. Already, the priests were quarreling among themselves. Nevertheless, the expedition got under way, arriving at the designated site on the San Sabá river on 15 April 1757. Despite the assurances of the Lipans in San Antonio, not a single Indian was there to meet them (Weddle, 44–50).

To the suspicious Colonel Parilla, the absence of the Indians indicated a fool's errand, and he urged the abandonment of the project. The priests, however, overruled him, and construction began on the mission, officially christened Santa Cruz de San Sabá, and the fort, designated the Presidio of San Luis de las Amarillas in honor of the reigning viceroy, the Marqués de las Amarillas. The priests were as suspicious of the soldiers as Parilla was of the Apaches. A few years earlier, a mission on the San Xavier (now San Gabriel) river had failed, in part because the soldiers, inspired by their commander, had appropriated the wives and daughters of the Indian neophytes. To guard against such abuses, the new mission was located 5km (three miles) downstream, and on the opposite side of the river from the presidio. While this might prevent military corruption, it also placed the mission too far away for aid when the time came.

About mid-June, some 3,000 Apaches appeared. They advised the priests, however, that they had not come to congregate, but were hunting buffalo. Their mood was sullen, and they spoke of war against the Comanches and the Hasinais (Weddle uses the term "Tejas" for Hasinai throughout, but "Tejas" is a colloquial term and specifically denotes a branch of the Hasinais living in the Neches-Angelina area of east Texas, far removed from the area under consideration (see Bolton, 53)) to avenge a recent attack against them. They advised the priests, however, that they planned to return and congregate, once the hunt was over and the Comanche–Hasinai raid had been avenged. No one is certain what the Apaches did during their absence, but they may have boasted of an alliance with the Spaniards, and during fighting may have lost some articles the Spaniards had given them. Whatever the case, their enemies believed the Spaniards had thrown in with the Apaches, and this sealed the doom of San Sabá. At the mission, meanwhile, the lack of Indian neophytes made it increasingly obvious the project was failing. Several of the priests returned to Mexico, and those remaining felt Terreros, the mission president, had deceived them. As autumn approached, various bands of Apaches came through, paused long enough to take advantage of the mission hospitality, and continued southward, giving the impression of fleeing. Rumors reached Terreros and Parilla that the northern tribes were banding together to destroy the Apaches, erroneously presuming that they had congregated at the mission (Weddle, Part 2).

As time passed, a respect grew between Parilla and Terreros, and they increasingly consulted each other on their respective goals which, in Parilla's case, was pacification, and in Terreros', the saving of souls. The priests ministered to the neophytes, while Parilla made it evident that the ministry could be backed by military force, if necessary. Although Terreros complained to the viceroy that the Indians' "promises of submission are sometimes pretexts for delay" he added that Parilla's "personally directed management … has protected them and decreased their antagonism." Nevertheless, he and Parilla believed that they personally should appear at court to explain to the viceroy the requirements necessary for a complete subjugation. Terreros' letter was dated 13 February 1758. By the time it reached the court in Mexico City, it was a moot point. Terreros was dead and the mission destroyed (Terreros to Amarillas, in Simpson, 1–3).

On 25 February, Indians stampeded the horses in the presidio pasture. Sergeant Francisco Yruegas took 14 soldiers in pursuit, but after 12 days recovered only one live horse. Upon returning, he reported large numbers of Indians armed for battle. Parilla sent a detail to warn the escort of a supply train bound for San Antonio. The detail was attacked and four soldiers wounded, but they managed to reach the train. Smoke signals were seen in the north and east. On 15 March Parilla urged the priests to come to the presidio for protection. Terreros refused, apparently convinced the raid on the pasture and the attack on the troops were isolated incidents. Parilla left a guard of eight soldiers with two light cannon, ammunition, and muskets, then returned to the presidio.

At dawn the next day about 2,000 Comanches, Hasinais, Tonkawas, Bidais, and other allied tribes rushed the mission. They were painted for war, many carried modern firearms, sabers, and lances, and some were dressed in the style of the French military. Some 300 managed to get into the courtyard. Terreros and another priest, Fray José de Santiesteban, were killed, along with a soldier and two civilians. The others fought their way to the buildings, where they barricaded themselves in while the Indians plundered the mission. Then, the raiders set fire to the stockade, hoping it would consume the survivors in their refuges.

A relief column from the presidio encountered a band of heavily armed Indians on the road, and three soldiers were killed in the first volley of musket fire. Returning to the fort, they encountered mission Indians with a tale of slaughter. Convinced the mission was beyond aid, Parilla prepared the presidio for defense. That night, a sergeant took a detail to the mission, but found the Indians alert. Nevertheless, the soldiers rescued the survivors, who had managed to slip out of the buildings in small groups under cover of darkness. Two days later, the Indians withdrew (Weddle, Part 2).

The exact number of people killed at San Sabá is not known, but probably did not exceed 10 (Weddle, 88–89). This was small as massacres go, but the impact was great. The mission was doomed from the start, the victim of intertribal conflicts and the rivalries of empires. The organization and arms of the Indians left no doubt in anyone's mind that they were, in the words of the governor of Coahuila, "instigated by foreign political agents," specifically the French (Angel de Martos y Navarrete to Toribio de Guevara, in Simpson, 17).

The disaster marked the limit of Spain's imperial ambitions. It also inaugurated full-scale warfare between Indians and whites on the Southern Plains. Fighting would continue, passed on from Spain to other powers, for almost 120 years.

The Northern Plains

For the purposes of this book, the domain of the Northern Plains Indians extends from the Canadian border to the Platte river of Nebraska, and from the Rocky Mountains to approximately the Mississippi river. In fact, the Northern Plains extend well into Canada, and the Indians of the United States crossed over frequently. To them, Canada was "Grandmother's Land," so-called because of the portraits of an aging Queen Victoria that stared down at them from the walls of government outposts. Canada was a refuge in times of trouble with the United States, because US troops were hesitant to risk British wrath by crossing the border, nor was Great Britain likely to permit it. Thus, the boundary became a "Medicine Line,"

that offered a sort of magical protection once the Indians crossed it.

The most powerful of the Northern Plains tribes were the Western, or Lakota Sioux and their allies, the Cheyennes. The Lakotas, perhaps the largest Indian nation in the United States, were divided into seven tribes, Oglala, Brulé, Hunkpapa, Miniconjou, Blackfeet, Two Kettles, and Sans Arcs. Each had its own specific territory, although each summer they all met for an annual council that brought thousands of people together.

The Lewis and Clark expedition established a permanent contact between the Indians and outsiders from the east. The age of the mountain man, which came in the wake of Lewis and Clark, introduced the Plains tribes to a plethora of newcomers. The effect was unnerving to the Indians, who resented the intrusion of trappers into their territories. Ambushes became common, and a trapping brigade's horse herd offered an incentive for theft. The mountain men themselves relied on old tribal grievances, often allying with one tribe against another (Hanson, 7).

One of the first tribes to react was the Arikara (or Ree) of the Upper Missouri river. In the spring of 1823, a group of Rees got into a dispute with a band of Missouri Fur Company traders, and two Indians were killed. In retaliation, on 2 June 1823, several hundred Rees attacked a trapping expedition led by William H. Ashley, about 950km (600 miles) upriver from Council Bluffs, Iowa. Fifteen trappers were killed and 12 others wounded. Forced downriver, Ashley sent a message to Fort Atkinson, Nebraska, and a punitive expedition was mounted under Colonel Henry Leavenworth. The expedition, consisting of 200 infantrymen with artillery, about 700 Sioux allies, and 100 or more trappers, bombarded the Ree village, but Leavenworth allowed the inhabitants to escape. His failure to pursue and destroy the Indians was a serious loss of prestige for the whites among the Upper Missouri tribes, who thereafter were less hesitant to attack and, for a time, even managed to close the upper river

The Presido de Nuestra Senora de Loreto, better known as La Bahia, in Goliad, was one of the strongest Spanish frontier defense works, and the best preserved Spanish interior fort in the United States. The chapel is original, as are the lower portions of most of the walls. (Author's collection)

to American trade (Utley, *Encyclopedia*, 16–17; Anonymous, 157–58).

While the trappers fought the Upper Missouri tribes, the Indians of the Platte valley and surrounding region resented the mass movement of whites across the plains toward Oregon and California. By the early 1840s, the sheer numbers of transients became threatening, particularly to the great Lakota Sioux tribes, who were accustomed to dominating by sheer number. Francis Parkman, Jr, who visited the Lakotas at the time, wrote (137):

Until within a year or two, when the emigrants began to pass through their country on the way to Oregon, they had seen no whites except the handful employed about the Fur Company's posts. They esteemed them a wise people, inferior only to themselves ... But when the swarm of Meneaska, with their oxen and wagons, began to invade them, their astonishment was unbounded. They could scarcely believe that the earth contained such a multitude of white men. Their wonder is now giving way to indignation; and the result, unless vigilantly guarded against, may be lamentable in the extreme.

This large movement of people actually threatened the Indian way of life. It drove game away from traditional hunting grounds, forcing the tribes to move farther afield in search of food. By 1845, much of the buffalo had been driven out of the Platte valley, requiring the Lakotas to hunt west of the Laramie Mountains and in the range of their traditional enemies, the Utes and the Shoshones. Another point of contention was settlement. On the eastern edge of the Great Plains, the encroachment of permanent white residents forced more Indians into smaller areas, throwing mutually antagonistic tribes into close contact with each other. War became inevitable (DeLand, 15:33–34; Myers, Folder 10).

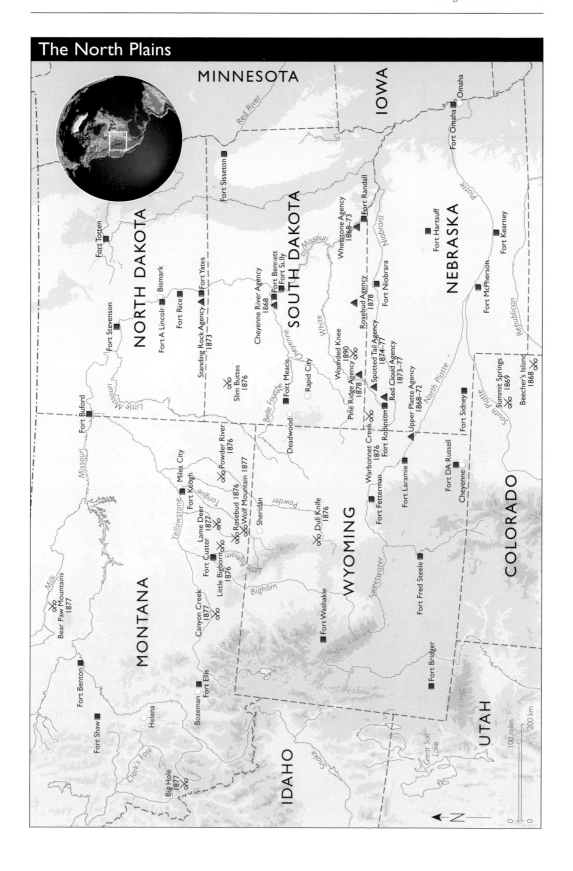

The North Plains

The soldier and the warrior

The Plains Indian mode of war

War was a means by which a warrior gained prestige, honor, and plunder. Individual combat was highly esteemed, and trophies of battle highly prized. Yet this individualism brought certain collective risk. Plains Indians were largely nomadic and tribal, and generally functioned in small bands. A dead warrior could not be replaced until a young boy reached fighting age, generally in his mid-teens. On the other hand, they realized that dead soldiers would be replaced immediately, often with a public outcry for vengeance. Consequently, in organized fighting, Indians preferred hit-and-run raids rather than open battle. Raiding itself was calculated on a cost–benefit basis. It was not worth losing several warriors just to obtain two or three scalps, but it was well worth the loss to obtain a herd of horses (Myers. Folder 10).

One best understands Indian thought when one looks at the exceptions, which is to say direct confrontations with the enemy. At Adobe Walls, Texas, in 1874, and the Rosebud, in Montana, in 1876, the Indians had a clear advantage. Yet each time, they broke off fighting when their losses began to mount. In the battle of the Little Bighorn, in which five companies of Seventh Cavalry were annihilated, the Indians were purely on the defensive.

There was no single standard for an Indian warrior. Each tribe or national group had its own customs and traditions. A Northern Cheyenne warrior generally retired from active combat about the age of 40, assuming of course, that he had a son who could take his place in the battle line. Although retired warriors would participate in battle as spectators, staying in the rear, singing war songs and shouting encouragement, actual fighting was left to younger men with more stamina and agility (Marquis, *n.d.*, 118–19). In other tribes, however, a warrior might fight well into old age. The Kiowa war chief Satank was in his 70s at the time of his last raid in 1871. Likewise, in 1876, the septuagenarian Washakie led his Shoshones as scouts for General Crook's Bighorn and Yellowstone Expedition, which culminated in the battle of the Rosebud.

Weapons

Traditional Indian weapons could be divided into five basic types – striking, cutting, piercing, defensive weapons, and symbolic weapons. Striking weapons included such things as clubs, tomahawks, axes, and whips, while knives were used as cutting weapons, and arrows and lances for piercing. In many cases, Indian warfare had a ritual as well as practical significance, so that Indians also had decorative ceremonial equipment, like headgear, war shirts, and even face and body paint, which would bring protection, enhance bravery, or otherwise give their wearers an edge. Somewhere in between the practical and the ceremonial were defensive weapons that included shields and armor (Taylor, 2001, 6–10). With the introduction of firearms and steel weapons, defensive gear became more symbolic than useful, although a hard, well-reinforced shield of smooth rawhide could still deflect a lance or even a ball from the early muskets (Simpson, xvi).

The Tonkawa chief Chiahook, also known as "Charley" or "Charley Johnson," headed the Indian scouts attached to Fort Griffin, Texas. Many Indians served the government in an effort to settle ancient grievances against other tribes. Tonkawas were especially hated because they cannibalized the bodies of slain enemies. (Texas State Library and Archives)

The ruthless Kiowa war chief Satank was arrested for his part in the Warren Wagon Train Massacre in Texas in 1871. Rather than return to Texas for trial, he jumped a guard at Fort Sill, Oklahoma, and was killed. (National Archives)

Like any warrior culture, Plains Indians often endowed their fighting equipment with special powers. Shields were thought to be particularly potent, and the men who made them were in touch with the spirit world. The Kiowa war chief Satanta, who died in 1878, carried a special "sun shield," one of six made in the 1790s by the powerful medicine man Black Horse, and the modern Kiowas still believe in its power (Grinnell, 1972, 1:192–93; Robinson, 1998, 24–26).

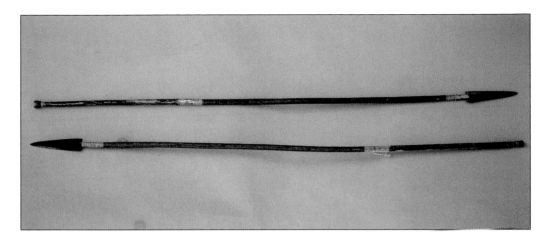

Plains Indian arrows with metal points probably obtained by trade. (Author's collection)

The government, through its Indian agents, issued guns for hunting, but unlicensed traders also made a lucrative business of selling the most modern firearms. Often, Indian warriors had better weapons than the soldiers had. Nevertheless, while an Indian was deadly with a bow, his aim with a firearm often was haphazard except at close range (Carleton, *Prairie Logbooks*, 271). Despite long familiarity with firearms, it was not until the latter part of the era that they became completely comfortable with them in combat, preferring instead the bow, lance, and shield for close-in fighting. A warrior gained battle honor by risking himself against the enemy. "Counting coup" – physically striking an enemy, living or dead – brought the greatest glory of all. Several warriors might "count coup" on the same enemy, but the supreme honor went to the one who struck first, and he vehemently defended his claim against any challenger (Grinnell, *Cheyenne Indians*, 2:30ff.).

The frontier soldier

The annexation of Texas in 1845 gave the United States Army an abrupt introduction into Plains Indian warfare with no time to prepare. Previously, as new areas were opened to settlement, the army went in, removed the local Indians, and concentrated them on reservations before serious clashes developed with incoming settlers. In Texas, however, the United States suddenly assumed responsibility for defending a heavily settled and populated state whose citizens viewed themselves as perpetually at war with the Plains tribes. The entire cavalry arm of the army consisted of two regiments of dragoons, and one of mounted rifles. The remainder of the troops was infantry and artillery. Consequently, infantry was sent to subdue mounted Indians, and with no previous experience, the US soldier had to improvise as he went along. Not until after the Civil War, which brought a reorganization and expansion of the cavalry arm, was the American soldier really able to meet an Indian on equal terms (Robinson, 2000, 105).

Officers had to contend with an enemy that did not fight by the generally accepted methods of war. West Point trained them to fight traditional battles against comparably trained field armies. This had served them well during the Mexican and Civil wars, and so they resisted change. One of Crook's aides, Lieutenant John Gregory Bourke, observed, "We have much to learn from the savage in the matter of Cavalry training; the trouble is our prejudices of education are so deeply rooted, common sense and observation have no permission to assert themselves" (Bourke, Diary, 6:597). Many officers were contemptuous of Indian hit-and-run tactics, later learning to their sorrow – that is not surviving to learn – how totally effective these tactics could be.

The Indian fighting soldier also faced public disdain. Americans, with their citizen-soldier heritage, have always been

suspicious of professionals. The soldier of the civil war was generally a member of a volunteer unit drawn from his home county or state. He had the support, indeed the blessing, of his community. The regular soldier, on the other hand, had no home but the army. Many were drawn from the urban poor, or from immigrants, some of whom had served in foreign armies, and others who were unable to find employment upon arrival in the United States. The bloody nature of Indian warfare was repugnant to the civilized Eastern press,

Model 1904 McClellan military saddle. The McClellan was introduced in 1859 and, in various modifications, continues to serve US mounted troops. (Author's collection)

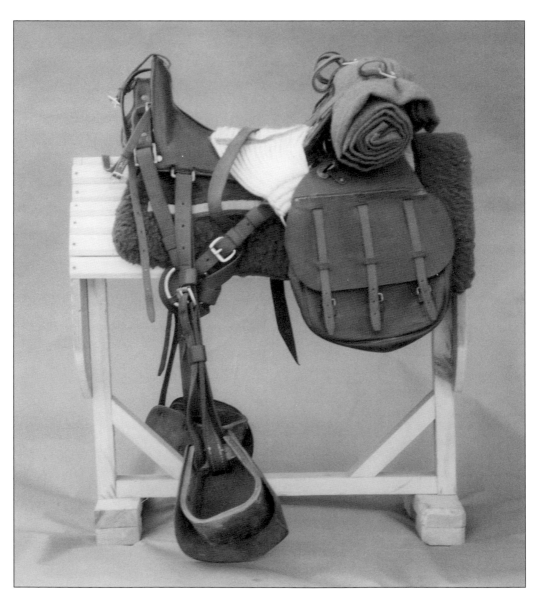

which often did not make the distinction between atrocities committed by vindictive local militias, and government policy executed by the regulars (Rickey, 24–25).

On post, bugles governed the soldier's life, with a specific call for each duty. A typical day might begin with reveille and stable call at daybreak. At 7.00 am the soldier had breakfast. Drill, which after stable call was the most hated part of the day, ran from 7.30 am to 8.30 am. Guard was mounted and 9.30 am, and those not on guard had fatigue duty for the remainder of the morning. There was another stable call at 4.00 pm, with retreat at sundown, fatigue at 8.15 pm, Taps at 8.45 pm. and guard inspection and mounting at 9.00 pm (Robinson, 1992, 43).

In his leisure time, a soldier might wander into one of the towns that frequently grew up in the vicinity of a military post. Sometimes these towns were well developed, with economic factors other than the army. Often, though, they were merely "hogtowns," shantytowns that existed solely to pander to the soldier's needs and vices. Either way, he could find gamblers, saloonkeepers, and "soiled doves," all willing to separate him from his hard-earned pay. The volatile combination of liquor, money, and women could lead to illness or violence. In March 1875, one post surgeon reported (United States Department of War, Office of the Surgeon General):

The habits of the Men might be materially improved, by the removal of the number of Lewd Women living in the vicinity of the post. The Soldiers not only become demoralized by frequenting these resorts but some of them have already contracted venereal diseases and one soldier was wounded by a pistol ball in one of these drunken haunts.

Arms and equipment

The US soldier on the frontier was poorly clad for the task facing him. When the Civil War ended, the government still had massive

The model 1878 infantry pack was typical of military issue designed by Ordnance officers in the East who knew little about Western field conditions. (Author's collection)

stores of uniforms and equipment. That, together with a reduction of the army by two-thirds within five years of the wars' end, convinced Congress there was no need to appropriate money for new clothing until the existing stockpiles were exhausted. Because of contractors profiteering during the war, however, much of it was ill-fitting or defective, and in 1872, a new, better quality was introduced. Nevertheless, Civil War stocks were not exhausted until about 1880, and government parsimony dictated that the transition period lasted years, rather than the months originally intended (McChristian, 37–42).

Another problem was equipment designed in total ignorance of frontier conditions. Infantrymen, for example, were issued a packing system based on weight distribution that was superbly suited for

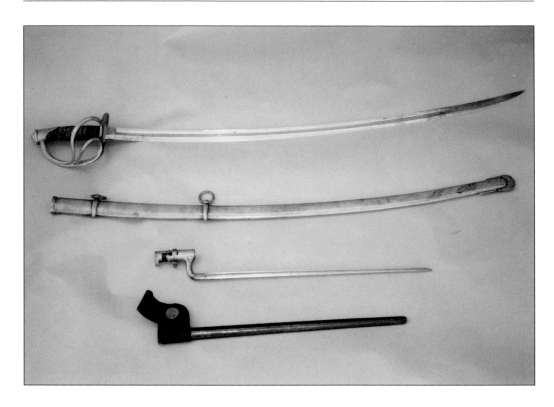

Useless accoutrements, the Model 1858 Cavalry saber and Model 1873 Infantry bayonet were regular issue during the Plains Wars, but were routinely left at post during field expeditions as they had no value in the hit-and-run fights with Indians. (Author's collection)

Europe and the American east. In the trackless expanses of the frontier, however, it only added a mass of additional field equipment that was an impediment for a foot soldier on a forced march. The average infantryman much preferred to roll up a few essentials in a blanket and sling it over his shoulder, with a haversack hanging down to one side. The army also insisted on cartridge boxes fastened to the waist-belt, a carry-over from the paper cartridge of muzzle-loading arms. The brass cartridge, however, made the box redundant, and soldiers often fashioned cartridge belts with loops on them, in the civilian style. Not until 1876, however, did the Bureau of Ordnance bow to reality, and issue a looped cartridge belt (McChristian, 178–79, 196–97; Utley, 1984, 75).

Cavalrymen were issued sabers, and infantrymen bayonets, but the nature of Indian warfare gave little opportunity to use them. They routinely were left on post as useless encumbrances more suited for guard duty or parade than combat (Utley, 1984, 76).

Given the myriad weapons used during the Civil War, the army made efforts to standardize. Not until 1873, however, was the goal realized for both cavalry and infantry. The sidearm was Colt's Model 1873 Single Action Army revolver in .45-caliber. The breechloading Model 1873 Springfield became the standard shoulder arm, in .45–70 long rifle for the infantry, and .45–55 carbine for the cavalry. Both the handgun and the shoulder arms had drawbacks. The Colt's cylinder, fixed in a one-piece frame, had to be rotated by hand each time a cartridge was ejected or inserted. The Springfield's single-shot hinged-block action made it effective at long ranges, but proved a hindrance in close-in fighting, especially as more Indians acquired Winchester or Henry repeating rifles (Utley, 1984, 70–72).

Bugle of the type used by troops in the Plains Wars during the second half of the 19th century. Indians, most notably the Kiowa chief Satanta, and the Cheyenne Dog Soldiers, also acquired bugles and, according to some contemporary accounts, learned to signal with military calls. This was not unique to the American Plains; during the siege of Khartoum in 1885, Major Gen. C.G. Gordon reported that Sudanese Madhists used Egyptian Army bugle calls to confuse and demoralize troops defending the city. (Author's collection)

Regardless of weaponry, marksmanship was at best indifferent, because the government begrudged money spent on ammunition for target practice. Indeed, many soldiers went into combat totally unfamiliar with their firearms. Only after the Custer disaster of 1876, and the heavy losses at Bear Paw Mountain during the Nez Percé War a year later, was a regular program of marksmanship enforced (Rickey, 100–12).

Wars handed down through generations

With the end of the Seven Years' War, France ceded Louisiana west of the Mississippi to Spain, removing the threat of French intervention on the Spanish frontier. The most serious danger in the north now became the Plains Indians, and this dictated a reorganization of Spanish defenses. In 1767, the Marqués de Rubí, a professional soldier and diplomat, inspected the northern provinces to consider improvements to frontier defense. On his recommendation, most of the presidios north of the Rio Grande, including the long-suffering San Luis de las Amarillas on the San Sabá, were closed. A new line of defense would follow the Rio Grande up to about the 30th parallel, then across to the Pacific. The only presidios above the line would be Santa Fe, San Antonio, and Loreto (better known as La Bahia) at Goliad. The area of extreme eastern Texas would be managed out of New Orleans (Jackson, 72, 79–81).

Although Rubí's policy made the line of defense more workable, depredations by the Lipan Apaches continued. In 1781, faced with increasing raids, Colonel Juan de Ugalde, governor of Coahuila, began a series of punitive expeditions that damaged, but did not stop, the Apaches. In 1785, with his authority expanded, he initiated a new, devastating campaign that forced the Lipans and their Mescalero Apache allies to cut back their raids. Finally, in 1789, he moved deep into central Texas, establishing headquarters in the old, abandoned presidio on the San Sabá. On 9 January 1790, he surprised a large Indian camp on the Sabinal river, killing nearly 40, and capturing women, children, and the Apache livestock herds. In honor of the victory, a nearby canyon was named Cañon de Ugalde, which the Texans render as Uvalde Canyon (Weddle, 188–89).

After Ugalde's campaigns, an uneasy calm settled on the frontier. Aside from occasional raids against the settlements, the Indians generally stayed out on the plains. In 1821, however, a new people began arriving, first in small groups, but within a few years numbering into the thousands. In the spring of that year, in the final months of colonial rule, the Spanish government granted Moses Austin the right to bring Americans colonists into the Brazos and Colorado river valleys. Within months, Austin was dead, and Mexico had become independent, but the new government reaffirmed the agreement with his son, Stephen F. Austin.

As the American settlers moved into the Texas interior, the Plains tribes began raiding their livestock. The settlers retaliated and soon the friction degenerated into bloodshed. In response to the settlers' pleas for assistance, the Mexican governor in San Antonio authorized them to establish a local militia. On 5 May 1823, the first company was organized – the birth of the Texas Rangers (Barton, 61–62; Barker, 1:672).

For the next 13 years, Indians and Texas settlers raided and counterraided. But as the 1820s drew to a close and the 1830s began, the most serious problem was deteriorating relations with the Mexican government. During the War of Independence in 1835–36, Rangers protected the frontier, allowing the army to concentrate on the struggle with Mexico. After independence, the Rangers functioned as needed, sometimes as frontier minutemen, called up to handle a crisis and returning to their homes when finished, and sometimes as a volunteer militia, called up for specific lengths of service.

The Mexican army had scarcely evacuated Texas when the new republic suffered one of its worst Indian raids, very similar to what had occurred at the San Sabá Mission 78 years earlier. The scene was Parker's Fort, a stockaded settlement in east central Texas, where the forests of the east begin to give way to the plains. It was a religious community consisting of 21 adults and 13 children, many of whom were related to the Reverend James W. Parker, the leader. On 19 May 1836, most of the men were out working in the fields, and the gates of the stockade were open to admit the breeze. A band of about 500 Comanches and allies approached the settlement under a flag of truce. Upon reaching the gate, they rushed in. The fort was plundered. Five were killed, and five others were captured.

Eventually, the captives were ransomed except James Parker's niece, Cynthia Ann, and nephew, John, who were children at the time. John was raised as a warrior, and eventually moved to Mexico. Cynthia Ann was recovered in 1860, after 24 years captivity. She now was 33 years old, and remembered little of her former life besides her name. She existed as a virtual prisoner with her relatives. She left behind a son, Quanah Parker, the last great Comanche war chief (Plummer, 322ff.).

The raid on Parker's Fort inaugurated depredations that lasted the remainder of the decade. The Comanches destroyed isolated farms and ranches, and carried large numbers of women and children into captivity. In January 1840, they proposed a peace council, and the Texas government agreed provided they brought their captives to San Antonio as a pledge of good faith.

The Comanche delegation appeared on 19 March, but brought only one captive, 15-year-old Matilda Lockhart, who carried the scars of intensive torture during her two years with the Indians. Twelve principal chiefs were taken into the old Spanish government house, while the others remained in the courtyard. Matilda told the government representatives that the Comanches planned to bring in the other captives one or two at a time in hopes of obtaining large ransoms. Troops then surrounded the building, and the Indians were told they would remain hostages until all captives were returned. The chiefs drew

their weapons, one stabbed a sentry, and the troops opened fire. When the fighting ended, 30 chiefs and warriors were dead, together with three women and two children. Twenty-seven women and children, and two old men were taken prisoner, while seven soldiers and citizens were killed, and eight wounded (Winfrey and Day, 1:101–2, 105–06; Brice, 22–25).

For months, the Comanches and their Kiowa allies held off retaliation, encouraged by Mexican agents to wait until the Texans had become complaisant. Then, in early August, they swept across Texas, striking the little seaport town of Linnville on 8 August. Some citizens were killed or captured, but most managed to escape to a steamer anchored in the harbor, where they watched the Indians plunder the warehouses (Brice, 28–33).

Elsewhere, Ranger companies and regular troops came together and, guided by Tonkawa Indian scouts, intercepted the Comanches at Plum Creek on 12 August. Ranger Robert Hall noted they were decked out in plunder from Linnville. "Many of them put on cloth coats and buttoned them behind," Hall remembered. "Most of them had on stolen shoes and hats. They spread the calico over their horses and tied hundreds of yards of ribbon in their horses' manes and to their tails." The Texans dismounted and opened fire. The second volley disorganized the Comanches, and the Texans charged in, routing them ("Brazos", 53–55).

One participant in the Plum Creek fight was a young ranger named Jack Hays who, four years later, gave the Indians their rudest shock of the era. Accustomed to single-shot muzzle-loading rifles and pistols, a band of Comanches attempted to ambush Hays and his rangers west of Austin on 8 June 1844. Instead, they ran into five-shot Colt revolvers, their first encounter with repeating weapons. About 30 warriors had been killed and wounded when they fell back (Robinson, 2000, 70–71).

A year later, the United States annexed the Republic of Texas. American jurisdiction would

LEFT Parker's Fort, reconstructed on the original site for the Texas Centennial in 1936, shows the type of dwellings used by settlers who "forted up" for defense. A stockade forms the rear wall of the cabins. (Author's collection)

become official on 19 February 1846. From that point onward, the US government would be responsible for defending the Texans against the Plains Indians. Whether the US was capable of doing so was another matter.

The Northern Plains

While the Texans battled Indians on the Southern Plains, more and more emigrants followed the Platte valley in their trek toward Oregon and California. In 1843, close to 1,000 men, women, and children passed a fur-trading post, known locally as Fort Laramie, near the confluence of the Laramie and North Platte rivers in what is now eastern Wyoming (Lavender, 48). To ascertain that emigrants could travel

unmolested, the government sent Colonel Stephen Watts Kearny with 250 dragoons to meet with the Indians in the vicinity. On 16 June 1845, Kearny held a council with about 1,200 Indians near Fort Laramie, explaining to them the meaning behind the white movement.

I am opening a road for your white brethren. They are now following after me, and are journeying to the other side of the great mountains. They take with them their women, their children, and their cattle. They all go to bury their bones there, and never to return. You must not disturb them in their persons, or molest their property; neither must you on any account obstruct the road which I have now opened for them. Should you do so, your great father would be angry with you, and cause you to be punished.

No punitive action would be taken against the Indians for past depredations and killings, Kearny said, but he expected them to cease immediately.

The Indians listened politely, and pledged friendship. Kearny distributed gifts, and then, to further impress them with the government's power, he ordered several rounds fired from howitzers. The traders at the post told Kearny that until his visit, the Indians believed that the only white people were emigrants. The arrival of the soldiers with their artillery, however, created fear and uncertainty (Carleton, 246–50). And while this may have had the desired effect of convincing some to acquiesce, it may have made others all the more determined to resist.

In 1846, Congress passed a bill authorizing the construction of military posts to protect the road to Oregon. The first of these, Fort Kearny, Nebraska, was established two years later, and in 1849, the War Department purchased Fort Laramie for $4,000. Work began immediately to expand

This view of Fort Laramie, Wyoming, shows the open layout of most Western military posts, which actually were cantonments rather than fortified installations. (Little Bighorn Battlefield National Monument)

the post out in front of the old traders' stockade (Lavender, 52–53, 57–59).

Meanwhile, the westward movement gained impetus. Besides the on-going trek to Oregon, the discovery of gold in California and the development of Utah by the Mormons added to the numbers coming up the Platte. In order to maintain peace, the government decided to issue annuities in the form of food and merchandize to the Indians in exchange for their good behavior. An ancillary plan called for tools, farming equipment, and education, in hopes of turning the Indians into (by white standards at least) productive citizens. The annuity issue was a major event, bringing thousands of Indians to the vicinity. The first attempt to implement this program with the northern tribes was a treaty signed at Fort Laramie in 1851. The government, however, labored upon the erroneous assumption that Plains society functioned like white society and that a treaty signed by the chiefs was binding on the tribe itself. Having failed to realize how little actual control the chiefs had over individuals and events, the government erred again, by not providing sufficient military force to impose the peace in exchange for annuities. The following year, some 60,000 people in perhaps 12,000 wagons passed Fort Laramie. Given the Indian weakness for white livestock, a major confrontation was only a matter of time (Lavender, 48, 69ff.).

The breaking point came on 18 August 1854, when, after a series of attacks on emigrants during recent weeks, the Indians were congregated in the vicinity of Fort Laramie for their annuities. A Mormon wagon train was moving toward the fort, and as it passed one of the Sioux camps, a warrior named High Forehead killed and butchered one of the oxen, driving off its owner. Realizing this could mean trouble, the paramount chief, Brave Bear, went to Fort Laramie and suggested waiting a few days until the agent arrived to sort the matter out. The officers of the post, however, believed that if nothing was done the Indians would get completely out of hand. The following day, Lieutenant John L. Grattan, a brash young officer fresh from West Point, took 29 soldiers, an interpreter, and two pieces of artillery to the Indian camps, to demand the surrender of High Forehead. When Brave Bear offered restitution, Grattan refused. High Forehead, meanwhile, had armed himself and, like Grattan, was ready to fight. After about 45 minutes, Grattan ran out of patience and ordered his men to open fire. Brave Bear was mortally wounded, but others began to fight back. Then several hundred mounted warriors charged, and Grattan's command was cut to pieces. Only one soldier survived, and he died shortly afterwards (Hyde, 1987b, 56ff.).

Although a calm descended on the area around Fort Laramie after the fight, a call went up in the east for retribution. Secretary of War Jefferson Davis believed the incident had been deliberately planned by the Indians in order to plunder the annuity stores. He ordered Brigadier General William Harney to organize a retaliatory campaign. The quarter-century of bloodshed collectively known as the Sioux Wars had begun (Utley and Washburn, 205).

Battle on the Plains

The Southern Plains, 1845–61

The US Army's first serious encounter with Comanches came when it was more preoccupied with the Mexican War than with Indians. The army was consolidating along the Rio Grande for a push into the Mexican interior when, on 22 July 1846, a runner came to the occupied town of Camargo with word that a band was raiding along the river. They were burning ranches, killing men, carrying off women and livestock, and had already attacked a Texas Ranger camp three miles away. A detachment of rangers under Captain Ben McCulloch spent several days tracking them down throughout the vicinity, and passing ranches that had been raided. He failed to overtake them, however, and they continued their depredations beyond the reach of the US troops (Robinson, 2000, 84–85).

Military posts constructed in Texas after the Mexican War were virtually useless because they were garrisoned by infantry, and the outbreak of depredations in 1848 prompted the Texas government to form new companies of mounted rangers. Within a year, however, the state had exhausted its own financial resources, and the US government agreed to defray expenses. Occasionally the army went so far as to request the state muster Ranger companies to serve with US regular troops. Rarely, however, did the federal government reimburse the state (Robinson, 2000, Chapter 7).

In 1853, federal officials called a meeting with the leaders of the major Southern Plains tribes at Fort Atkinson, Kansas (a different Fort Atkinson from the one mentioned in the Arikara War), in an effort to end the raiding. The government insisted on the right to establish roads and military posts in the Indians' country, and demanded the return of captives. In exchange, the Indians would receive $18,000 in annual annuities for 10 years, with an option for a five-year renewal. The Indians resented the roads and military posts, and would not discuss captives. In the end, the most the government could get was a promise that there would be no future raids for livestock or captives. They had no intention, however, of honoring this pledge or returning the existing captives, and within a year they denied making any pledges (Mooney, 173–74).

Although Indians raided all along the Texas frontier line, the most serious depredations were in the north-west, along the upper Brazos and Trinity rivers. The state established two reservations in the upper Brazos country near the military posts of Fort Belknap and Camp Cooper, and while the Indians on the reservation generally were peaceful, the reserves were used as a haven by marauding bands. White settlers failed to distinguish between friendly and hostile, and took revenge where they could find it, raiding the reservations and murdering agency Indians. This brought retaliatory raids, and some Comanches from Camp Cooper actively participated in general depredations. Ultimately, the state closed the reservations and relocated those tribes to the Indian Territory. Nevertheless, raiding continued unabated, with atrocities committed by both sides (Robinson, 2000, Chapter 7).

The Northern Plains, 1854–61

After the Grattan fight, some Brulés wanted to avenge the death of Brave Bear. In November 1854, one group attacked a mail wagon below Fort Laramie, killing three people, while another raided a trading post west of the fort. Winter was relatively

The battle of Washita, 27 November 1868

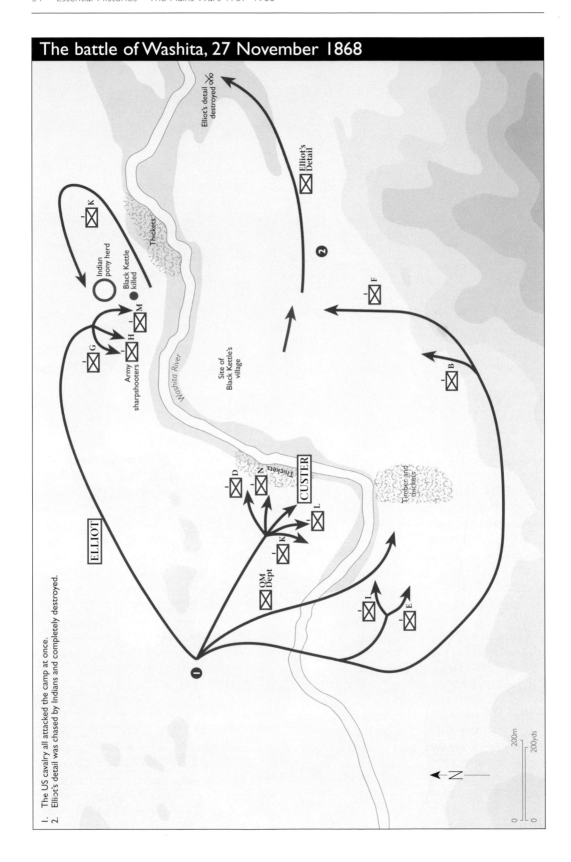

Elliot's detail
destroyed

-K

Indian
pony herd

Black Kettle
killed

-M

Thickets

-G   -H

Army
sharpshooters

Washita River

Site of
Black Kettle's
village

-N   -D

Thickets

CUSTER

-L

-K

QM
Dept

Timber and
thickets

-I

-E

-B

-F

ELLIOT

Elliot's
Detail

-X

1. The US cavalry all attacked the camp at once.
2. Elliot's detail was chased by Indians and completely destroyed.

200m

200yds

N

0

0

Battle of the Rosebud, 17 June 1876

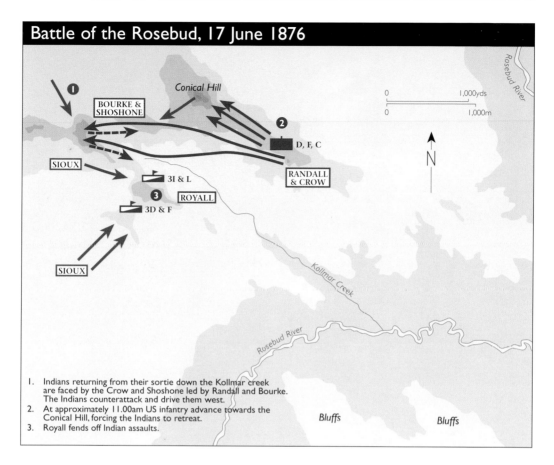

1. Indians returning from their sortie down the Kollmar creek are faced by the Crow and Shoshone led by Randall and Bourke. The Indians counterattack and drive them west.
2. At approximately 11.00am US infantry advance towards the Conical Hill, forcing the Indians to retreat.
3. Royall fends off Indian assaults.

peaceful, but the Brulés resumed their depredations again in the spring of 1855. The possibility loomed that the outbreak might spread to other tribes and bands, so the large freight companies that used the Platte road lobbied in Washington for some sort of decisive action.

In August, Thomas Twiss, a former army officer, assumed the agency at Fort Laramie for the specific purpose of coordinating with the military, and Brigadier General W.S. Harney was ordered to organize an expedition. Twiss ordered all Indians who wished to avoid trouble to remain south of the North Platte river, where they would find sanctuary. Despite his efforts, some Indians refused to move south, and at dawn on 3 September, Harney's infantry attacked a major Brulé camp under Little Thunder, near Ash Hollow, a few miles above the North Platte. Eighty-six people were killed, and 70 women and children were captured.

Harney then moved on to Fort Laramie, where he reassured the Indians who had accepted Twiss sanctuary. From there, he marched east to Fort Pierre, in what is now South Dakota, demonstrating that he could pass through the heart of Lakota country with impunity. At Pierre, the following spring, he bullied the chiefs into accepting government authority, and with the Platte road now apparently safe, the expedition was disbanded (Hyde, 1987a, 76–81).

The withdrawal of troops was premature. The Lakotas were humiliated by troops passing through their country, and even more by the treatment of their chiefs at Fort Pierre. They were also aware that, as settlers advanced into the Lower Missouri country, the Indians were being expelled, and realized that if this advance up the river continued, they could be next. From that point onward, the Lakota policy became one of war (1987a, 81–84).

The civil war

The federal government's failure to protect the frontier was one factor in Texas' decision to leave the Union in February 1861. Had the state chosen to reestablish itself as a sovereign republic, it might have succeeded. However, it opted to join the Confederate States of America which, within two months, became embroiled in a war to establish its independence from the United States. This war occupied the Confederate government's full attention, and it could spare no troops for frontier defense. In the meantime, federal troops – perhaps one-third of the entire strength of the US Army – were ordered to abandon their posts in Texas and withdraw. Although state troops tried to assume the responsibility for the frontier, the Confederacy's wartime demands quickly superceded the needs of the state (Robinson, 2000, Chapter 9).

Texas was not the only frontier state exposed by the war. In August 1862, the four-year-old Union State of Minnesota became the scene of one of the worst uprisings in US history. The eastern, or Santee Sioux had been dissatisfied since 1851, when they were pressured into ceding 24 million acres to the government in exchange for two reservations in the Minnesota Valley – designated upper and lower – and annuities spread over a 50-year period. The next step came in 1858 when, in response to settlers clamoring for more land, the government negotiated purchase of an additional million acres at 30 cents an acre (later reduced by half). In both the 1851 and 1858 treaties, Indian traders submitted claims that were deducted from payments. Agents were appointed under the patronage system, and enriched themselves at the expense of the Indians.

In 1861, the Indians' crops failed, and during the following winter, they grew hungry. They were also aware that the male white population of fighting age had been substantially reduced by the requirements of war. The breaking point came in the summer of 1862, when annuities payments and the

ration issue were delayed for a month by bureaucratic squabbling. The Indians grew increasingly hungry, but when Chief Little Crow demanded the traders extend credit, they refused. Trader Andrew J. Myrick went so far as to say, "If they are hungry, let them eat grass." That thoughtless remark was one remark too many (Carley, 1–6).

On 17 August, four Indians from the Upper Reserve killed five settlers at Acton Township, then took refuge in the Lower Reserve. At first, the Lower Reserve Sioux were undecided, but during a council at

Refugees from the upper Sioux Agency in Minnesota pause during their flight after the Indians rose up in 1862. The photograph was taken by Adrian J. Ebell, a member of the group. (Minnesota Historical Society)

Little Crow's house, the talk turned more toward war. Against his own better judgment, Little Crow ultimately agreed to lead a rising to expel the whites from the Minnesota valley.

At sunrise the following morning, the Indians attacked the settlement at the Lower Agency. Twenty whites were killed, and 10 captured. Forty-seven managed to escape while the Indians plundered the warehouses. Among the dead was Andrew Myrick, whose body was found with his mouth stuffed with grass. The war spread up the valley to the Upper Agency, leaving a wake of death and destruction. A detachment sent from Fort Ridgely was ambushed with a loss of 24 men. At the Upper Agency, several leaders opposed the war, and one, John Other Day, moved the whites into the brick warehouse. At daybreak 19 August, he managed to get 62 refugees across the river to safety.

The Minnesota Uprising 1862

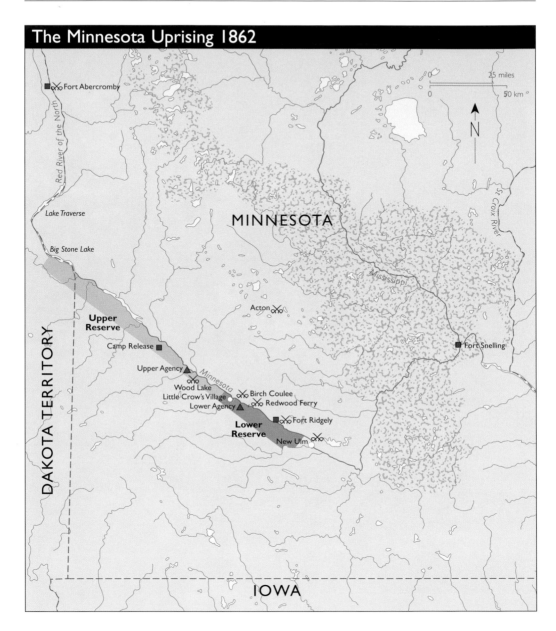

The Indians raged through the area destroying homesteads, killing, and carrying people into captivity. Refugees poured into Fort Ridgely, an open cantonment without defensive works, and a courier was sent for help. Both the fort and the town of New Ulm were attacked several times, but managed to hold with severe losses.

The failure to take Fort Ridgely and New Ulm was the turning point. Troops were dispatched to the area, along with citizen volunteers. The Indians were defeated at

Wood Lake on 23 September, and three days later surrendered. Some 269 white and mixed-blood captives were released. Over the next six weeks, a military tribunal hastily tried 392 Indians for their part in the uprising, hearing as many as 40 cases in a single day. When it adjourned on 5 November, 307 had been sentence to death, and 16 to prison. Brevet Major General John Pope, commander of the military division, commuted one death sentence to prison. As the condemned prisoners were marched through New Ulm en route to internment, troops had to protect them from angry mobs.

At the behest of Episcopal Bishop Henry Whipple, President Lincoln reviewed and commuted the death sentences of all but 39 prisoners who could be definitely established as having committed murder or rape. One of these was later reprieved because the testimony against him was questionable. The others were hanged in a mass execution in Mankato, Minnesota, on 26 December. Two leaders of the rising who had fled into Canada later were kidnapped, spirited back to the United States, tried, and hanged. The hapless Little Crow fled into Dakota Territory, but returned a year later, and was killed by a farmer (Carley).

No one will ever know the exact number of soldiers and settlers killed in the rising. Estimates range from 450 to 800, but 500 seems to be a reasonable estimate. The Indians later indicated their losses in the actual fighting were about 21 (Carley, 1).

Several leaders besides Little Crow fled into the Dakotas, where they told their stories to the Plains Sioux. The latter, already angered by prospectors crowding through their territory en route to newly discovered Montana gold fields, were ready to listen. The situation was aggravated by military expeditions into the Dakotas led by Brigadier-Generals Henry Hastings Sibley and Alfred Sully. Sully campaigned as far as the Yellowstone river, pursuing not only fleeing Santees from Minnesota, but also the Lakotas through whose territory he marched. The final blow to their dignity came in July 1864, when Sully founded Fort Rice in what is now North Dakota, establishing a permanent military presence on the Upper Missouri. War spread across the Northern Plains (Utley and Washburn, 231–32).

Like the Santee Sioux in Minnesota, the Kiowas and Comanches of the Southern Plains were aware that trouble between the whites had caused a withdrawal of troops. Both Union and Confederacy tried to enlist the Indians in their cause. Confederate Brigadier General Albert Pike, who commanded the Department of the Indian Territory, advised a group of Indians that he had "no objection" if they attacked federal wagon trains. "To go on the warpath somewhere else is the best way to keep them from troubling Texas," he explained to President Jefferson Davis (United States Department of War, *War of the Rebellion*, 4 May 1862, Series 1, 13:822). Federal officials, on the other hand, encouraged the Kiowas "to do all the damage they could to Texas …" (Mooney, 179).

Being opportunists, the Kiowas and Comanches raided both sides. The Texas frontier was particularly vulnerable. Men were loath to enlist for Indian fighting when the Confederate government might conscript frontier defense units for the war in the East. Only when they were assured they would be exempt from the Confederate draft would they join Texas's Frontier Regiment, preferring to risk their lives for their homes rather than the Southern Cause. Although a smallpox epidemic among the Indians in 1862 gave the state a reprieve, the closing weeks of 1863 and the year of 1864 witnessed the worst depredations in Texas history.

The most devastating raid came on 13 October 1864, when several hundred Comanches and Kiowas swooped down on Young County, about 160km (100 miles) west of Fort Worth. The settlers were completely surprised. Some were killed or captured, while others fled to the wellbuilt home of a rancher named George Bragg, where they held off a six-hour siege. Still others reached the ranch too late, and hid in the brush along Elm Creek, listening to the fighting only a few yards away. By the time help arrived the next day, the Indians had retreated, leaving behind 11 dead settlers, and carrying with them seven women and children – white and black – as captives. They also took over 1,000 head of cattle (Hamby; United States Department of War, *War of the Rebellion*, Series 1, Vol. 41, 1:885–86). (Over the next year, all the captives were ransomed except an 18-month-old girl who was never seen again).

Thirty-eight Sioux involved in the rising are executed in a mass hanging at Mankato, Minnesota, on 26 December 1862. More than 300 were condemned, but President Abraham Lincoln commuted the sentences of all those not actually guilty of murder or rape. (Minessota Historical Society)

The Indians took their captives to a group of winter camps situated along the Canadian river in northern Texas, near the ruins of an abandoned trading post called Adobe Walls. Once they had settled in, the younger warriors went out raiding again, this time moving into Colorado and New Mexico. At Adobe Walls, however, they were exposed to attack by troops from Union-held forts in New Mexico. On 24 November, Indian scouts attached to the First New Mexico Volunteer Cavalry located the camps, and informed their commander, Colonel Christopher (Kit) Carson, one of the era's greatest frontiersmen. After a night march, Carson's troops overran the westernmost camp, occupied by the Kiowas, shortly after 8.00 am the next day.

The warriors gave ground slowly over the 6.5km (4 miles) between their camp and the ruins. At Adobe Walls, however, they turned and made a stand. Finally, a pair of mountain howitzers was brought up, and the Indians were driven out. Carson halted at the ruins to rest and feed his men. Downriver, Dohasen, the aging paramount chief of the Kiowas, managed to round up about 1,000 warriors from the main camp, who rode back and attacked. After fierce fighting, the howitzers opened up with explosive shells, and the Indians abandoned the field. Carson destroyed about 150 lodges, with stores and munitions. Believing it unsafe to remain in the area, he withdrew back to New Mexico, unaware of the recent Young County raid, or that the captives had been driven into the brush and hidden when the fighting started (United States department of War, *War of the Rebellion*, Series 1, Vol. 41, 1:842; Mooney, 315–17).

The cumulative raiding elsewhere frightened the citizens of Colorado. Most of the tribes in the vicinity admitted that the Lakotas were trying to unite them into attacking travelers on the Platte and Arkansas roads, and the local Cheyennes were restless. Territorial Govenor John Evans hoped to negotiate a new treaty placing them on a reservation, but they refused, saying they had been swindled out of enough land. Evans, who was looking for an excuse to seize what he could not obtain by treaty, was ready to believe that the Cheyennes were plotting with the Lakotas to clear the region of whites. Colonel John M. Chivington, commander of the Military District of Colorado, was prepared to agree. The Cheyennes themselves were divided. The militant Dog Soldier Society wanted war, but so far, a group of peace chiefs headed by Black Kettle maintained the upper hand (Hoig, 1961, 31–34).

In spring 1864, Indians ran off some cattle, and troops were ordered out on punitive expeditions. On 12 April, they clashed with a small band of Cheyennes, setting a new war into motion. A few weeks later, soldiers attacked and destroyed a Cheyenne camp in a canyon near Cedar Bluffs. A third fight occurred on 16 May, when a military detachment engaged Cheyennes about 4.5km (3 miles) from the Smoky Hill river, and the well-known peace chief Lean Bear was killed.

The local raids, combined with regular reports of Lakota depredations along the Platte road, created a panic in Colorado. Indians were not the only threat. Two years earlier, a Confederate advance on the territory had been thrown back, but many feared another attempt. As much as anything else, however, was the underlying fear of a general uprising that would turn Colorado into another Minnesota. To counter the supposed threat, Evans raised a regiment of 100-day volunteers, the Third Colorado Cavalry (54–55).

Among the Cheyennes, Black Kettle and the peace faction were no longer able to restrain the Dog Soldiers or the young warriors from raiding. Soon Lakotas, Arapahos, Kiowas, and Comanches joined. Most of the depredations were in Kansas or southern Nebraska, but there was a real possibility of their spreading into Colorado. As winter approached, however, the peace faction began reasserting itself, and on 28 September, Black Kettle and other

Cheyenne and Arapaho peace chiefs met with Evans and Chivington, and came away with the idea that if they settled in the vicinity of a military post, they would be safe. In November, Black Kettle and about 600 followers moved their camp to the Sand Creek valley, about 65km (40 miles) from Fort Lyon. Relations with the soldiers were good, and Black Kettle assumed he was safe.

Elsewhere, however, the men of the Third Colorado, recruited from the lower echelons of society, were complaining that they would not have a chance to kill Indians before their enlistments expired. Chivington led them to Sand Creek where, on 29 November, he deployed 700 men and four howitzers around the camp. Black Kettle ran up a US flag and a white flag over his tipi, but the soldiers charged. Chivington, who had remarked that he hoped to be "wading in gore," wanted no prisoners, and men, women, and children were killed indiscriminately. Children's brains were literally beaten out with guns. Men's testicles were removed to make pouches, pregnant women were ripped open, and women's pubic areas were "scalped." Black Kettle managed to escape, but some 200 – mostly women and children – were killed and mutilated. The Third Colorado returned triumphantly to Denver where 100 scalps were exhibited on the stage of the local theater (Hoig, 1961, United States Congress; Utley and Washburn, 234–35).

If the citizens of Denver were ready to greet Chivington as a conquering hero, others were not. Even in Colorado, there was enough outrage to reverberate to Washington, where the Joint Committee on the Conduct of the War launched an investigation. Although the committee's main purpose was to investigate the myriad blunders and accusations that arose from the Civil War, any military action during that period, including fighting, Indians was subject to inquiry. The final report assigned varying degrees of blame, but singled out one special villain. Chivington, the report said, wearing the uniform of the United States and with the honor of the nation in his trust, "deliberately planned and executed a foul and dastardly massacre which would have disgraced the veriest savage among those who were the victims of his cruelty." It concluded "for the purpose of vindicating the cause of justice and upholding the honor of the nation, prompt and energetic measures should be at once taken to remove from office those who have thus disgraced the government ... and to punish, as their crimes deserve, those who have been guilty of these brutal and cowardly acts." Due to a legal technicality, however, Chivington could only be censured, and no one ever came to trial (Hoig, *1961*, 165–69; United States Congress, V–VI).

Repercussions spread across the plains. The Southern tribes burned for revenge, and the Northern tribes were still smoldering over their conflicts with Sibley and Sully. Indians devastated the Platte valley, and on 26 July 1865, hundreds of warriors fell on the military post at the Upper Platte bridge, severely beating a cavalry detachment, and wiping out a supply train. In response, Sully and Brevet Major General Patrick E. Connor mounted a two-pronged expedition. Sully took his troops into Dakota Territory with little result, but Connor met with more success in Wyoming, carrying the war deep into Lakota country. Eventually, however, the campaign failed because of distance from support, unfamiliarity with the terrain, bitterly cold weather, and food shortages. The government directed that henceforth, efforts should be directed at defending the roads (Utley and Washburn, 235).

The Southern Plains 1861–77

As the Civil War drew to a close, an uneasy calm settled on the Southern Plains. Kit Carson's fight at Adobe Walls had shaken the Indians, who were not accustomed to the military being able to reach so deep into their territory. They asked for peace and, in response, the government appointed a treaty commission to meet with the Indians at the mouth of the Little Arkansas river, at the present site of Wichita, Kansas, in mid-October 1865. Although the Kiowas

attended, many Plains tribes, including powerful elements of the Southern Cheyennes, boycotted the council because of suspicion and outrage stemming from the Sand Creek Massacre. By 18 October, most of the leaders present signed (Mooney, 179–80).

The Kiowas agreed to a reservation south of the Arkansas river, with an agency at Fort Zarah, Kansas. Dohasen did much of the negotiating on their behalf, but it was increasingly obvious the old chief would not live much longer, and already factions were vying for leadership after his death. The main contenders were the powerful war chiefs Satanta and Lone Wolf. There was, however, a new contender, the younger chief Kicking Bird, who, although a valiant war leader, realized that the sheer demographic and technological superiority of the whites meant that they ultimately must prevail. Thus, while Satanta and Lone Wolf competed for leadership of the tribe as a whole, and the war faction in particular, Kicking Bird began forming a peace faction (Robinson, 1998, 43–44).

For the time being, at least, the Little Arkansas Treaty allowed travelers and freight to follow the Santa Fe Trail, the Smoky Hill road to Denver, and journey up the Platte without serious incident. Nevertheless, the region of the Smoky Hill and Republican rivers in western Kansas remained a trouble spot. The Cheyenne Dog Soldiers, who had boycotted the treaty council, resented the government's insistence that they give up their hunting grounds along the Smoky Hill. Even more ominous, the Red Cloud War, then being waged along the Bozeman Trail of Wyoming and Montana, was beginning to spill over into the Southern Plains. Already, there had been raids along the Republican river in Kansas, and the Cheyennes, though still peaceful, were restless. Major Henry Douglass, commander of Fort Dodge, advised his superior, Major General Winfield Scott Hancock, that large, well-armed bands of Sioux, Cheyennes and Arapahos were moving south, and he expected trouble (Leckie, 30 33).

In April 1867, Hancock went to Fort Larned, Kansas, where he met with four

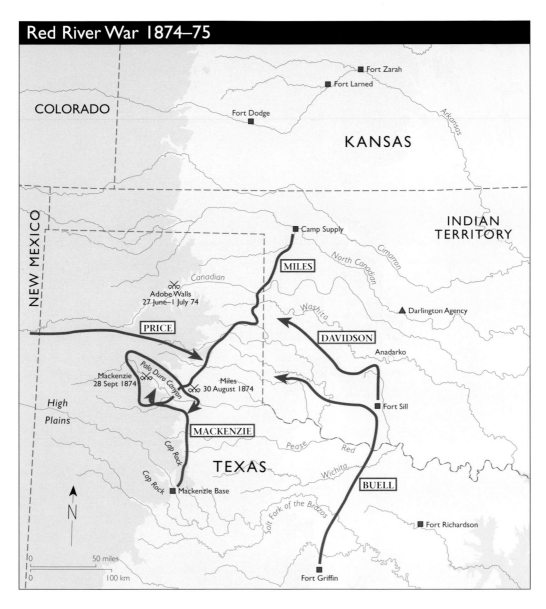

Red River War 1874–75

COLORADO

KANSAS

NEW MEXICO

INDIAN
TERRITORY

■ Fort Zarah

■ Fort Larned

Fort Dodge ■

Arkansas

■ Camp Supply

North Canadian

Cimarron

MILES

Canadian

Adobe Walls
27 June–1 July 74

Washita

▲ Darlington Agency

PRICE

DAVIDSON

Anadarko

Mackenzie
28 Sept 1874

Palo Duro Canyon

Miles
30 August 1874

■ Fort Sill

High
Plains

MACKENZIE

Pease

Red

Cap Rock

TEXAS

Wichita

Cap Rock

■ Mackenzie Base

BUELL

Salt Fork of the Brazos

■ Fort Richardson

N

0   50 miles
0   100 km

■ Fort Griffin

chiefs from a Cheyenne–Oglala camp about
45km (30 miles) away. Failing to bully them
into submission, he marched on the village
on 15 April. Fearing another massacre like
Sand Creek, the Indians fled, and Lieutenant
Colonel George Armstrong Custer took a
cavalry detachment in pursuit. It was
Custer's first Indian expedition. He noted
depredations along the Smoky Hill road, and
that many people had been killed. Although
Hancock had no evidence the same Indians
were involved, he ordered the camp
destroyed (Hancock).

Now he sent Custer to seek out and
destroy any hostile Indians, and Custer spent
the first half of the summer chasing them to
no avail. The only engagements of any real
significance were an attack on his supply
train, which was beaten back, and the
complete destruction of a 10-man detail
under Lieutenant Lyman S. Kidder. Ironically,
Kidder and his men were wiped out by
Oglalas under the chief Pawnee Killer,
who had spent the spring and summer
convincing Custer and Hancock of his
good will.

Major General Winfield Scott Hancock's troops, camp outside Fort Harker, Kansas, as they prepare for the first post-Civil War expedition against Southern Plains Indians in April 1867. The conflict, known as Hancock's War, proved farcical, and created more problems than it solved. (Kansas State Historical Society)

Hancock's War, as it came to be called, was the first concerted military action against Plains Indians after the Civil War. Its failure filled the various Sioux bands with contempt for the military, and convinced many erstwhile Cheyenne peace chiefs that they had no alternative but war (Robinson, 1993; Utley and Washburn, 241, 244).

The specter of new bloodshed in the wake of a bloody civil war prompted public pressure on the government to negotiate a solution. On 19 October 1867, a treaty council convened between representatives of the federal government and leaders of the major Southern Plains tribes at Medicine Lodge, Kansas. The commissioners tried to impress on the Indians that the advance of white civilization meant they would have to give up their warrior/hunter way of life, settle down, and become assimilated.

In the end, the Indians grudgingly agreed to the treaty. The Kiowas and Comanches would settle on a reservation near what would become Fort Sill, Oklahoma; the Caddoes, Wichitas, and affiliated tribes about 100km (60 miles) to the north at Anadarko; and the Southern Cheyennes and Arapahos farther north at what would become

Darlington. They would be allowed to hunt buffalo unmolested south of the Cimarron river, meanwhile establishing farms and permanent homes, and sending their children to government schools at the agencies. The government would provide rations to supplement the buffalo diet for an indefinite period until they were firmly established. How the government expected the Indians to make a 180-degree reversal of their ancient culture in only a few years was not explained (Robinson, 1998, Chapter 5).

Although many Indians attempted to congregate at the agencies, the government procrastinated in carrying out the treaty provisions. As the months passed, the Indians grew increasingly destitute and restless. In early 1868, the Kiowas and Comanches began plundering into Texas. Hancock's successor, Major General Philip H. Sheridan, hoped to alleviate some of the problem by issuing rations from army supplies, but these were limited, and congress still procrastinated, not authorizing an Indian appropriation until late July. By then, it was too late. A Cheyenne war party attacked their ancient enemies, the Kaw Indians, and ransacked a few settlers' houses in the process. Throughout the remainder of the summer, clashes between Indians and whites accelerated.

Cavalry detachments patrolled the region of the Saline, Solomon, and Smoky Hill rivers with little results, although after one fight, a troops expedition recovered two captive women. Sheridan instructed his aide, Major George A. (Sandy) Forsyth, to take Lieutenant F.H. Beecher, nephew of the renowned minister Henry Ward Beecher, and 50 handpicked frontiersmen and look for the Indians. Forsyth departed Fort Hays, Kansas, on 29 August. On the morning of 17 September, the expedition suddenly found itself confronted by hundreds of Cheyennes and Oglalas. Forsyth led the men to a small island in the Arickaree river, where they entrenched among the low trees and bushes.

For seven days the whites held off a siege, eating horse meat and drinking water scooped from the sand, until the Indians departed and a relief column arrived from Fort Wallace. The fight subsequently became known as Beecher's Island, after the lieutenant, who was mortally wounded. Forsyth lost five others and 15 wounded who

One of the last photographs of Lieutenant Colonel George Armstrong Custer, taken in the spring of 1876, shows him with the shorter hair he preferred later in life. In the field, Custer tended to keep his hair cut close to his scalp for ease of cleanliness. (Author's collection)

recovered, including himself. The Indians lost at least 32 killed, including the great Cheyenne chief Roman Nose, and many more wounded (Leckie, Chapter 3).

Forsyth's fight, and a futile Indian hunting expedition by Sully, convinced Sheridan to wage a winter campaign, when lack of forage for their ponies would pen the Indians into winter camps in river valleys. He planned to drive the tribes onto their reservations, and kill any that held back. To command his cavalry, he retrieved Custer from Michigan, where he was whiling away an enforced suspension under sentence of court-martial.

The Kiowas and Comanches sensed that something was afoot, and began moving in toward the agency at Fort Cobb, in southwestern Oklahoma, which was declared a refuge for non-hostile bands. General Sherman, however, had declared all Cheyennes and Arapahos collectively hostile, regardless of whether or not they had actively participated in depredations. When Black Kettle and several other Cheyenne peace chiefs tried to bring their bands to Fort Cobb, they were told to camp elsewhere until notified otherwise (Leckie, 88–92; Hoig, 1976, 73–74).

On Sunday, 22 November 1868, the Seventh Cavalry marched out of the military depot of Camp Supply in heavy wind and snow, provisioned for 30 days in the field. Four days later, an advance party sent word that it was following a large Indian trail. By late 27 November, scouts investigating the Washita river had found a Cheyenne camp under the hapless Black Kettle. The Seventh divided into four units, all of which hit camp simultaneously at dawn the following day. Within 10 minutes, the troops controlled the camp, and the warriors retreated among the trees and ravines to begin a return fire. The soldiers dismounted and moved against the Indian position for hand-to-hand fighting. This time, Black Kettle's luck ran out. He and his wife were killed as they crossed the river trying to escape. The fighting began to die down, and Major Joel Elliott took a detachment of 17 men to round up fleeing warriors (Hoig, 1976).

Custer's troops attack a Cheyenne village on the Washita river in Oklahoma in November 1868. Among the dead was the Cheyenne peace chief Black Kettle, who had survived the Sand Creek Massacre almost exactly four years earlier. (Author's collection)

About 10.00 am, large numbers of Indians counterattacked, and Custer realized this was one of several major camps along the river. Pickets ran in saying they had been driven from their positions, and a patrol was driven back by Arapahos. In the distance, they heard gunfire, but did not realize that Elliott's detachment was being massacred. Late afternoon, Custer ordered a withdrawal without bothering to check on Elliott's situation. Not until 10 December were the bodies discovered. Although extensive mop-up operations remained, the Winter Campaign had proven itself, and ultimately the Southern Plains Indians were driven into their agencies (Hoig, 1976, 134–40; Leckie, 133).

When President Grant implemented his Peace Policy late the following year, the Indians initially appeared cooperative, but their interest was short-lived. Already, in the spring of 1869, raiding parties were slipping into Texas, and that year would prove to be one of the bloodiest in the history of the state. In June, the Kiowas held their annual Sun Dance, which was attended by the Comanches, Kiowa-Apaches, and Southern Cheyennes. When it ended, raiders dispersed in all directions. The Cheyennes even attacked Camp Supply, and the Kiowas took 73 mules from the quartermaster's corral at newly established Fort Sill. In Texas, 15 people were killed in Jack County alone in a single month (Leckie, 136ff.).

The year 1870 was little better, and in 1871, the raiding began earlier than normal. On 18 May a band of about 150 Kiowas, Kiowa-Apaches, and Comanches attacked a wagon train carrying corn from Weatherford, Texas, to Fort Griffin. Seven teamsters were killed, and over 40 mules were driven off as plunder. (The incident is known to history as the Warren Wagon Train massacre, after the owner of the train, freight contractor Henry Warren of Weatherford). When the survivors reached Fort Richardson that night, they were personally interviewed by General Sherman, who was on an inspection tour of Texas, and had passed over the same spot only a day earlier. He dispatched Colonel Ranald Mackenzie and a detachment of Fourth Cavalry to hunt down the Indians.

A fanciful woodcut shows the death of teamster Samuel Elliott during the Warren Wagon Train Massacre. In reality, Elliott was not tied to a wheel, but was strapped to a wagon tongue and roasted over a fire. (Author's collection)

Continuing on to Fort Sill, Sherman learned that the raiders, who were attached to the agency, had arrived almost simultaneously, and Satanta had boasted about it to Agent Lawrie Tatum, naming himself, the old chief Satank, Eagle Heart, and Big Tree as leaders. Tatum requested the Indians be arrested and sent to Texas for trial, and Sherman was happy to comply. Although Eagle Heart managed to slip away, the others were arrested, and turned over to Mackenzie, who had followed them to Sill. As the troops prepared the Indians for the trip to Texas, Satank jumped a guard and was killed. Satanta and Big Tree were confined at Fort Richardson, and tried for seven counts of murder in civil court in adjacent Jacksboro. They were sentenced to death, but Govenor Edmund J. Davis, on advice of Tatum, commuted their sentences to life in prison as hostages for Kiowa good behavior (Robinson, 1997). This infuriated Sherman, who remarked, "Satanta ought to have been

hung and that would have ended the trouble ..." (Quoted in Nye, 147).

Despite Tatum's hopes, the effect was only marginal. The Quahadi Comanches, under Cynthia Ann Parker's son, Quanah, continued to raid. Meanwhile, the imprisonment of Satanta and Big Tree had cost the Kiowa war faction prestige, and the war chiefs were out to regain it with new depredations. Although Mackenzie led campaigns during the summer and fall of 1871, he failed to suppress the Indians, and in 1872, the raids grew worse. In April, Kiowas attacked a wagon train at Howard's Wells in west Texas. Seventeen teamsters were killed, and the train was plundered (Nye, 152–54). On 22 June, Mackenzie reported, "There have been more depredations lately than ever before – four murders in the last week that are really true and since [then], nine more reported, of the truth of which I am not yet convinced" (United States Department of War, Office of the Adjutant General, record group 391).

On 29 September, however, Mackenzie captured a major Comanche camp on the North Fork of the Red river, destroying 262 lodges, and taking over 120 women, children,

Colonel Ranald S. Mackenzie was beset by bouts of insanity that eventually forced him out of the army. Nevertheless, he built the Fourth Cavalry into a first rate mobile assault force, and was victorious in both the Red River War and the Great Sioux War. (Author's collection)

Lone Wolf was one of the heads of the Kiowa war faction, and a leader in the Red River War of 1874–75. (Oklahoma State Historical Society)

and wounded as prisoners. They were interned at Fort Concho as hostages for the release of white captives. This was a shock for the Indians, who were not accustomed to having to bargain for the release of their own people. The raiding essentially ceased as they pondered their next move. The Kiowas, meanwhile, had settled down, because some of their chiefs had recently traveled to Washington and seen first hand the real power of the government. In consequence, the Friends Committee, the Quaker organization that supervised the agencies in Kansas and the Indian Territory, were advocating the release of Satanta and Big Tree as both reward and incentive to good behavior, and the Comanche captives became part of the bargain.

Eventually, the Fort Concho prisoners were released to their people. After some

argument, Govenor Davis agreed in 1873 to parole Satanta and Big Tree, subject to stringent conditions of enforcement by the federal government (Robinson, 1997).

Prison had taken much of the fight out of Satanta, and the much younger Big Tree had quickly grasped the reality of the situation. Even the militants, like Lone Wolf, had begun to settle. The Comanches, however, resumed raiding, and on 30 November, James Haworth, who had succeeded Lawrie Tatum as agent, was told to withhold rations. The decision angered those who were not involved, and was made worse when the government rescinded the order. Contemptuous of the vacillation, the Comanches resumed their raiding, joined by young Kiowa warriors (Leckie, 181–82).

Even when issued, the rations were not adequate because the amounts had been predicated on the idea that the Indians would continue hunting buffalo for subsistence. In 1870, however, buffalo hides suddenly became valuable when a means was found to tan them for industrial leather. A skilled buffalo hunter could make substantially more than an eastern factory worker could, and in considerably less time, and soon the plains echoed with the booming of heavy-caliber rifles. Within three years, the buffalo were virtually exterminated north of the Cimarron River in Oklahoma, and the hide hunters moved south, deep into the Indian Territory and Texas, into the region that the Indians considered their exclusive hunting domain.

Besides buffalo, the Cheyennes and Arapahos were losing livestock to white horse and cattle thieves, who were raiding the herds and driving them into Kansas. Whiskey peddlers took advantage of the desperation, and alcoholism was becoming chronic. The breaking point came in

Hunters skin a buffalo near what is now Abilene, Texas, in 1874. The market for buffalo hides led to massive slaughter in the early 1870s, and was a major cause of the Red River War. (Texas State Library and Archives)

May 1874, when white raiders stole 43 ponies. A pursuit party of warriors attempted to recover them, but failing, ran off a herd of cattle near the Kansas line, where they clashed with federal cavalry. Fighting broke out in Kansas and the Indian Territory, and Indians began attacking buffalo hunters in northernmost Texas.

Raiding into Texas was increasingly dangerous. Mackenzie's highly mobile and skilled Fourth Cavalry had set the standard, and the departmental commander, Brigadier General Christopher C. Augur, kept scouting expeditions more or less constantly in the field. In his report for the period of 30 September 1873 to 28 September 1874, General Augur reported that although 60 citizens had been killed by Indians, 32 warriors were also known to have been killed, a heavy loss by Indian standards. Lone Wolf's son had been killed in one such raid, and the old war chief brooded over it throughout the winter and spring. On 1 May 1874, he joined a raiding party that went south to recover his son's body and devastate the Texas frontier (Leckie, 185ff.; Wallace, 103–04).

Among the normally secular, pragmatic Comanches, the desperation was such that a prophet appeared among their ranks for perhaps the only time in recorded history. His name was Isa-tai, and although a young man, barely out of his teens and unproven in battle, people were ready to believe his claim that he could vomit forth bullets by the wagon load. He had lost a favorite uncle during a raid in Texas, and burned for vengeance. Among his early converts was Quanah Parker. In May, Isa-tai organized a Sun Dance, common enough among other Plains tribes, but totally alien to Comanche culture. He used the gathering to reinforce his power as a messiah, and to whip up enthusiasm for war. Before the ritual was finished, Quanah had devised a plan that other chiefs approved. They would destroy a buffalo hunter settlement at Adobe Walls, near the site of Kit Carson's fight with the Kiowas 10 years earlier (Haley, 52–55).

At dawn on 27 June, the Indians gathered on the ridges overlooking Adobe Walls, whose total population was 28 men and one woman, all hunters or suppliers. The men, however, had been up since 2.00 am, shoring up the heavy sod roof of one of the buildings where they slept. Thus, when the Indians swept down, all but two managed to reach the safety of the buildings alive. The initial assault was driven back by the deadly fire of the hunters with their heavy buffalo rifles. The Indians then settled down for a siege, but by mid-afternoon, discouraged by mounting losses, they withdrew. Three hunters were killed, and 13 Indian bodies were found (Leckie, 191–93).

The Comanches and Cheyennes were ready for war, but to mount it on the scale they desired, they needed the Kiowas. Lone Wolf advocated war, but was opposed by Kicking Bird and the powerful peace faction. Many Kiowas waited to see which group would prevail. One by one, the leading chiefs and medicine men opted for peace, and the war faction collapsed. Kicking Bird led three-quarters of the Kiowa nation to Fort Sill to enroll as neutrals, leaving Lone Wolf and his supporters to do as they pleased (Robinson, 1997, 170–71).

Sheridan, who now commanded the Military Division of the Missouri encompassing the entire plains region, ordered five columns of troops to converge on the region where the hostiles were active. (Sheridan had been promoted to Lieutenant General in keeping with his new responsibilities). Colonel Nelson A. Miles would move south from Kansas with cavalry and infantry; Major William R. Price east from New Mexico with cavalry; Mackenzie northward, and Col. George Buell northwest into the high plains of Texas, with cavalry; and Lt. John W. Davidson west from Fort Sill. The Indians would be run down and battered back and forth between the military columns until subdued (Haley, 105).

At Darlington, little more than 10 percent of the Cheyennes remained on the reservation, and the situation was so tense

A self-made soldier, Colonel Nelson A. Miles was a martinet in his own right, but with little regard for the army and its formalities. In later life, he was the last general-in-chief of the army before the position was abolished in favor of an army chief of staff. (Little Bighorn Battlefield National Monument)

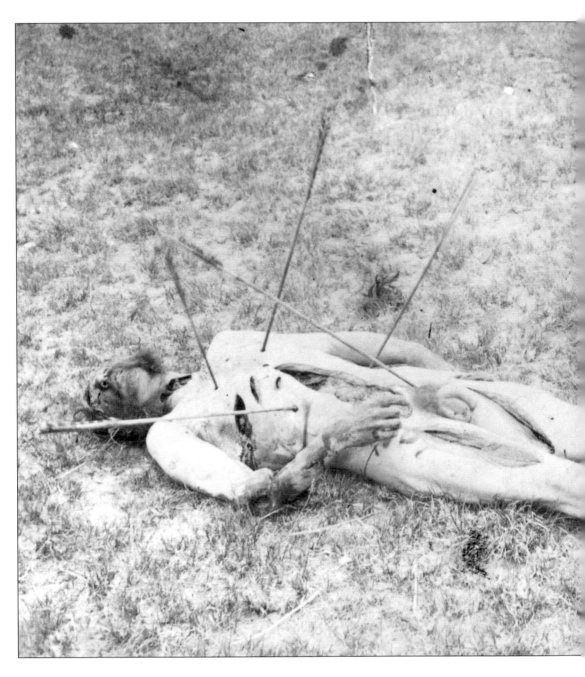

that the agent asked for military protection. A company arrived simultaneously with several bands of Comanches, and Lone Wolf's Kiowas were also known to be in the vicinity. The commander, Captain Gaines Lawson, requested reinforcements, and Colonel Davidson brought four companies of cavalry. Although the Comanches initially intended to surrender, Lone Wolf's arrival initiated fighting, and eventually the Indians scattered out onto the plains (Leckie, 200–04).

From the north, Miles' infantry marched into Texas, where they struck a large Indian trail that led an advance unit into a Cheyenne ambush along Prairie Dog Fork of the Red river. When the main body of troops arrived, the Cheyennes broke and fled, and a

A victim of Hancock's War, the mutilated body of Sergeant Fred Wyllyams lies dead on the Kansas Plains in 1867. Indians mutilated the bodies of their enemies in the belief that their souls likewise would be crippled, thus negating their fighting ability in the afterlife. They did not always wait until the victim was dead, however, and many soldiers set aside one bullet for suicide if capture became inevitable. (Kansas State Historical Society)

that no Indian could have slipped past Miles. The mutilated bodies of the party were found later, prompting General Augur's acid comment, "A Commander against hostile Indians is never in such imminent danger as when fully satisfied that no Indians can possibly be near him" (Haley; quoted in Wallace, 81).

The Indians suffered one of their most crushing blows early 28 September, when Mackenzie's cavalry, leading horses down a cliff-face in near darkness, attacked a string of winter camps in Palo Duro Canyon. Although most of the Indians managed to escape, the camps with their stores, and more than 1,000 captured ponies were destroyed. The Indians, now dismounted and destitute, slowly began drifting back to the agencies to surrender. Satanta turned himself in at Darlington on 4 October. Although here is no evidence that he personally took part in any hostilities, he admitted to being at the Wichita Agency when fighting broke out, and had associated with hostile leaders. These were deemed parole violations, and he was returned to prison where he committed suicide four years later (Wallace, 124–27; Robinson, 1998, 188–92).

There was never any question of the outcome of the Red River War. Although the region was brutally hot, and water a constant issue (at one point Miles' men opened the veins of their arms to suck the blood and reduce the swelling of their tongues), the troops still had adequate mobility, along with overwhelming numerical superiority. Much of the region was heavily settled, and the soldiers were never critically far from support. There were few obstacles that the military could not overcome. The Indians, on the other hand, were never completely organized, and without the support of the majority of

running fight ensued for about 32km (20 miles) before the Indians managed to vanish among the canyons leading up to the high plains. Miles' presence in Texas, however, left too few troops to defend southern Kansas, and the Indians raided with virtual impunity. He was also overconfident. When a surveying party asked for military protection, it was refused on the grounds

the Kiowas, their fighting ability was limited. By 2 June 1875, when Quanah Parker's surrender officially ended the war, the leading chiefs had already been transported to Fort Marion, Florida, where they were interned for four years. Mop-up operations continued against small, isolated bands for another couple of years, but the 150-year conflict in the Southern Plains essentially had ended.

The Northern Plains 1861–77

The Northern Plains provided a totally different scenario. Much of the region was unsettled and, to a large extent, unknown. Military expeditions might range hundreds of miles from support. In winter, snow blocked travel over the open country, and in summer, temperatures could soar to over 100 degrees.

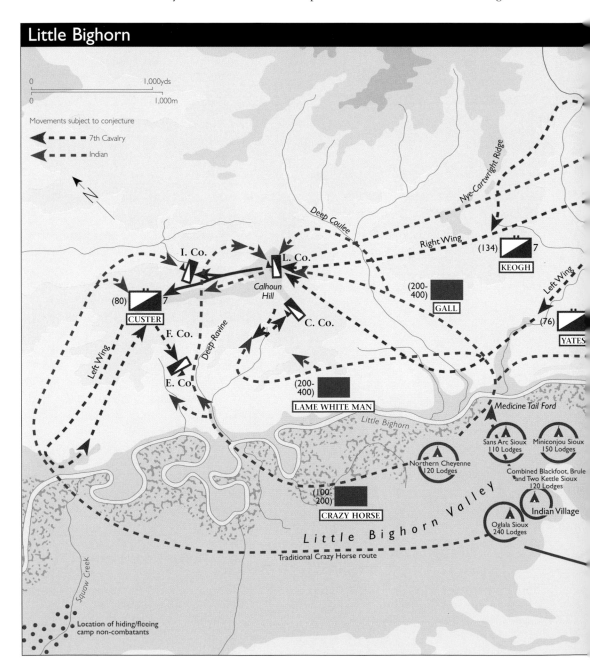

Little Bighorn

The Indian tribes were powerful, militant, and, in the case of the Lakotas, could count their warriors in the thousands. It is significant that the greatest "massacres" of entire military units occurred in this region.

In 1865, while government commissioners negotiated what they thought were peace treaties with the Upper Missouri tribes, the bulk of the Lakota fighting power was in the Powder river country of Wyoming, celebrating its latest round of victories against the whites. In June 1866, their leaders finally appeared at Fort Laramie, but when they heard the government wanted roads across their country, they balked. A gold strike in western Montana in 1862 had led to the establishment of a government road, better

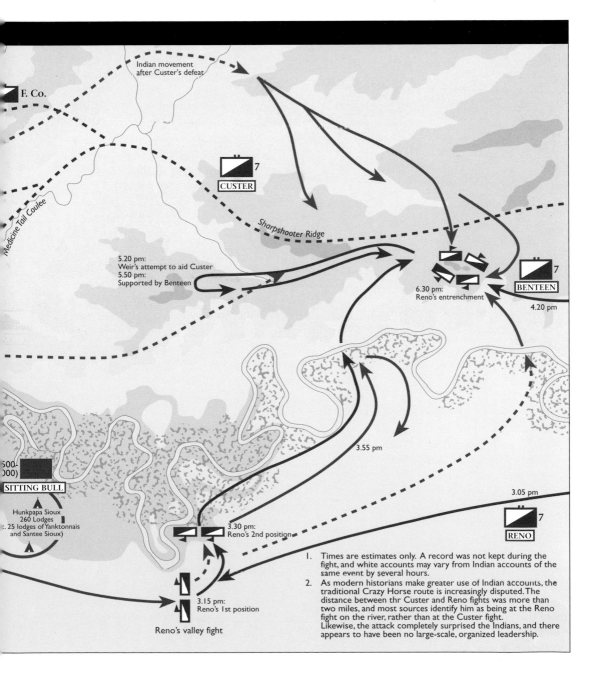

Indian movement after Custer's defeat

F. Co.

7
CUSTER

Medicine Tail Coulee

Sharpshooter Ridge

5.20 pm:
Weir's attempt to aid Custer
5.50 pm:
Supported by Benteen

6.30 pm:
Reno's entrenchment

7
BENTEEN

4.20 pm

3.55 pm

3.05 pm

500-
000)

SITTING BULL

Hunkpapa Sioux
260 Lodges
c. 25 lodges of Yanktonnais
and Santee Sioux)

3.30 pm:
Reno's 2nd position

7
RENO

1. Times are estimates only. A record was not kept during the fight, and white accounts may vary from Indian accounts of the same event by several hours.
2. As modern historians make greater use of Indian accounts, the traditional Crazy Horse route is increasingly disputed. The distance between thr Custer and Reno fights was more than two miles, and most sources identify him as being at the Reno fight on the river, rather than at the Custer fight.
    Likewise, the attack completely surprised the Indians, and there appears to have been no large-scale, organized leadership.

3.15 pm:
Reno's 1st position

Reno's valley fight

The Oglala chief Red Cloud fought the government to stand during the Red Cloud War of 1866–68. Although he sympathized with the hostilities during the subsequent Great Sioux War, he stayed out of the conflict. He remained a powerful force among the Lakota Sioux until his death in 1909. (Little Bighorn Battlefield National Monument)

known as the Bozeman Trail, from Fort Laramie to Montana, and the extensive travel on that road was a sore point. Not only were they determined to keep any new roads from being built, they also wanted the Bozeman closed. At a critical moment, a large number of new troops appeared, and the influential chiefs Red Cloud and Man Afraid of His Horses, suspecting a trick, departed with their followers. Discussions with the hostile Lakota bands collapsed (Hyde, 1987a, 137–39).

The arrival of these troops was nothing more than unlucky coincidence. Their leader, Colonel Henry B. Carrington, had been appointed commander of a military district to

guard the Bozeman Trail. With his troops, he was to garrison General Connor's post of Fort Reno, and construct two new forts, designated as Phil Kearny and C.F. Smith, farther up the trail. It was a sign of the government's post-Civil War economy that Carrington had only 700 infantrymen and a handful of cavalry to maintain order in a region where Connor had been given 3,000 cavalry.

Red Cloud was determined not to allow the military into the area. On 17 July 1866, Indians infiltrated a picket line at the Fort Phil Kearny construction site, and stampeded the horses. Luring a pursuit party beyond immediate support, they turned on it, and the soldiers barely escaped annihilation. En route back to the fort, they came upon a trader's wagon with six dead and mutilated white men. This inaugurated what became known to history as the Red Cloud War (Hyde, 1987a, 139–40; Brown, 77–78).

Throughout the summer and fall, Carrington sent messages to his superiors asking for cavalry. Meanwhile, depredations continued and the cemetery at Fort Phil Kearny began to fill even as the buildings were being constructed. Red Cloud had rallied his own Oglalas, together with Hunkapaps, Brulés, Miniconjous, Cheyennes, Arapahos, and Gros Ventres.

On 3 November, cavalrymen arrived, among them Captain William J. Fetterman, an ambitious young officer with an enviable combat record in the Civil War. Like many such officers, however, he was contemptuous of Indians, and bragged that with 80 men he could subdue the entire Sioux nation.

For defensive purposes, Fort Phil Kearny was built on an open plain. Wood for construction was provided from a heavily guarded saw mill several miles away. The most vulnerable point was the wood train carrying lumber to the fort from the mill. The train had been attacked several times, and Carrington determined that the Indians hoped to lead a relief column away from support and massacre it. On 21 December, the train again was attacked. Fetterman demanded that he lead the relief column, and Carrington ordered him to rescue the

Members of the Fort Laramie Treaty Commission pose with a Lakota woman during negotiations in 1868. Among the key members were (from left to left center), Brigadier General Alfred H. Terry, commander of the Department of Dakota; Brigadier General William Harney, an experienced Plains Indian fighter; and Lieutenant General W. T. Sherman who, the following year, became general-in-chief of the army. (Little Bighorn Battlefield National Monument)

train and return immediately. Instead, Fetterman chased the Indians several miles beyond a line of hills. There, he found himself surrounded by masses of warriors who massacred the entire column. By coincidence, it consisted of 80 men (Brown).

The Red Cloud War lasted another 18 months. Again, however, the government was unwilling to undertake a major Indian campaign so close to the end of the Civil War. Consequently, a treaty commission met with Red Cloud and other chiefs at Fort Laramie in 1868, and negotiated a treaty that effectively ended the Sioux Wars for the time being. The Indians were given a massive reservation encompassing the entire western half of the modern state of South Dakota, including the Black Hills. Northeastern Wyoming and southeastern Montana were designated unceded Indian lands off the reservation, where they might roam as they pleased. Except for necessary government military, civil, and scientific expeditions, no outsider would be permitted on the reservation or the unceded lands without joint permission of the Indians and the

government. The Bozeman Trail would be closed, and Forts Reno, Phil Kearny, and C.F. Smith would be abandoned. Finally, the government would provide annuities, rations, job training, and schools (DeLand, 15:125–27; Lazarus, 433ff.).

For a while, the treaty appeared workable. However, the completion of the first transcontinental railroad in 1869 opened up the plains, and initiated a railroad construction boom. Other lines began moving across the region, through Kansas and the Dakotas, stirring resentment among the tribes. Surveying crews laying out the routes required military protection. Rations and annuities were often late, and the Indians on the reservation began to

Custer's two-mile wagon train passes through Castle Creek Valley during the 1874 Black Hills Expedition. Custer confirmed the existence of gold in the hills, initiating a rush that led to the Great Sioux War of 1875–76. (Little Bighorn Battlefield National Monument)

suffer. Resistance centered around the Hunkpapa chief Sitting Bull, who refused to accept the treaty, and remained in the unceded lands, encouraging others to leave the reservation and join him.

In 1874, Custer led a surveying expedition into the Black Hills that confirmed the existence of gold. This information arrived in the east at a time of severe economic depression, and soon the hills were flooded with miners and prospectors. This was in clear violation of the Fort Laramie Treaty, and

that all Indians would have to be within their reservations on or before 31 January 1876, or be declared hostile. The deadline came and went, and on 1 February, the matter was turned over to the War Department.

General Sheridan believed that a winter campaign involving a three-pronged attack, similar to the tactics on the Southern Plains, would be effective against the Northern tribes. Accordingly, he notified the two generals in whose jurisdictions the war would be waged, Crook in the Department of the Platte in Omaha, Nebraska, and Alfred Terry of the Department of Dakota in St. Paul, Minnesota. A column of Crook's troops would more north from Wyoming, while one column of Terry's would move east from western Montana, and a second column from Terry would move west from Dakota. The three columns would batter the Indians back and forth between them, and force them onto the reservations. Colonel John Gibbon was designated to lead the Montana column, while Custer would lead the Dakota column. Crook would make his own arrangements, but given his preference for field service, it was presumed he would have a heavier hand in the Wyoming column than Terry would have in his.

Unfamiliar with the northern climate, Sheridan did not realize until too late that it would be well into spring before either Gibbon or Custer could move. Crook, meanwhile, went to Wyoming, where he began to organize his troops. Nominal command of the expedition fell to Colonel Joseph J. Reynolds, with Crook along as an "observer." Nevertheless, there was little question in anyone's mind that Crook was actually in charge, and this seriously undermined Reynolds' position.

The result was a fiasco. Reynolds attacked a village, which Crook insisted to his dying day belonged to Crazy Horse, but in fact was a Cheyenne village. The attack itself was bungled so badly that Crook, looking for scapegoats, court-martialed Reynolds and two other officers. The Cheyennes, who until now considered the war a Lakota problem, turned hostile. Together with Crazy Horse's Oglalas,

when the military proved inadequate for the task of eviction, the Indians took matters into their own hands and began attacking the intruders. The government then attempted to buy the hills from the Indians, and failing that, to lease them. But when the Indians refused to agree to either, it became obvious the hills would have to be taken by force. On 6 December 1875, Indian agents were directed

they combined with Sitting Bull's Hunkpapas in a massive, constantly moving Indian camp. In Montana, Gibbon's column finally got under way in late March. Twice his scouts found the giant camp and, each time, Gibbon did nothing. Not until 17 May did the Dakota column get moving, and then with General Terry in charge. Custer was relegated to a subordinate role, because earlier in the year, he had publicly humiliated President Grant, and only Terry's intervention saved his career.

On 28 May, Crook took to the field again. Establishing a base camp at Goose Creek, in the foothills of the Bighorn Mountains, he hunted and fished, waiting for the Crow and Shoshone Indian scouts that finally joined him in mid-June. At 5.00 am, 16 June, the column moved north again (Robinson, 2001, Chapter 10). One officer, however, commented, "I did not think that General

Last Stand Hill at Little Bighorn Battlefield National Monument is dotted with white government markers approximating where the bodies of Custer and his immediate command were found. The large shaft on the crest marks the mass grave of soldiers after they were removed from makeshift graves and reinterred. (Author's collection)

Crook knew where [the hostile Indians] were, and I did not think our friendly Indians knew where they were, and no one conceived we would find them in the great force we did" (Mills, 398).

The next morning, during a break in the march for coffee along the Rosebud River, Crook's Indian scouts prowling the hills collided with hunters from the vast hostile camp that now was just a few miles away. Crook's scouts hurried back to the soldiers, followed by masses of hostiles. The ensuing battle lasted several hours, as the hostiles tried to draw the individual companies of soldiers into the hills, cut them off, and destroy them piecemeal. Finally, as their losses mounted, they broke off and returned to their camp, leaving Crook in possession of the battlefield, but so badly mauled that he had no choice but to withdraw back into Wyoming. Although he claimed victory until he died, in fact, he had barely averted disaster. The Indians, meanwhile, broke camp and began moving toward the Little Bighorn river (Robinson, 2001, 182–84).

Meanwhile, on the Yellowstone, Terry's forces had finally linked with Gibbon's.

to fight, the two converging columns would block a successful retreat and bring them under control (Terry, 4).

The Seventh departed about noon 22 June, moving down along the Rosebud. Over the next two days, the column found signs of the great Indian camp. At dusk on 24 June, Lieutenant Charles Varnum took some of the Crow Indian scouts to a height overlooking the Little Bighorn Valley, and saw the camp some 30km (18 miles) away along the Little Bighorn. Custer got his men moving again. He hoped to conceal them in the hills dividing the Rosebud and Little Bighorn valleys, rest them, scout the Indian camp, and then attack at dawn, 26 June.

At daylight, Sunday, 25 June, he ordered a halt for coffee, while he joined Varnum and the scouts on the height. As they pointed out the camp, they also noticed Indians from the village watching them. Custer decided to attack immediately. Moving his troops into the Little Bighorn Valley, he divided them into three battalions, sending one under Captain Frederick W. Benteen up the valley to cut off retreat, and one, under Reno, across the river to attack the village from the front. He would follow the ridges and hit from the rear.

After a forced march over rough terrain, Reno charged the village shortly before 3.00 pm. Before reaching it, however, his exhausted, thirsty horses became unmanageable, forcing him to dismount and form a line. Taken by surprise, the Indians quickly recovered and organized a counterattack, and Reno was forced back into some timber near the river. As the hostiles began moving in among the trees, he realized he was vulnerable, and organized a retreat across the river and up into the ridges. The retreat fell apart at the riverbank. Hostile Indians moved in among the soldiers, cutting them into small groups, knocking them from their horses and killing

On 16 June, a scouting detail of six companies of Seventh Cavalry under Major Marcus A. Reno found one of the campsites of the giant village, and soon located the trail. The next day, they followed the trail up the Rosebud, unaware of the battle Crook was then fighting 100km (60 miles) upriver. Finally, Reno turned back toward the Yellowstone, reporting the information to Terry on 20 June. Terry decided to send Custer with the cavalry to circle around and press the Indians from the south, while Gibbon's infantry pressured them from the north. Thus if one column actually became embroiled in a fight, the other would be close enough to assist – assuming, of course, that Custer would allow the infantry time to get into position. If the Indians decided not

Only six months after the Custer disaster at Little Bighorn,
Frederick Whittaker published a highly romanticized
biography of his former Union Army commander that
served as the basis for much of the Custer mystique. This
illustration from the book was one of the first to depict
the so-called "Last Stand," but like so many of the era, is
totally imaginary. (Author's collection)

them. Reno managed to reach the top of a
ridge with the remnants of his battered
command, where he found a natural
depression to serve as a makeshift fort.

Benteen, meanwhile, determined that he
was on a fool's errand. Receiving a message

Reno rather than continuing on to Custer. Together the two officers began building a defense (Overfield, 40–41).

Custer was unaware of what had befallen Reno. The last thing he had seen was Reno charging across the plain toward the village. A short time later he sent a courier to Benteen with a message to join him with the ammunition packs. Then, after a probe at the center of the village, he returned to the ridges, leaving three companies under Captain Myles Keogh overlooking the village near that point, while Captain George W. Yates took two companies to the far end. Custer set up headquarters on a rise between the two groups.

The first attack came against Keogh's line, which appears to have collapsed. Yates placed one of his companies in line, and detached the other to support Keogh. Then his line collapsed, and the Indians moved in among the troopers with knives, hatchets, and clubs. The survivors gathered on the rise around Custer, where the officers seemed to have restored some sort of order. By then, however, it was too late. The five companies were annihilated.

Several miles upriver, Reno's men dug in. Sniping continued until nightfall, and throughout the next day. Late Monday, the Indians finally broke camp, separated into individual bands, and began moving out of the valley. On Tuesday, 27 June, Gibbon's column, accompanied by General Terry, found the bodies of Custer's troops, and rescued Reno's beleaguered command. (The disaster at the Little Bighorn is one of the most heavily discussed subjects. Among the many recent works are Fox; Gray; Robinson, 1995; Sklenar; and Utley, 1988).

News of the disaster arrived in the East amid the celebration of the nation's centennial. It cast a pall of gloom over the celebration, created a furor, and the public demanded vengeance. On Sheridan's orders, Miles and Mackenzie were transferred north with their regiments. The government authorized the construction of two new military posts, and the army was expanded. Sherman instructed Sheridan to remove the

from Custer to return to the main column with the ammunition packs, he turned about and arrived at the river just as Reno's men were fleeing up on the ridge. Believing that his own inexperienced troops would have no chance against so many warriors, he consolidated with

The powerful Brulé Lakota chief Spotted Tail grudgingly supported the government during the Great Sioux War of 1876–77. Appointed head chief of all the Sioux, he held that position until his assassination during a tribal political dispute in 1881. (Smithsonian Institute)

agents of Red Cloud and Spotted Tail, and replace them with local military commanders. Food and equipment could only be issued to Indians actually present for roll call, and any that were either absent or subsequently left would be treated as enemies. "We must not have another massacre like Custer[']s," Sherman said, "and Congress is now in session willing to give us all we want" (United States Department of War, record group 393, Special File, Sioux War).

There was one bit of good news. The Fifth Cavalry under its new commander, Colonel Wesley Merritt, was marching to join Crook when it encountered a large hostile band at Warbonnet Creek, Nebraska, on 16 July. The Indians were beaten and scattered. Although the fight was little more than a skirmish, it was the first real victory of the war and,

coming on the heels of the Custer debacle, gave public morale a much-needed boost (Robinson, 1995, Chapter 22).

After spending much of the summer since the Rosebud fight hunting and fishing at Goose Creek, Crook finally broke camp on 5 August, and headed north with almost 2,000 men. To move rapidly, they left their wagons, bedding, baggage, and all but the most basic food and equipment. Despite the time of year, an early winter was setting in. The temperature dropped alarmingly, and rain was almost continuous. The troops were cold, wet, and hungry. Five days later, they linked with Terry, and the two columns followed the Indian trail from the Rosebud over to the Tongue river. As time passed, it grew increasingly obvious that almost 5,000 men commanded by two brigadier-generals would never catch roaming bands of Indians. Crook's horses were giving out, and many of the cavalry had to lead them on foot through the mud. Although Terry's men were well provisioned, Crook's rations were reduced to sugar, bacon, and hardtack, and men had only enough coffee to brew one cup at a time (King, 18 August 1876; Finerty, 255–56; Robinson, 1995, 237–38).

On 24 August, the command reached the Yellowstone, where Crook replenished from steamboats that supplied Terry. Then he struck out on his own, on an ordeal known to history as the Horse Meat or Starvation March. By the time he had reached the Heart River, 320km (200 miles) north of the Black Hills, he could feed his troops only two more days on half-rations. Nevertheless, he opted to march to the Black Hills, where he believed the settlements were threatened with attack.

The rain continued. Mud balled up around the hooves of the horses and mules, damaging their feet. Every time an infantryman took a step, several pounds of muck stuck to his shoes. One of Crook's aides, Lieutenant Walter S. Schuyler, wrote to his father, "I have seen men become so exhausted that they were actually insane, but there was no way of carrying them, except for some mounted officer or man to give

This drawing of Crook's fight at the Rosebud is romanticized, but nevertheless shows the desperate nature of the struggle, which nearly resulted in Crook's annihilation. These same Indians destroyed Custer only eight days later. (Author's collection)

them his own horse ... I saw men who were very plucky, sit down and cry like children because they could not hold out." As for meals, he said, "water and tightened belts" (Schuyler, 1 November 1876, 87).

Worn-out horses and mules were shot and butchered for food. On 7 September, Crook ordered Captain Anson Mills to take 150 men and escort the Commissary Department to the Black Hills settlements. Mills departed that evening. As Crook resumed the march the next morning, a courier arrived with the message that Mills had engaged a large village at Slim Buttes. When he arrived, he found Mills' troops had taken the village and driven the Indians down into a ravine, where many more were killed. The men resupplied from Indian provisions, which would ration them for another two days, and destroyed the village. On 13 September, the exhausted, hungry command collapsed near Bear Butte, not far from Deadwood, and

soon, wagons loaded with food were rumbling in (Robinson, 2001, 192–97).

Although Crook's men were suffering, the Indians were even worse off. The constant pressure from the soldiers forced them to keep moving, and stay close to their camps. They were unable to hunt and lay in supplies of food for winter, and their own ponies began to starve. Many realized their situation was hopeless, and started back toward the reservations (Neihardt, 134).

At the agencies, meanwhile, the Indians were placed under military rule. On 15 August, congress approved an ultimatum that forced them to surrender the unceded lands of Montana and Wyoming, as well as the entire Great Sioux Reservation west of the 103rd meridian, which included the Black Hills. They would receive no further rations until they agreed. They were also expected to draw rations on the Missouri River, where they would be controlled, and to become self-supporting by white standards. In other words, they would surrender or starve (Gray, 260–62).

Although Red Cloud did not openly join the hostiles, he was sympathetic. He and another chief, Red Leaf, took their bands and

LEFT (BOTH) Crook's horsemeat march. (US Military
Academy Library, West Point, New York)

moved to Chadron Creek, about 32km
(20 miles) northeast of Camp Robinson.
Determined to make an example of Red
Cloud, Mackenzie's men surrounded their
camps, and marched them to Camp
Robinson, where they were disarmed and
unhorsed. Then Crook formally deposed Red
Cloud as head chief of the Lakotas, and
appointed Spotted Tail in his place
(Robinson, 1995, 264–67).

Crook organized yet another expedition,
with the cavalry arm commanded by
Mackenzie, and the infantry by Lieutenant
Colonel Richard Irving Dodge. On
25 November 1876, five months to the day
after the Little Bighorn, Mackenzie's troops
attacked a major Cheyenne village on the
Red Fork of the Powder river. After hard
fighting, the Indians retreated into the
surrounding hills, leaving the soldiers in
possession of the camp, where many
souvenirs of the Little Bighorn were found.
The lodges and winter stores were destroyed,
leaving the Cheyennes completely destitute
and effectively knocking them out of the war
(Robinson, 1995, 296–301).

In Terry's department, meanwhile,
conduct of the war now was left exclusively
to Miles. Despite the problems other officers
experienced during the previous winter, he
was determined that "if the Indians could
live in that country in skin tents in winter ...
we, with all our better appliances could
be so equipped not only to exist in tents,
but also to move under all circumstances."
Accordingly, he planned carefully, and

Crook's horsemeat march. (US Military Academy Library,
West Point, New York)

requisitioned adequate equipment to chase the Indians down regardless of season or weather (Miles, 1:218–19).

Miles' main opponent was Sitting Bull, whose disillusioned chiefs were growing tired of the war. After an abortive attack on a government wagon train, Sitting Bull met with Miles on 21 October. Nothing was settled, but Miles' knowledge of Sitting Bull's plans, obtained through Indian spies, unnerved the chief. The two met again the following day, and Miles gave Sitting Bull an ultimatum: he could return to his camp unmolested, but if he had not submitted to the government in 15 minutes, the troops would open fire. As the Indians withdrew, they set fire to the grass to cover their movements. Miles sent scouts to stop them, and fighting began. After outflanking the Indians, the infantry formed into classic squares, forcing the Indians out on a plain where artillery opened up. Finally the Indians retreated and the soldiers went into camp, although sniping continued back and forth all night (Miles, 1:121ff.; Greene, 83ff.).

For many of the chiefs in Sitting Bull's camp, this was enough. They broke away, and began heading to the agencies and military posts to surrender. Sitting Bull and about 400 followers started north, eventually seeking refuge in Canada.

With Sitting Bull neutralized, Miles turned his attention to Crazy Horse. On 7–8 January 1877, his soldiers attacked Crazy Horse's camp at Wolf Mountain in southern Montana. The second day of the fight, the Indians took refuge among the bluffs, forcing the infantry to charge. Hand-to-hand fighting ensued, just as a blizzard blew in which, according to Miles, "added an inexpressible weirdness to the scene." With resistance effectively smashed, he started his troops back north, to get them into the shelter of their post (Miles, 1:238).

Throughout the spring, Indians sought out the officers they felt would give them the best terms for surrender. Miles, a self-made soldier who disdained the military obsession with regulation and policy, was determined to be magnanimous and immediately enlisted surrendered warriors as army scouts, before the government could

Miles (4) stands with members of his staff as he prepares for a march that resulted in the defeat of Crazy Horse in January 1877. Miles sports a beard against winter cold, and wears his distinctive bearskin coat. The Indians called him "Bearcoat" and referred to his hard-driving Fifth Infantry as the "Walk-a-Heaps." (Little Bighorn Battlefield National Monument)

1. Eng.
2. Dr. Tilton
3. Pope
4. Gen. Miles

Miles' infantrymen level their long Springfield rifles during a raging snowstorm at the battle of Wolf Mountain, in January 1877, in this drawing by Frederick Remington. (Author's collection)

otherwise dispose of them. Although Crook sympathized with the Indians, he was a West Pointer and a career soldier who ultimately obeyed the government mandate of removal. Those who surrendered to him often found themselves transported to the Indian Territory for internment on the reservations there (Robinson, 2001, 214, 226).

On 7 May 1877, Miles' troops captured a large camp of Miniconjous under the chief Lame Deer, who was killed in the fight. This action essentially ended the Great Sioux War although, as with the Red River War, mop-up operations would continue for another year or so. Now, with the great tribes of both the Northern and Southern Plains broken, the complete government control of the central two-thirds of the United States was assured. Part of that control was the policy of removal and concentration of the tribes to the Indian Territory.

Survivors

The battle of the Little Bighorn was a pivotal event. For the Indians, it was perhaps their greatest single victory, one in which they completely annihilated five companies of a modern army. Yet it was a hollow victory because it outraged the nation, and assured the ultimate destruction of the Indian way of life. As such, the Little Bighorn left an indelible imprint on those who fought there. Well into the 20th century, both Indian and white survivors had vivid recollections of that day. Among them were the Cheyenne warrior Wooden Leg (1858–1940), and Sergeant Charles Windolph (1851–1950), Company H, Seventh Cavalry, who is believed to have been the last white survivor.

Wooden Leg

Wooden Leg began relating his story to Dr. Thomas Marquis, former physician to the Northern Cheyenne Agency in Montana, in the 1920s. Although Marquis did not speak Cheyenne, he was reasonably fluent in Plains sign. This was the primary means of communication, although Wooden Leg sometimes would emphasize a point with words from his limited English vocabulary, and augment his gestures with pencil sketches. Other Cheyennes who were either present at the fight, or among the bands hostile to the government in 1876, often participated in the discussions, corroborated Wooden Leg's experiences, and offered their own views on the subject (Marquis, n.d., vii–ix).

Wooden Leg was born on the Cheyenne river in the Black Hills of South Dakota in 1858. His name referred to physical stamina – the ability to walk long distances without tiring as though his legs were made of wood. He earned it when he and some companions lost their mounts to Crow horse thieves. On foot, they overtook two of the Crows, rushed and killed them, and recovered their horses (Marquis, n.d., 1–5).

Growing up, Wooden Leg was typical of a Cheyenne boy training to be a warrior and provider. He learned to ride and hunt, and through painful experience of snowblindness and frostbite, how to handle himself outdoors. The only hostile encounter with whites came when he was about seven or eight years old, when members of his band fought soldiers – probably Connor's – on Lodgepole Creek near its confluence with the North Platte. His own first combat experiences were against Crows and Shoshones, the traditional enemies of the Cheyennes. When Wooden Leg was about eight, his older brother, Strong Wind Blowing, and another Cheyenne were killed in the Fetterman massacre.

"There was rejoicing in our camp on account of the victory," he said, "But our family and all relatives of the two dead Cheyennes were in mourning. We wept and prayed for the spirits of our lost ones" (Marquis, n.d., 14–15).

Wooden Leg was in Two Moon's camp when Reynolds attacked it on 17 March 1876. He had no ammunition for his old muzzle-loading rifle, and had loaned his revolver to his cousin, who had gone out with the scouts the night before. He did have a borrowed bow and arrows, and grabbed the first pony he saw, to go out and fight. It soon became obvious that the camp was lost, so he returned to his lodge to gather his valuables. As he rode out, he picked up two children, carried them to safety, and then went back into the fray. When he and three companions killed and stripped a soldier, he came away with the man's blue coat. From a distance, they watched as the soldiers burned their village. Later, they recovered what they could

Wooden Leg, a Cheyenne warrior shown here in 1927, participated in virtually every major battle of the Great Sioux War, including the Rosebud and the Little Bighorn. (Little Bighorn Battlefield National Monument)

from the wreckage, and that night, Wooden Leg was among the group that stampeded the horses (Marquis, n.d., 165–69).

The Cheyennes joined Crazy Horse's Oglalas, and together the two groups traveled up and joined the giant camp of the Hunkpapas under Sitting Bull. Wooden Leg participated in the battle of the Rosebud, after which the camp moved toward the Little Bighorn. The Cheyenne camp circle was at the north end, downriver from Reno's attack, and so these warriors were primarily concerned with Custer. Describing the fight, Wooden Leg recalled (Marquis, n.d., 230, 234):

Most of the Indians were working around the ridge … occupied by the soldiers. We were lying down in gullies and behind sagebrush hillocks. The shooting at first was at a distance, but we

kept creeping in closer around the ridge. Bows and arrows were in use much more than guns. From the hiding-places of the Indians, the arrows could be shot in a high and long curve, to fall upon the soldiers or their horses. An Indian using a gun had to jump up and expose himself long enough to shoot …

I saw one Sioux walking slowly toward the gulch, going away from where were the soldiers. He wabbled [sic] dizzily as he moved along. He fell down, got up, fell down again, got up again. As he passed near to where I was I saw that his whole lower jaw was shot away. The sight of him made me sick. I had to vomit.

After the battle, the tribes split up. In November, while the main Cheyenne band camped on the Red Fork of the Powder river, Wooden Leg and nine other warriors went out searching for Crow Indians. They passed through the Little Bighorn, and collected unfired cartridges and souvenirs scattered about the battlefield. As they headed back toward their camp, they encountered their people who, during their absence, had been attacked by Mackenzie.

"They had but little food," Wooden Leg said. "Many of them had no blankets nor robes. They had no lodges. Only here and there was there one wearing moccasins. The others had their feet wrapped in loose pieces of skin or of cloth. Women, children and old people were straggling along over the snow-covered trail down the valley" (Marquis, n.d., 282–86).

Following the surrender, Wooden Leg was among the group exiled to the Indian Territory. He did not, however, join Dull Knife or Little Wolf in the outbreak, but waited until he and other Northern Cheyennes were allowed to repatriate. He later became a baptized Christian and a judge of the Indian Court (Thrapp, 3:1594).

Sergeant Charles Windolph

Wooden Leg's army counterpart, Sergeant Charles Windolph, was with Captain Frederick Benteen's battalion at the Little

Infantrymen and Indian scouts mop up Dull Knife's camp on the Powder river on 25 November 1876, after Mackenzie's cavalry captured it. The fight destroyed Cheyenne military power forever. This drawing is by famous Western artist Frederick Remington. (Author's collection)

Bighorn. He was in his 80s and living in Lead, South Dakota, when historian Frazier Hunt first contacted him in the mid-1930s. Over the next 10 years, until 1946, he related his story to Hunt and his son, Robert. The following year, it was published "with explanatory material and contemporary sidelights on the Custer Fight," as *I Fought With Custer*. Although Windolph commented that the 70 years since the fight had given him plenty of time to remember the details and fix them in his mind, he acknowledged his account might not match those of other survivors. "Even the men who were with Benteen and Reno and lived to tell the tale, didn't come anywhere near telling the same stories about what they did, and what they saw," he explained, adding, "I had only one pair of eyes, so, of course, all I can tell is what I saw myself" (Hunt and Hunt, 1–2).

Windolph was born in Bergen, Prussia, on 9 December, 1851. He reached military age as Prussia was preparing to go to war with France, and to avoid the draft, he escaped first to Sweden, and later to the United States. Like many other young German draft dodgers, he found it difficult to earn a living in the United States, and so ended up with the only job available – enlistment in the US Army (Hunt and Hunt, 3–4).

Company H, Seventh Cavalry, was posted to Nashville, Tennessee, when Windolph joined in 1870. Three years later, his battalion was sent to Dakota Territory (North Dakota), where he took part in the Yellowstone Expedition, to explore a route for the railroad into Montana. He was not present in the expedition's only Indian fight on 4 August, because Company H had been left behind to guard the supply depot on the lower Yellowstone. The following year, he participated in Custer's Black Hills Expedition. After a brief stint in New Orleans during the winter of 1875–76, his company was sent to Fort Abraham Lincoln.

On 17 May, the Seventh rode out of Fort Abraham Lincoln as part of General Terry's

Dakota Column. Windolph remembered the day (Hunt and Hunt, 53):

You felt like you were somebody when you were on a good horse, with a carbine dangling from its small leather ring socket on your McClelland [sic] saddle, and a Colt army revolver strapped on your hip; and a hundred rounds of ammunition in your web belt and in your saddle pockets. You were a cavalryman of the Seventh Regiment. You were a part of a proud outfit that had a fighting reputation, and you were ready for a fight or a frolic (Hunt, 53).

The Dakota Column linked up with Gibbon's Montana Column, and on 22 June, the Seventh separated and started on its scouting expedition. Windolph recalled that although the men expected a hard fight, they were not particularly worried. Each man believed that if anyone died, it would be someone else, not himself. On 25 June, after a hard three days, Seventh located the Indian village and prepared to attack.

About noon, Benteen took his battalion, including Company H, up the valley and scouted the hills, while Custer and Reno moved down the valley toward the village. After about two hours, Benteen ordered the battalion to turn about and rejoin the others. As they drew closer, they heard gunfire, Benteen ordered his men to draw pistols, and they charged up the bluffs at a gallop to find Reno and his men fleeing up the hill.

"I'll never forget that first glimpse I had of the hilltop," Windolph said. "Here were a little group of men in blue, forming a skirmish line, while their beaten comrades, disorganized and terror stricken, were making their way on foot and on horseback up the narrow coulee that led from the river, 150 feet (30m) below" (Hunt and Hunt, 96).

For the next several hours until sundown, the two battalions held off the Indians, all the while wondering why Custer didn't come to support them. It never occurred to them that Custer and the remaining five companies of the Seventh were already dead. After a cold, rainy night, the shooting began again. By now the wounded were crying for water, and Benteen called for volunteers to make the near suicidal rush to the river. Windolph was one of 17 who came forward, and Benteen detailed him and three other good marksmen to draw fire and keep the Indians distracted while the others went for water. Several of the water party were wounded, but Windolph and his three German countrymen emerged unscathed. All four received the Medal of Honor (Hunt and Hunt, 104–05).

After the Indians withdrew, and Terry and Gibbon arrived, the men learned of Custer's fate. Windolph was a member of the detail that buried Custer and his brother, Tom.

After the Great Sioux War, Windolph participated in the Nez Percé campaign of 1877. He left the army in 1883, and worked for Homestake Mining Company in Lead, for 49 years. He died on 11 March 1950, at the age of 98 (Thrapp, 3:1582).

The slow move toward Indian rights

During the period immediately following the Civil War, the majority of the American people, which is to say those living east of the Mississippi, were relatively indifferent to the conditions on the plains. The Indian situation was a mere abstraction. The four exhausting years of internal conflict, the horrendous drain of blood and treasure, and the devastation in the South and the border states, were a reality. The reaction to the Red Cloud War demonstrated the public's lack of enthusiasm for an Indian campaign. Indian fighting would be bloody and expensive (the Great Sioux War alone ultimately cost $2,312,531.24, a staggering figure for the time). The government was pressured to develop the nation, and do whatever was necessary to encourage that development while avoiding conflict. Indeed, one of the reasons a commission was appointed to negotiate the Medicine Lodge and Fort Laramie Treaties was to convince the Indians to allow development to proceed unmolested.

When conflicts did occur, life in the East went on, often oblivious to the fact that a war was even under way. In 1876, the year the Great Sioux War began, Alexander Graham Bell invented the telephone, Samuel L. Clemens, better known as Mark Twain, published *The Adventures of Tom Sawyer*, and professional baseball teams organized the National League. Colorado became a state, joining the existing plains states of Kansas, Nebraska, Nevada, and Texas. John D. Rockefeller was busy consolidating the oil industry, and the dominant economic force was steel (Robinson, *Good Year to Die*, xxi–xxii).

Canada was settling its great plains simultaneously with the United States, but the history of the two movements could not have been more opposite. When the North West Mounted Police was organized in 1873, many predicted it would have the same bitter experience as the US Army south of the border. The 300,000 square miles under its jurisdiction had problems identical to those of the United States, i.e. tens of thousands of disenchanted Indians, whiskey peddlers who profited from Indian discontent, and a large helping of American badmen who had fled across the border to escape prosecution in their own country. Many of the Indian tribes were related to, or allied with, the American Lakotas, who themselves frequently fled north across the "medicine line" to take refuge in British territory. However, the Mountie had an advantage over his American counterpart in a rigorous training program that prepared and conditioned him for his assignment. Other factors were stringent discipline and careful attention to equipment necessary for the job ahead.

The first encounter between Mounties and Plains Indians came on 13 August 1874, when a detachment en route to Fort Edmonton, Alberta, encountered about 30 dirty, hungry Sioux. The men's reaction was more of curiosity than hostility, and soon the Mounties and Indians were sitting together, smoking and exchanging pleasantries through their Indian and Métis (mixed-blood) scouts. The Indians were told that Queen Victoria was the mother of all Canadians, regardless of race, that she loved all her children equally, and would not allow any of her children to take unfair advantage of the others. This meeting set the pattern for their future relations with any Indians. Thus, the Canadian Plains were settled without a shot ever being exchanged between Mountie and Indian (Tanner, Chapter 5).

If Canada resolved its Indian question peacefully, Mexico was an entirely different matter. As noted earlier, the US conflict with the Southern Plains Indians was inherited from Spain and Mexico. The Kiowas especially were notorious for raiding into that country, and Mexican captives were even adopted into the tribe. One reason for the failure of the Fort Atkinson Treaty was the US insistence that raids into Mexico cease, and that all Mexican captives be repatriated (Mooney, 173).

During the first four decades of its independence, Mexico failed to achieve political stability. The country was divided between a conservative faction centered in Mexico City and consisting of the large landholders, clergy, and army, and the liberals who dominated the provinces. Although the country's first president, Major General Guadalupe Victoria, managed to finish his term, few, if any, of his successors did. In 1858, the country was plunged into a vicious three-year civil war between the Mexico City conservatives and the liberal reformers. No sooner was that resolved and the reformers gained power than Mexico was invaded by the French, who, in concert with the conservatives, installed the Austrian Archduke Maximilian on the throne. With the ousting of the French and the execution of Maximilian, the country was devastated and needed complete internal reorganization. Mexico was unable to defend its own frontier from Indian raids from the United States, nor was it capable of preventing Indians from Mexico from raiding into the US (Parkes).

The border between the US and Mexico was not a "medicine line," as was the border with Canada. US troops had little compunction about chasing Indians well into Mexico. And because the Indians routinely raided there, they were in enemy territory regardless of which side of the border they were on, and behaved accordingly. The establishment of the authoritarian regime of Porfirio Diaz at the end of 1876 inaugurated more than three decades of relative stability, and Mexican troops began actively suppressing Indian outbreaks. As time passed, the US and Mexican governments reached an accommodation whereby the military of either country could cross into the other in "hot pursuit" of raiding Indian bands. From the US viewpoint, the term "hot pursuit" became so broadly defined that American troops sometimes employed scouts to lead them to major Indian camps deep in the mountains of Mexico.

One reason for public ignorance of events on the plains was lack of reliable and reasonably current information. Not until the late 1860s was there serious newspaper coverage of Indian fighting. Instead, eastern editorial staffers who never left their offices wrote largely imaginary accounts. This began to change in 1867, when Joseph Wasson, co-owner of the Silver City, Idaho, *Owyhee Avalanche*, accompanied then-Lieutenant Colonel George Crook on an expedition against the Indians of the Pacific northwest. Wasson's dispatches were reprinted in the *San Francisco Evening Bulletin*, giving metropolitan readers their first eyewitness reports of an Indian campaign. Aware that a well-cultivated public image might lead to advancement (it did), Crook continued to encourage correspondents, not only in the northwest, but also during his campaigns in Arizona and on the plains. Soon, professional correspondents from New York, Chicago, Denver, and elsewhere accompanied expeditions against Indians, and soldiers augmented their meager army pay by selling their accounts to the newspapers. Correspondents Wasson and Robert Strahorn took an active part in the fighting during Crook's campaigns, and Mark Kellogg died with Custer at the Little Bighorn (Knight, 31–32; 2001, 94, 164–65).

The Indian Wars reached their climax during the decade of the 1870s, but during much of that time, the eastern part of the nation was preoccupied with the economic depression, known to history as the Panic of 1873. The crisis began on 18 September 1873, when the New York banking firm of Jay Cooke & Co. went bankrupt. Cooke's interests were extensive, including control of the Northern Pacific Railroad, then under construction across the Northern Plains. Two

Brigadier General George Crook (seated second from right) poses with staff, scouts, and friends outside Fort Fetterman, Wyoming, during a lull in the fighting in 1876. Crook, who eschewed military formality, preferred a civilian suit and white sun helmet in the field, and rarely wore a uniform even at his headquarters. (US Army Military History Institute)

days later, the New York Stock Exchange was forced to suspend trading. Over the next six years, more than a million people – one-fortieth of the entire population – lost their jobs. For those still employed, wages fell 20 percent although there was no significant reduction in the cost of living (McFeely, 392–93). Many took to the roads, and when word reached the East about the discovery of gold in the Black Hills, they headed for the Dakotas in hopes of a fresh start.

Arriving in Wyoming at the height of the rush, in February 1876, Bourke wrote (Diary, 3:2–3):

In Cheyenne, we could see and hear nothing but "Black Hills." Every store advertises its inducements as an outfitting agency, every wagon is chartered to convea [sic] freight to the new Pactolus. The Q[uarter]. M[aster]. Dept. experiences grave difficulty in finding the transportation needed by the Army at the different camps. Everything is bound for the Black Hills. Cheyenne is full of people and her merchants and saloon keepers are doing a rushing business. Great numbers of new buildings, mostly brick, have been erected during the past six months, giving the town a bustle and activity as well as an appearance of advancement in favorable contrast with Omaha, Denver and Salt Lake … I saw many adventurers journeying to the Black Hills; their wagons and animals looked new and good as a general thing and the supplies carried ample in quantity. However, there were many on foot and without adequate sustenance and some begging their way from ranch to ranch along the trail … It is strongly suggestive of the want and misery of the Eastern states that so many people should rush upon slight stimulus towards the new El Dorado.

Gold and goldrushes were among the most obvious signs of advancing technology that was pushing the Indians aside. Prior to the Civil War, however, the great concern of Eastern reformers was the abolition of slavery. Once that was accomplished, they turned their attention westward, and President Grant's Board of Indian Commissioners and his Peace Policy were among the results. However, there was no serious, coordinated plan or effort. The movement gained impetus in 1879, when a group of Ponca Indians took their grievances to court. The problem had its origins nine years earlier when in the Fort Laramie Treaty, by bureaucratic error, Ponca lands on the Missouri river were ceded to the Lakotas as part of the Great Sioux Reservation. When the government decided to relocate the Lakota Agencies to the Missouri river in 1876, it was deemed expedient to remove the Poncas to the Indian Territory. Interior Secretary Carl Schurz rationalized that, because the Lakotas and Poncas were ancient enemies, this would be in the best interests of the latter tribe.

Relocation began during the spring of 1877, and many Poncas died en route. Many more died in the hot, malarial climate of Oklahoma. In early spring 1879, the only son of the Ponca chief Standing Bear died of malaria. Standing Bear, who had already lost two daughters in the relocation, decided to bury the boy in his old country. Thirty others joined him on the march from Oklahoma, across Kansas and Nebraska, walking along behind a wagon carrying the boy's coffin. On reaching their home country, the Omahas welcomed them on their reservation, allowing them to settle and plant crops. The government, however, was unwilling to tolerate this breach of established policy, and ordered General Crook to arrest the Poncas and send them back to the territory (Howard, 32–36).

Crook was less than enthusiastic. With his connivance, and perhaps even at his suggestion, the Poncas' story was sent to metropolitan newspapers from Chicago to New York. Citizens' committees formed in Omaha, where the Poncas were interned, and in Yankton, capital of Dakota Territory (South Dakota). The case demonstrated that the government's solution – relocation from ancient lands and concentration in the Indian Territory – was a failure, and galvanized the Eastern humanitarians into action (Mardock, 173).

The guiding forces were General Crook and Thomas Henry Tibbles, former abolitionist and preacher who now was assistant editor of the *Omaha Daily Herald*. Tibbles believed the case hinged on whether the equal protection guarantees under the Fourteenth Amendment to the Constitution applied to American Indians. At his behest, two of the Midwest's leading attorneys took the case *pro bono* and filed a writ of *habeas corpus*.

United States ex. rel. Ma-chu-nah-zah (Standing Bear) vs. George Crook was heard before US District Judge Elmer Dundy in Omaha on 30 April 1879. Crook was named as defendant in his capacity as the officer responsible for enforcing the government edict, but made no secret of his sympathies with the Poncas. The government's response was that an Indian was a ward of the government, and therefore had no legal standing in court (Tibbles, 1973, 199–200, and 1995, 34ff.).

After all the arguments were heard, Standing Bear addressed the court. His simple statement, that he was a human being with the same feelings, hopes and dreams of any human being, reduced Judge Dundy to tears. A week later, he issued his ruling – just as Indians were expected to obey the laws of the United States, so were they entitled to the protection of those laws. The detention of the Poncas, he declared, was in violation of that protection, and they were ordered released (Tibbles, 1995, 108–11; Robinson, 2001, 238–39).

Riding the momentum, Tibbles arranged for Standing Bear to make a speaking tour of the eastern states, attracting more people to the Indian cause. The activists found an ally in Crook. Like many soldiers, he had initially viewed them as naive busybodies who knew nothing of the situation, and had advocated a military solution. Yet, from the beginning of his career as a young lieutenant on the

West Coast, he had always believed that the settlers and government had provoked much of the trouble that required military action. Even before the Ponca case, he had commented to Tibbles, "The buffalo is gone, and an Indian can't catch enough jack rabbits to subsist himself and family, and then there aren't enough jack rabbits to catch. What are they to do? Starvation is staring them in the face ... I do not wonder, and you will not either, that when these Indians see their wives and children starving, and their last sources of supplies cut off, they go to war. And then we are sent out there to kill them. It is an outrage" (*Army and Navy Journal*, 29 July 1878). The Standing Bear case, where Indians had used the legal system to achieve their goals, convinced him that there were alternatives.

Unfortunately the Indian rights activists never could agree on an agenda. An extreme faction believed the Indians should be given immediate citizenship under the Fourteenth Amendment, after which the need for assimilation into 19th-century society could be considered. Moderates agreed with Secretary Schurz that there would have to be a long period of government stewardship to ease the Indians away from tribal life in slow stages. Ultimately, the basic question of a future for the Indians became lost in rhetoric and ideology (Robinson, 2001, 239–40).

The Ponca chief Standing Bear initiated a legal case that was one of the first steps in establishing the rights of Indians as residents of the United States. (Nebraska State Historical Society)

Women and children

The brutal realities

There was nothing romantic or noble about Plains Indian life. It was a life of hardship, and a struggle for survival from dawn to dark, with each person doing his or her assigned task.

The role of the women was only dimly understood by whites, who often used the standards of their own civilization as a measure of Indian life. An officer posted to Fort Sill, Indian Territory, in the 1870s wrote that Kiowa women were little more than "slaves" (Myers, Folder 10). In fact, the relationship was not bondage so much as a division of labor. The warrior fought the wars, conducted the raids, made and repaired weapons, undertook the often grueling and dangerous task of hunting for food, and raised ponies, the commodity by which Plains Indians reckoned wealth. The women gathered plant foods, cooked the meals, prepared the hides of animals killed by their male relatives, made and repaired the clothing and tipis, tended the children, and whatever other tasks were to be done around camp.

Although the Indian women rarely were combatants, they often accompanied their men into battle or on raids. During the Warren Wagon Train Massacre in Texas in 1871, two Kiowa women stood off to one side, encouraging the warriors with shrill tongue-rattling (Nye, 129). At the battle of the Little Bighorn in 1876, a Cheyenne woman known as Kate Bighead remained on the fringes, singing war songs to encourage her nephew who was in the fight (Marquis, 1987, 89).

With some exceptions, such as the Minnesota uprising, Indian prisoners usually received consideration from regular soldiers, who viewed Indian fighting simply as a duty. Military prisoners were interned at a fort, then placed on a reservation, and those considered most incorrigible might be sent to Fort Marion. Those who fell into the hands of citizens or local volunteer troops, however, were not always so fortunate. The ongoing raids back and forth kindled deep hatreds among the settlers, who were not always concerned about distinguishing between friendly and hostile bands. The vicious mutilation of the Indian bodies following the Sand Creek Massacre demonstrated what whites were capable of.

Nelson Lee

Among white settlers and travelers, one of the greatest fears was being taken alive. With few exceptions, captivity for adult males meant a slow, hideous death, while women and even young girls might be gang-raped. One of the few adult males to survive was Nelson Lee, a former Texas Ranger, who spent three years as a captive. In the spring of 1855, Lee joined a company formed by William Aikens, to drive mules from Texas to the California market. Shortly after midnight on 3 April, Comanches attacked their camp, and all were killed except Lee, Aikens, Thomas Martin, and John Stewart. The Indians stripped them, tying them spread-eagle between posts, in pairs facing each other. Lee and Aikens were forced to watch while Stewart and Martin were scalped alive, then their bodies repeatedly slashed for about two hours, before the Indians finally put an end to their misery by splitting their skulls with hatchets. Then for whatever reason Lee and Aikens were allowed to dress and return to their tents. Aikens later was sent away with another band, while Lee continued on with his captors to their main camp. Here, he forestalled any thoughts of killing him by making himself useful, to the point they nicknamed him *Chemakacho* meaning Good White Man (Lee, 104–08, 115).

Several months later, three white women were brought into camp. They identified themselves as Mrs Henrietta Haskins, and her daughters, Margaret, and Harriet. They were survivors from a party of English Mormon emigrants which had been massacred two or three years earlier. The mother, who was feeble and rheumatic, served as "a common drudge," while the daughters were "slaves and wives" of two warriors. During their stay in Lee's camp, Mrs Haskins' health broke, and she was scalped and slashed to death while her daughters were forced to watch (Lee, 144).

If a female child was captured at an early enough age, she often adapted readily to her situation, grew up as a member of the tribe, and came to identify with the Indians and share their animosity toward her own race. Indians frequently adopted captive children, both boys and girls, especially on the Southern Plains, where their birthrate was low and the infant mortality rate high. During his captivity, Nelson Lee recalled meeting four white girls, ranging in age from 12 to 18 (Lee, 123):

They knew no other than the language of the Comanches, and in all respects conformed to their manners and customs. It was, therefore, evident to me they had been captured in early childhood and remember no other life than that they were then leading.

Adolescent boys, with their tendency toward rebellion, and desire to assert themselves, often had little trouble adapting to the ways of the Indian warrior. The story of Theodore Adolphus (Dot) Babb, who was captured by Comanches in Texas in September 1865, at the age of 13, is not unusual. With Babb's father and older brother driving cattle to Arkansas, the household consisted of himself, his mother, nine-year-old sister, an infant sister, and a Mrs Luster, a young Civil War widow who was living with the family. The Indians attacked late in the afternoon, breaking down the door of the house, mortally wounding Mrs Babb, and carrying off Mrs Luster and the two older children. That night, Mrs Luster escaped, although she later was captured by a party of Kiowas. The Comanches, meanwhile, had ascertained that Babb assisted in the escape, and decided to kill him. The boy's defiance, however, won their respect, and they carried him back to their main camp to raise him as a warrior. He adapted readily, participating in raids on other tribes. After two years, he and his sister were ransomed and returned home, although he maintained close ties with his adoptive Comanche family for the rest of his life (Babb, 20–36, 58).

The "glittering misery" of army wives

Although General Sherman believed officers should marry young so their wives might help relieve the isolation of frontier duty, government indifference made life almost unendurable for military dependents. As the wife of one junior officer commented (Boyd, 136):

It is notorious that no provision is made for women in the army. Many indignation meetings were held at which we discussed the matter, and rebelled at being considered mere camp followers. It is a recognized fact that a woman's presence – as a wife – alone prevents demoralization, and army officers are always encouraged to marry.

The most famous army wife of all, Elizabeth Bacon Custer, complained that while the regulations might go into minute detail on such mundane things as how to boil bean soup, wives were totally ignored (Stallard, 16).

The use of the term "camp follower" was no exaggeration. According to army regulations, dependents of soldiers and officers had no legal status other than that of camp followers. Unlike laundresses, who were considered military personnel and entitled to quarters, rations, and the services of the post surgeon, wives were left to their own devices. And where the laundresses had certain specified legal rights, which they invoked with a vengeance, wives were subject to the whims of the post commander, who could even ban them from the post if it suited him. Frequent cuts in military spending led to regulations designed to discourage enlisted men from marrying. Consequently, many enlisted men's wives served as laundresses, and enlisted men sometimes married laundresses. Either arrangement brought the family extra income and rationing (Stallard, 16, 57–59).

The wife of an officer went west for love of her husband, a sense of duty, and a certain amount of romantic idealism about the region. The latter notion was quickly dispelled by reality. At best, their lives involved inconvenience, and at worst, total misery. They left large, comfortable homes in the east, often to live in tents and hovels. Even when reasonably decent housing was available, their positions were not always secure because their husbands could be "ranked out" by senior officers. Frances Boyd, wife of a cavalry lieutenant at Fort Clark, Texas, described the procedure:

I was ill at the time, confined to my room; and messages were brought at intervals from six different officers, who all outranked Mr. Boyd, that each had selected our house. Ridiculous as it may seem, every one was outranked by another. Finally, a captain of the infantry chose our quarters, and then the doctor declared I could not be moved ….

The following day, Mrs Boyd gave birth to her third child, who immediately contracted whooping cough. Both her other children also came down with it, and she herself was ill from childbed fever. "For a week I was at death's door with fever; and yet the very day baby was four weeks old we were obliged to move, that the captain, who demanded his house without further delay, might be accommodated" (Boyd, 270–72).

For the next two years, the five members of the Boyd family occupied a one-room shanty,

while the captain, a bachelor, kept the house. Still, Mrs Boyd felt better off than another wife who was forced to live in the hallway that separated the duplex quarters of two other officers and their families. One morning her husband was advised that a superior officer wanted the hallway. In disgust, he resigned from the army (Boyd, 273).

When soldiers were in the field in hostile country, wives never knew whether they would see them again. Elizabeth Custer, whose husband died along with half his regiment at the Little Bighorn, wrote of "the terrible parting which seemed a foreshadowing of all the most intense anguish that our Heavenly Father can send to his children" (Custer, 182). As if to aggravate their unhappiness, wives visiting the East during their husbands' campaigns sometimes found that the public was not even aware that a military expedition was under way (Custer, 88).

The uncertainty especially increased if the Indians attached to the post began to get uneasy. Many army wives were aware of the incredible efficiency of the so-called "moccasin telegraph," that still-unfathomable means by which Indians received news from throughout the plains much more quickly than government couriers could carry it. Although the details might vary as they circulated from one group of Indians to the next, the basic information generally was reliable. In early July 1876, at Fort Rice, one of two stations of the Seventh Cavalry, the Indians began talking about a massacre involving the entire command. The wives of the officers gathered together in one of the quarters for a sleepless night, waiting for some sort of word. Early the next morning, the Missouri river steamer arrived with mail from the war zone. "Unwashed, uncombed, the thud-thud of our hearts almost suffocating, we dashed to the trader-store post office," the wife of Lieutenant Francis M. Gibson remembered. "All those from forlorn old Fort Rice were safely accounted for – all but one, our dear Jack [Lieutenant Jack Sturgis], so very young, so beloved by us all" (Fougera, 265–66).

Further north, at Fort Abraham Lincoln, the Seventh's headquarters post, the wives were not so fortunate. Twenty-six women learned that day that they were widows.

Often bodies could not be recovered immediately, and sometimes not at all, denying the widows the comfort of seeing proper funerals and burials. Adding to the emotional pain, the army assumed no responsibility for the widow, who was expected to vacate quarters as soon as possible. The benefits paid to the widow and surviving children were so paltry that Congress considered that it was doing Indian Wars widows a favor in 1908, when it increased their pensions to $12 a month (Stallard, 42).

Martha Summerhayes, herself a soldier's wife, summed up the feelings of all when she wrote, "I fell to thinking: was the army life, then, only glittering misery…?" (Summerhayes, 45).

An unresolved legacy

On 11 November 1865, two Santee chiefs, Medicine Bottle and Shakopee, who had been kidnapped and smuggled out of Canada, were hanged at Fort Snelling, Minnesota, for their part in the 1862 uprising. According to legend, as Shakopee mounted the gallows, he heard the whistle of a railroad locomotive and remarked, "As the white man comes in the Indian goes out" (Carley, 75).

If the story is apocryphal, it was nevertheless prophetic. To some extent, the so-called "Indian Question" went all the way back to Columbus, when the rest of the world learned for the first time that there were other people on the planet besides conventional Europeans, Africans, and Asians. This raised the dilemma of what sort of people they might be, and how to deal with them. The United States inherited the British policy of treating them as sovereign nations. Alone among the people of the United States, Indians were specifically exempted by the Constitution from obligations and benefits of citizenship. And while Judge Dundy's ruling in the Standing Bear case essentially gave them protection under the Fourteenth Amendment, it did not establish citizenship, nor could it. Decades earlier, Chief Justice John Marshall had defined the Indian tribes as "domestic dependent nations," with the power to enter into treaties with the federal government. Even that ended in 1871, in part because of the House of Representatives' jealousy of the Senate's treaty-making authority. Henceforth, Indians were wards of the government, subject to the joint decisions of both houses of congress. This created yet another bureaucratic stumbling block that was beyond the Indian cultural comprehension (Utley and Washburn, 194; Robinson, 2001, 113).

One of the most devastating government programs was the removal of Indians from their home territories, and their concentration in the Indian Territory, without consideration of how the change in environment would affect them. Such was the case with the Northern Cheyennes, who were concentrated with their Southern cousins around Darlington where they could be watched and regulated. The Northern Cheyennes, accustomed to the mountains and valleys of Montana and Wyoming, were not acclimatized to the heat and humidity of the Southern Plains, and within two months of their arrival, nearly two-thirds were ill.

On 9 September 1878, a large band under Dull Knife and Little Wolf broke camp and started home. After driving off a detachment of soldiers, they crossed into Kansas, where some warriors went on a rampage of murder, rape, and plunder. Above the North Platte river, they split into two groups, with Little Wolf leading his people to Montana where the ever-insubordinate Nelson Miles allowed them to settle quietly. Dull Knife, meanwhile, was forced to surrender his band near Fort Robinson, Nebraska, where they were interned pending transportation back to the Territory. Determined to die rather than return, they barricaded themselves in a barracks. With the tacit consent of Crook and Sheridan, the commanding officer, Captain Henry Wessells, cut off their food and water to force them into submission. The Cheyennes, however, had firearms concealed in pieces in their clothing, and on 9 January 1879, they began reassembling them. Late that night, they attacked the guards and fought their way out. Over the next few weeks, they were hunted down, and most were recaptured. Some were allowed to settle at Pine Ridge, just south of the Black Hills. Others were returned to the Territory,

Dull Knife (seated) and Little Wolf were leaders of the Cheyenne Outbreak of 1878–79. They were two of the four "old men" or senior chiefs of the Northern Cheyennes. (Smithsonian Institute)

although eventually they, too, were allowed to go to Pine Ridge or Montana (Monnett).

Another group pushed beyond endurance was the White River Utes of western Colorado. When silver was discovered in the San Juan Mountains in their territory, they were forced to surrender one-fourth of their reservation. This was followed by pressure from local citizens to seize the rest of their reservation and remove the Utes to the Indian Territory. Matters came to a head with the appointment of a totally incompetent agent, Nathan C. Meeker, who insisted they plow up their pony pastures and turn to agriculture. A confrontation between Meeker and a Ute medicine man called Johnson led to a scuffle and Meeker sent for troops. A detachment sent from Fort Fred Steele, Wyoming, the nearest post, was blocked at Milk river, and pinned down in a week-long siege before a relief column arrived. The Utes, meanwhile, had risen up, burned the agency, killed Meeker and nine employees, and carried off their families.

To avoid possible harm to the hostages, Interior Secretary Schurz enlisted the aid of Charles Adams, a former agent whom the Utes trusted, and Ouray, the powerful chief of the Uncompahgre Utes. Faced with Ouray's threat to unite all the other Ute tribes against them, the White River band surrendered and returned the hostages. The incident accelerated demands for removal of all Utes. Although some retained a small reservation in southwestern Colorado, the rest were removed to Utah (Utley and Washburn, 306–10).

The Cheyenne Outbreak and the Ute Rising signaled the end for the Plains Indians. Isolated incidents might occur here and there, but in reality the Indian Wars on the Great Plains were over, and the region rapidly developed. The Great American Desert, as it once had been called, was no more. In 1889 alone, Wyoming, Montana,

and Idaho were admitted as states, and Dakota Territory was divided into North and South to create two states. Utah followed in 1896, the delay caused primarily because the Mormon theocracy that governed the territory had to readjust to accommodate federal law and policy. Then, in 1906, the Indian Territory was consolidated with the Territory of Oklahoma, which was admitted as a state one year later.

The reality of the situation was summed up by Schurz, who wrote in the *National Review* that every part of the country was becoming accessible by railroad, and that gave the land conventional economic value. The Indians, he said, would have to face that reality. Meanwhile, because many whites still advocated extermination, the Indians needed government protection ("Present Aspects").

In 1887, Congress approved the General Allotment Act, better known as the Dawes Act, after its sponsor, Senator Henry Laurens Dawes of Massachusetts. The Act terminated tribal ownership of reservation lands, allocating .65km2 (160 acres) to every Indian head of household, 0.3km2 (80 acres) to single persons over 18 years old and orphans under 18, and 0.15km2 (40 acres) to all others under 18. Citizenship was offered to those who accepted the allocation and abandoned tribal life. The result of the act was two-fold: first, it attempted to destroy the base of tribalism by abolishing communal lands, and second, once the lands were allocated to all Indians on a reservation, many reservations would still have a vast amount of unallocated land that would be opened to settlement. This led to the loss of almost 0.5 million km² (100 million acres) of Indian land, some 80 percent of what they held before the act went into effect (Utley, 1997, 121–22).

One of the reservations broken up under the act was the remnant of the Great Sioux Reservation created under the Fort Laramie Treaty. A commission composed of Govenor Charles Foster of Ohio, chairman, Senator William Warner of Missouri, and Crook, now major-general and commander of the Military Division of the Missouri, met with the Lakotas in the spring and summer of 1889. Although Crook used diplomacy, he also led the Indians to understand that if they did not agree to hand over the land, the government would take it anyway. Adding insult to injury, once they signed away their land, the government reduced their appropriation. In desperation, many joined the Ghost Dance movement, which had originated in Nevada that year, and now was rapidly moving eastward across the plains (Robinson, 2001, 299–300).

An early Ghost Dance movement had originated among the Paiutes and was active in California and Oregon in the 1860s and 1870s before gradually fading away. It was revived in 1889 by a Paiute named Wovoka, who preached the dawn of a new era in which the Indian lands would be restored, and people would be reunited with their dead ancestors. Wovoka's message stressed peace, and the performance of a circular dance.

The very technology that the Indians had opposed for so long – telegraph and railroads – aided its spread, and soon it was embraced throughout the plains. Ancient tribal enemies set aside their animosities, and joined together in a religious euphoria, preparing for a world to come. It became particularly popular among the Lakotas, now reduced to total desperation. The government, sensing the threat of rising Indian nationalism, determined to stop it. At the Standing Rock Reservation, North Dakota, the movement centered on Sitting Bull. When tribal police went to arrest him on 15 December 1890, fighting broke out. Sitting Bull, several of his followers, and some of the Indian police were killed.

The Dakota Reservations were occupied by troops, and Oglala leaders at the Pine Ridge Reservation, in South Dakota, managed to contain the Ghost Dancers. At Cheyenne River, South Dakota, a large group of Ghost Dancers under Chief Big Foot panicked at the arrival of troops and fled westward toward the Badlands. They were rounded up and brought to Wounded Knee Creek on 28 December. The army planned to march them to Pine Ridge the next morning, and put them on the train for Cheyenne River.

On the morning of 29 December, the warriors were separated from the women and children, and searched for weapons. The soldiers were nervous, and many had been drinking the night before. A scuffle broke out over a rifle, a shot was fired, and the Indians began pulling out concealed weapons. The soldiers leveled their rifles and opened fire at point-blank range, killing about half the warriors in the first volley. Then four rapid-fire Hotchkiss cannons opened up with shrapnel. When it ended, the bodies of 146 men, women, and children were buried in a mass grave. However, many wounded later died, and relatives recovered the bodies of other dead, so the actual toll may have reached 300. The Indian way of life also died at Wounded Knee (Hoxie, 223, 694–97).

The Plains Wars now entered the realm of legend. Just as whites have mixed emotions over Custer, so too Indians have mixed emotions over their chiefs. Among the Kiowas, the animosity between the Satanta adherents and Kicking Bird adherents lingers to some extent even today. Quanah Parker, who after his surrender prospered as a rancher, businessman, and ultimately federal judge, remains a controversial figure among the Comanches. Red Cloud's grudging accommodation after the close of the Plains Wars causes some Oglalas to question his integrity. The defiant chiefs, however, have become symbols, particularly if they died resisting the government, or at least under questionable circumstances. Such were the cases of Crazy Horse, who was bayoneted to death at Camp Robinson in 1877, and Sitting Bull, both of whom had assumed almost mythical proportions even among the troops during the Great Sioux War.

After interviewing many Indian combatants for a final report to General Crook, Lieutenant Philo Clark noted (United States Department of War, record group 393, Sioux War, 14 September 1877):

Great prominence has been given Crazy Horse and Sitting Bull in this war; the good fighting strategy and subsequent muster by retreats being attributed to them, whereas they are really not entitled to more credit or censure than many others so far as plans and orders were concerned ....

There is no question that during this war, the two chiefs were, in fact, respected and charismatic leaders, Sitting Bull perhaps a little more than Crazy Horse. Dead, however, they have assumed cult status, as symbols of Indian resistance. The Lakotas, particularly the Oglalas of Pine Ridge, South Dakota, have cited the "Spirit of Crazy Horse," in asserting their identity, and their right to exercise their own way of life.

Today, the Indian continues to trouble the national conscience. Although all Indians born in the United States are citizens, in many cases they have been relegated to a secondary status, reduced to a permanent dependency on the federal government. Part of this is because a massive government bureaucracy exists on managing Indian affairs. "The fact is," General Crook once observed, "there is too much money in this Indian business ...." (Crook, 28 November 1871, Collection). That still holds true. Casino gambling has been extolled as the great cure for all Indian ills, but it is a mixed blessing. Some tribes have grown wealthy, but others have suffered. In 1999, an Oglala leader observed that the casinos at Pine Ridge bring large amounts of money to a tribal benevolent fund, but because so many members of the tribe gamble, the draw on that fund has increased proportionately.

No one seems sure how to address the situation of the Indians, and the Indians themselves are divided. Some insist that all reservations, government relief, and other programs separating them from the mainstream should be completely abolished, and the Indians should take their place as co-equal citizens, to succeed or fail on their own. Others contend that they cannot exist without government help, and assistance is the least the government can do.

Mass grave at Wounded Knee. (Author's collection)

The question facing the United States is the same question facing any nation, where an alien people have displaced but have not assimilated or been assimilated by the indigenous people. It is a question that also faces Canada, Brazil, South Africa, Australia, and many other nations. The indigenous people are human beings with the power of conscious thought and action; they cannot be placed on a reserve and preserved unchanged forever as though they were a species of wildlife. Yet neither can the indigenous people withdraw from a modern, ever advancing world. How to assimilate them into the modern world, yet preserve their rights as human beings is the great question. So far, there have been no answers.

Principal Indian characters

Big Tree (c. 1852–1929), Kiowa subchief, convicted with Satanta of murder for his part in the Warren Wagon Train Massacre of 1871, was later paroled. Became a Baptist deacon, and a prominent leader of his community.

Black Kettle (c. 1810–68), Cheyenne peace chief, and leader of the band massacred by Colorado troops at Sand Creek in 1864. Killed by regular troops in the battle of the Washita in the Indian Territory.

Brave Bear (d. 1854), Lakota paramount chief, mortally wounded in the Grattan Massacre.

Crazy Horse (c. 1840–77), Oglala Lakota war leader, famed for his charisma, and for his pale complexion and red hair. Killed during a scuffle at Camp Robinson, Nebraska.

Dohasen (d. 1866), Kiowa paramount chief.

Dull Knife, also known as Morning Star (c. 1810–83), Northern Cheyenne senior chief, one of the leaders of the 1878–79 outbreak. Allowed to live near Pine Ridge, South Dakota, until his death.

Isa-tai (c. 1842–1914), Comanche prophet, one of the instigators of the Red River War of 1874–75.

Kicking Bird (c. 1835–75), Kiowa peace chief, kept the bulk of his people neutral during the Red River War. Died under mysterious circumstances, possibly of poisoning by the war faction.

Little Crow (c. 1803–63), leader in Minnesota Uprising of 1862. Killed by a citizen a year later.

Little Wolf (c. 1820–1904), Northern Cheyenne senior chief, led the Outbreak of 1878–79. Surrendered to Col. Nelson Miles, and lived quietly in Montana until his death

Lone Wolf (c. 1820–79), Kiowa war leader, succeeded Dohasen as paramount chief.

Interned at Fort Marion, Florida, after the Red River War, died of malaria shortly after his release.

Medicine Bottle (d. 1865), leader in the Minnesota Uprising. Hanged at Fort Snelling, Minnesota.

Ouray (1820–80), autocratic paramount chief of the Uncompahgre Utes, ended the White River Ute uprising by threatening to unit all the other Utes against the White River band.

Parker, Quanah (c. 1845–1911), Comanche war chief, son of Peta Nacona and Cynthia Ann Parker. After the Red River War, he became a cattleman, businessman, and judge.

Red Cloud (1822–1909), Oglala war chief who fought the government to a standstill in 1866–68. He succeeded Spotted Tail as head chief of the Lakotas, and was prominent in tribal affairs until his death.

Satank (c. 1797–1871), Kiowa war leader. Arrested with Satanta and Big Tree after the Warren Wagon Train Massacre, he was killed by a guard at Fort Sill, Indian Territory.

Satanta (c. 1816–78), Kiowa war leader and diplomat, committed suicide in the Texas State Penitentiary, Huntsville.

Shakopee (d.1865), leader in the Minnesota Uprising. Hanged at Fort Snelling, Minnesota.

Sitting Bull (c. 1834–90). Hunkpapa political chief and leader of resistance in the early 1870s. Killed in a fight with tribal police.

Spotted Tail (c. 1823–81), Brulé leader, appointed by the government as head chief of the Lakotas in 1876. Assassinated during internal Lakota political dispute.

Standing Bear (c. 1829–1908), Ponca chief, initiated a landmark legal case that established Indian status as residents of the United States.

Washakie (c. 1804–1900), Shoshone
  paramount chief allied with the federal
  government during the Great Sioux War.
  Fort Washakie, Wyoming, was named in
  his honor.

Wooden Leg (1858–1940), Northern
  Cheyenne warrior, was prominent in the
  Great Sioux War. He later served as an
  army scout and a judge.

Further reading

Government documents and publications

United States

Barker, Eugene C., ed. *The Austin Papers.* Annual Report of the American Historical Association for the Year 1919. 2 vols. Washington: Government Printing Office, 1924.

Hancock, Winfield Scott. *Reports of Major General W.S. Hancock Upon Indian Affairs, With Accompanying Exhibits.* Washington: Government Printing Office, n.d. (1867).

Howard, James H. *The Ponca Tribe.* Smithsonian Institution Bureau of American Ethnology Bulletin 195. 1965. Reprint: Lincoln: University of Nebraska Press, 1995.

Lavender, David. *Fort Laramie and the Changing Frontier.* Washington: United States Department of the Interior, 1983.

Overfield, Loyd J., II, comp. *The Little Big Horn, 1876: The Official Communications, Documents and Reports with Rosters of the Officers and Troops of the Campaign.* 1971. Reprint: Lincoln: University of Nebraska Press, 1990.

United States Congress. *Report of the Joint Committee on the Conduct of the War, at the Second Session Thirty-eighth Congress. Massacre of Cheyenne Indians.* Washington: Government Printing Office, 1865.

United States Department of the Interior. Second Annual Report, Office of the Kiowa and Comanche Agency, Fort Sill, August 12, 1870. Manuscript copy in Myers.

United States Department of War. Office of the Adjutant General. Record Group 391 Series 757, Fourth Cavalry Expedition Records, Letters and Endorsements Sent and Orders Issued.

— Record Group 393. Special File. Military Division of the Missouri. National Archives Microfilm Publication 1495. Washington: National Archives, n.d. As follows:

Rolls 2–4. Sioux War, 1876–77.

— Office of the Surgeon General. Post Medical Report. Fort Griffin, Texas, 1867–1881.

— *The War of the Rebellion: A Compilation of the Official Records of the Union and Confederate Armies.* 130 vols. Washington: Government Printing Office, 1881–1898.

Wallace, Ernest, ed. *Ranald S. Mackenzie's Official Correspondence Relating to Texas, 1873–1879.* Museum Journal 10. Lubbock: West Texas Museum Association, 1968.

Individual states

DeLand, Charles E. *The Sioux Wars.* South Dakota Historical Collections 17. Pierre, S.D.: State Department of History, 1930.

Winfrey, Dorman H., and James M. Day, eds. *The Indian Papers of Texas and the Southwest, 1826–1916.* 5 vols. 1966. Reprint. Austin: Texas State Historical Association, 1995.

Spain

Jackson, Jack, ed. *Imaginary Kingdom: Texas as Seen by the Rivera and Rubí Military Expeditions, 1727 and 1767.* Austin: Texas State Historical Association, 1995.

Simpson, Lesley Byrd, ed., and Paul D. Nathan, trans. *The San Sabá Papers: A Documentary Account of the Founding and Destruction of San Sabá Mission.* 1959. Reprint. Dallas: Southern Methodist University Press, 2000.

Manuscripts

Bourke, John Gregory. Diary. 124 vols. United States Military Academy Library, West Point, NY.

Crook, George. Collection. Microfilm edition. Rutherford B. Hayes Library, Rutherford B. Hayes Presidential Center, Fremont, Ohio.

Hamby, Thorton K. "An Indian Raid in Young County, Texas, Oct. 13th, 1864." Elm Creek Raid Statements. Earl Vandale Collection. Center for American History, University of Texas, Austin.

King, Rufus, and Charles King. Collection. State Historical Society of Wisconsin. Madison.

Myers, James Will. Papers. Panhandle-Plains Historical Society. Canyon, Texas.

Schuyler, Walter Scribner. Papers. Henry E. Huntington Library and Art Gallery, San Marino, California.

Books

Primary sources

Babb, Theodore Adolphus. *In the Bosom of the Comanches: A Thrilling Tale of Untamed Indian Life, Massacre, and Captivity Truthfully Told by a Surviving Captive.* 1912. Reprint. Azle, Tex.: Bois d'Arc Press, 1990.

Bourke, John Gregory. *On the Border With Crook.* 1891. Reprint. Alexandria, Va.: Time-Life Books, 1980.

Boyd, Mrs. Orsemus B. *Cavalry Life in Tent and Field.* 1894. Reprint. Lincoln: University of Nebraska Press, 1982.

Carleton, James Henry. *The Prairie Logbooks: Dragoon Campaigns to the Pawnee Villages in 1844, and to the Rocky Mountains in 1845.* 1943. Reprint. Lincoln: University of Nebraska Press, 1983.

Custer, Elizabeth Bacon. *"Boots and Saddles" or, Life in Dakota with General Custer.* New York: Harper Brothers, 1885.

Finerty, John F. *War-Path and Bivouac: The Big Horn and Yellowstone Expedition.* 1955. Reprint. Lincoln: University of Nebraska Press, 1966.

Fougera, Katherine Gibson, *With Custer's Cavalry.* 1942. Reprint. Lincoln: University of Nebraska Press, 1986.

Hunt, Frazier, and Robert Hunt. *I Fought With Custer: The Story of Sergeant Windolph, Last Survivor of the Little Big Horn.* New York: Charles Scribner's Sons, 1947.

Lee, Nelson. *Three Years Among the Comanches: The Narrative of Nelson Lee, the Texas Ranger.* 1859. Reprint. Norman: University of Oklahoma Press, 1991.

Marquis, Thomas B., (comp.) 1987. *Custer on the Little Big Horn.* Second rev. ed. Algonac, Mich.: Reference Publications, Inc., 1987.

— n.d. Int. *Wooden Leg: A Warrior Who Fought Custer.* Originally published as *A Warrior Who Fought Custer.* 1931. Reprint. Lincoln: University of Nebraska Press.

Miles, Nelson Appleton. *Personal Recollections and Observations of General Nelson A. Miles.* 1896. Reprint. 2 vols. Lincoln: University of Nebraska Press, 1992.

Mills, Anson. *My Story,* 2nd. ed. Washington: Press of Byron S. Adams, 1921.

Neihardt, John G., comp. *Black Elk Speaks, Being the Life Story of a Holy Man of the Oglala Sioux.* 1932. Reprint. Lincoln: University of Nebraska Press, 1965.

Parkman, Francis, Jr. *The California and Oregon Trail: Being Sketches of Prairie and Rocky Mountain Life.* 1849. Reprint. Alexandria, Va.: Time-Life Books, 1983.

Sherman, William Tecumseh. *Memoirs of General W.T. Sherman.* Rev. ed. 1886. Reprint. New York: Library of American, 1990.

Summerhayes, Martha. *Vanished Arizona: Recollections of the Army Life of a New England Woman.* 1908. Reprint. Tucson: Arizona Silhouettes, 1960.

Tatum, Lawrie. *Our Red Brothers and the Peace Policy of President Ulysses S. Grant.* 1899. Reprint. Lincoln: University of Nebraska Press, 1970.

Terry, Alfred Howe. *The Field Diary of General Alfred H. Terry: The Yellowstone Expedition – 1876.* 2nd ed. Bellevue, Nebr.: The Old Army Press, 1970.

Tibbles, Thomas Henry. *Buckskin and Blanket Days: Memoirs of a Friend of the Indians.* 1957. Reprint. Lincoln: University of Nebraska Press, 1973.

— *Standing Bear and the Ponca Chiefs.* 1880. Reprint. Lincoln: University of Nebraska Press, 1995.

White, David A., comp. *News of the Plains and Rockies, 1803–1865: Original narratives of overland travel and adventure selected from the Wagner-Camp bibliography of Western Americana*. 8 vols. and supplement. Spokane: The Arthur H. Clark Company, 1996–2001.

Secondary sources

Bolton, Herbert Eugene. *The Hasinais: Southern Caddoans as Seen by the Earliest Europeans*. Norman: University of Oklahoma Press, 1987.

"Brazos" (pseud.). *The Life of Robert Hall, Indian Fighter and Veteran of Three Great Wars. Also Sketch of Big Foot Wallace*. 1898. Reprint. Austin: State House Press, 1992.

Brice, Donaly E. *The Great Comanche Raid: Boldest Indian Attack of the Texas Republic*. Austin: Eakin Press, 1987.

Brown, Dee. *The Fetterman Massacre*. 1962. Reprint. Lincoln: University of Nebraska Press, 1971.

Carley, Kenneth. *The Sioux Uprising of 1862*. St. Paul: Minnesota Historical Society, 1976.

Fontana, Bernard L. *Entrada: The Legacy of Spain and Mexico in the United States*. Tucson: Southwestern Parks and Monuments Association, 1994.

Fox, Richard Allan, Jr. *Archaeology, History, and Custer's Last Battle: The Little Bighorn Reexamined*. Norman: University of Oklahoma Press, 1993.

Greene, Jerome A. *Yellowstone Command: Colonel Nelson A. Miles and the Great Sioux War 1876–1877*. Lincoln: University of Nebraska Press, 1991.

Grinnell, George Bird. 1956. *Fighting Cheyennes*. 1915. Reprint. Norman: University of Oklahoma Press.

— *The Cheyenne Indians*. 2 vols. 1923. Reprint. Lincoln: University of Nebraska Press, 1972.

Gray, John S. *Centennial Campaign: The Sioux War of 1876*. 1976. Reprint. Norman: University of Oklahoma Press, 1988.

Haley, James L. *The Buffalo War: The History of the Red River Indian Uprising of 1874*. 1976. Reprint. Norman: University of Oklahoma Press, 1985.

Hoig, Stan. *The Sand Creek Massacre*. Norman: University of Oklahoma Press.1976, 1961

— *The Battle of the Washita*. Garden City: Doubleday & Company, Inc.

Hoxie, Frederick E. *Encyclopedia of North American Indians*. Boston: Houghton Mifflin Company, 1996.

Hyde, George. *Red Cloud's Folk: A History of the Oglala Sioux Indians*. Norman: University of Oklahoma Press, 1937, Reprinted 1987.

— *Spotted Tail's Folk: A History of the Brulé Sioux*. New ed. Norman: University of Oklahoma Press, 1974. Reprinted.

Lazarus, Edward. *Black Hills/White Justice: The Sioux Nation Versus the United States, 1775 to the Present*. New York: HarperCollins Publishers, 1991.

Leckie, William H. *The Military Conquest of the Southern Plains*. Norman: University of Oklahoma Press, 1963.

McChristian, Douglas C. T*he U.S. Army in the West, 1870–1880: Uniforms, Weapons, and Equipment*. Norman: University of Oklahoma Press, 1995.

McFeely, William S. *Grant, A Biography*. New York: W.W. Norton & Company, 1981.

Mardock, Robert Winston. *The Reformers and the American Indian*. Columbia, Mo.: University of Missouri Press, 1971.

Monnett, John H. *Tell Them We Are Going Home: The Odyssey of the Northern Cheyennes*. Norman: University of Oklahoma Press, 2001.

Nye, Wilbur Sturtevant. *Carbine and Lance: The Story of Old Fort Sill*. 3rd ed. Norman: University of Oklahoma Press, 1969.

Parkes, Henry Bamford. *A History of Mexico*. 3rd ed. Boston: Houghton Mifflin Company, 1960.

Priest, Loring Benson. *Uncle Sam's Stepchildren: The Reformation of United States Indian Policy, 1865–1887*. 1942. Reprint. New York: Octagon Books, 1992.

Robinson, Charles M., III. 1992. *The Frontier World of Fort Griffin: The Life and Death of a Western Town*. Spokane, Wash.: The Arthur H. Clark Co.

— *A Good Year to Die: The Story of the Great Sioux War*. New York: Random House, 1995

— *The Indian Trial: The Complete Story of the Warren Wagon Train Raid and the Fall of the Kiowa Nation*. Spokane: The Arthur H. Clark Co., 1997

— *Satanta: The Life and Death of a War Chief*. Austin: State House Press, 1998

— *The Men Who Wear the Star: The Story of the Texas Rangers*. New York: Random House, 2000

— *General Crook and the Western Frontier*. Norman: University of Oklahoma Press, 2001

Sklenar, Larry. *To Hell With Honor: Custer and the Little Bighorn*. Norman: University of Oklahoma Press, 2000.

Tanner, Ogden, and the Editors of Time-Life Books. *The Canadians*. Alexandria, Virginia: Time-Life Books, 1977.

Taylor, Colin F. *Native American Weapons*. Norman: University of Oklahoma Press, 2001.

Thrapp, Dan L. *Encyclopedia of Frontier Biography*. 3 vols. 1988. Reprint. Lincoln: University of Nebraska Press, 1991.

Utley, Robert M. 1988. *Cavalier in Buckskin: George Armstrong Custer and the Western Military Frontier*. Norman: University of Oklahoma Press.

— *Frontier Regulars: The United States Army and the Indian, 1866–1891*. 1973. Reprint. Lincoln: University of Nebraska Press, 1984

— (ed.) *Encyclopedia of the American West*. New York: Wing Books, 1997

— and Wilcomb E. Washburn. *The American Heritage History of the Indian Wars*. 1977. Reprint. New York: Bonanza Books, 1982.

Stallard, Patricia Y. *Glittering Misery: Dependents of the Indian Fighting Army*. Fort Collins, Colo.: Old Army Press, 1978.

Weddell, Robert. *The San Sabá Massacre: Spanish Pivot in Texas*. Austin: University of Texas Press, 1964. Reprinted 1988.

Articles

Primary sources

Anonymous. "Ashley-Ricaree Fight, 1823." 1823. Reprint. White, *News of the Plains and Rockies 1803–1865*. Vol. 1 (1996): 152–60.

Plummer, Rachel. "Narrative of Twenty-one Months Servitude As a Prisoner Among the Comanchee [sic] Indians." 1844. Reprint. White. *News of the Plains and Rockies 1803–1865*. Vol. 3 (1997): 321–35.

Schurz, Carl. "Present Aspects of the Indian Problem." *North American Review*. Vol. 133, no 296 (July 1881): 1–24.

Secondary sources

Barton, Henry W. "The Anglo-American Colonists Under Mexican Militia Laws." *Southwestern Historical Quarterly*. Vol. 65, no. 1 (July 1961): 61–71.

Hanson, Charles. "Thoughts on the Mountain Man and the Fur Trade." *Museum of the Fur Trade Quarterly*. Vol. 35, no. 4 (Winter 1999): 2–8.

Robinson, Charles M., III. 1993. "Blundering on the Plains: Hancock's War." *Old West*. Vol. 29, no. 4 (Summer): 28–34.

Newspapers

Army and Navy Journal
St. Louis *Missouri Democrat*

Index

Figures in **bold** refer to illustratiions

Adams, Charles 85
Adobe Walls, Texas, battle of 20, 40, 42, 51
Aikens, William 79
Almazon, Juan Antonio Perez de 13
Amarillas, Marqués de las 15, 16
Apache tribe 13, 14, 15, 16, 28
Arapahos tribe 42, 44, 46, 47, 50, 56
Arikara or Ree tribe 9, 17
Ash Hollow 35
Ashley, William H. 17
Atkinson, Fort, Treaty 75
Auger, Brigadier General Christopher C. 50, 53
Austin, Moses 28
Austin, Stephen F. 28

Babb, Theodore Adolphus (Dot) 80
Beecher, Henry Ward 46
Beecher, Lieut. F.H. 46
Beecher's Island 46
Bell, Alexander Graham 74
Benteen, Frederick W. 61, 62–3, 71, 72, 73
Bidais tribe 16
Big Foot, Chief 86
Big Tree, Chief of Kiowa tribe 49, 88
Bighorn and Yellowstone Expedition 20
Black Hills, South Dakota 70
Black Hills expedition, South Dakota 58, 72
Black Horse 22
Black Kettle, Chief of Cheyenne tribe 41, 46, 88
Board of Indian Commissioners 10, 77
Bourke, Lieut. John Gregory 23–4
Boyd, Frances 81
Bozeman Trail 56, 57
Brave Bear, Chief of Sioux tribe 32, 88
Brulé tribe 32, 35, 56
Buell, Colonel George 51
buffalo hunting 50, **50**
Bustillo, Juan Antonio

California 18
Camp Robinson 67
Canada 17, 74
Canadian mounted police 74
Carrington, Colonel Henry B. 56
Carson, Colonel Christopher (Kit) 40, 42
Castle Creek Valley **58**
Cavelier, René Robert 13
Cedar Buffs 41
Chadron Creek 67
Chaihook, Chief of Tonkawa tribe 20, **21**
Cheyenne Dog Soldiers see Dog Soldier Society
Cheyenne tribe 9, 17, 20, 40–1, 42, 44, 46, **47**, 50, 51, 52, 56, 59, 67, 70, 83
Chivington, Colonel John M. 41–2
Church involvement in Indian affairs 10, 15–16
Civil War 23, 24, 25, 26, 36, 39, 41, 57
Clark, Lieut. Philo 86
Cobb, Fort 46
Colorado 19, 40–1, 74
Comanche tribe 13, 14, 16, 29, 33, 39, 44, 45, 46, 48, 49, 51, 52, 80
Concho, Fort 49
Confederate States 36, 39, 41
Connor, Brevet Major General Patrick E. 42, 56
Cooke, Jay & Co. 75
Coronado expedition 13
Crazy Horse, Chief of Oglalas tribe 59, 68, 71, 86, 87, 88
Crook, Brigadier General George 9, **10**, 20, 59, 60, 61, 64, 67, 69, 75, 77–8, 83, 85–6, 87
Crow tribe 9, 60, 70, 71
Custer, Elizabeth Bacon 80, 81
Custer, Lieut. Colonel George Armstrong **10**, 43, **46**, 46–7, 59, 60, 61, 63, 73, 75, 86
    Black Hills expedition **58–9**
    'Last Stand' **62–3**

Darlington 45, 51, 53, 83
Davidson, Lieut. John W. 51, 52
Davis, Jefferson, President of the Confederate States 32, 39, 49
Dawes Act 85
Day, John Other 37
Dcnvcr 41
Diaz, Porfirio 75
Dodge, Colonel Richard Irving 67
Dodge, Fort 42
Dog Soldier Society 41, 42

Dohasen, Chief of Kiowa tribe 40, 42, 88
Douglass, Major Henry 42
Dull Knife, Chief of Cheyenne tribe 71, 72, 83, **84**, 88
Dundy, Judge Elmer 77, 83

Elliott, Major Joel 46–7
Elliott, Samuel 48
Evans, John 40–1

Federal States see Union States
Fetterman, Captain William J. 56
Fetterman massacre 70
First New Mexico Volunteer Cavalry Regiment 40
Forsyth, Major George A. (Sandy) 46
Fort Atkinson Treaty 75
Fort Laramie Treaty 58, 74, 77
Fort Laramie Treaty Commission **57**
Foster, Charles 85
Fourth Cavalry Regiment 47, 50
French colonialism 9, 13, 17

General Allotment Act 85
Ghost Dance movement 86
Gibbon, Colonel John 59, 60, 61, 63, 73
gold and gold rushes 55, 58, 76–7 see also silver
Goose Creek 60, 64
Grant, General Ulysses Simpson, 18th President of the United States 10, 60, 77
Grattan, Lieut. John L. 32
Great Britain 17
Great Sioux War (1876–77) 7, 64–9, 864
Gros Ventres tribe 56

Hancock, General Winfield Scott 42, 43
Hancock's War 44, **44–5**, 52
Harney, Brigadier General William S. 32, 35, **57**
Hasinai tribe 16
Haskins, Henrietta 80
Haworth, James 49
Hays, Fort 46
Hays, Jack 29
'Horse Meat March' 64–5, **66**, **67**
horses, introduction of 13
Howard's Wells 48
Hunkapap tribe 56, 60, 71
Hunt, Frazier 72

Idaho 85
Indians
    buffalo hunting 49–50
    communications 81
    executions of 39, **40**, 83
    fighting methods 20
    legal rights 77–8, 83
    peace chiefs 41
    present day status of 87
    reservations 44–5, 57–8, 65, 68, 77, 83, 85–6
    treaties with 44–5, 55, 58
    weapons 20, **22**, 22–3
    women's roles 79
Isa-tai 51, 88

Joint Committee on Conduct of the War 41–2

Kansas **14**, 41, 50, 51, 53, 57, 74, 83
Kaw tribe 45
Kearney, Colonel Stephen Watts 31
Kearney, Phil, Fort 31, 56, 57
Kellogg, Mark 75
Keogh, Captain Myles 63
Kicking Bird, Chief of Kiowa tribe 42, 51, 86, 88
Kidder, Lieut. Lyman S. 43
Kiowa tribe 20, 29, 39, 40, 42, 44, 45, 46, 47, 49, 51, 52, 54, 75, 86

Lakota Sioux tribe 9, 17, 18, 35, 39, 40–1, 55, 56, 77, 85, 86
Lame Deer, Chief of Miniconjous tribe 69
Laramie, Fort **31**, 31–2, 35, 55, 56, 57
Laramie, Fort, Treaty 58, 74, 77
Laramie, Fort, Treaty Commission **57**
Larned, Fort 42
Last Stand Hill, Little Bighorn **60**
Lawson, Captain Gaines 52
Lean Bear, Chief 41
Leavenworth, Colonel Henry 17
Lee, Nelson 79–80
Lewis and Clark expedition 17
Lincoln, Abraham, 16th President of the United States 39
Lincoln, Abraham, Fort 72
Linnville, Texas 29
Little Arkansas Treaty 42
Little Bighorn, battle of 20, **54–5**, **60**, 61–3, 70, 75
Little Bighorn National Monument **60**
Little Bighorn Valley 61

Little Crow, Chief of Sioux tribe 36–7, 39, **88**
Little Thunder, Chief of Brulé tribe 35
Little Wolf, Chief of Cheyenne tribe 71, 83, **83**, 88
Lodgepole Creek 70
Lone Wolf, Chief of Kiowa tribe 42, 49, **49**, 50, 51, 88

McClellan military saddle **24**
Mackenzie, Colonel Ranald S. 10, 47–8, **49**, 50, 51, 53, 63, 67, 71
Man Afraid of His Horses, Chief 56
Mankato, Minnesota 39, **40**
Marion, Florida, Fort 54, 79
Marquis, Dr. Thomas 70
Marshall, Chief Justice John 83
Maximilian, Archduke 75
Medicine Bottle, Chief of Santee tribe 83, 88
Medicine Lodge 44
Medicine Lodge Treaty 74
Meeker, Nathan C. 85
Merritt, Colonel Wesley 64
Mexican Civil War 75
Miles, Colonel Nelson A. 10, 51, **51**, 52, 63, 67–9, **68**, 83
Mills, Captain Anson 65
Miniconjoux tribe 56, 69
Minnesota refugees **37**
Minnesota uprising 36–9, **38**
Missouri Fur Company 17
Montana 19, 55, 57, 59, 60, 68, 83
Mormans 32, 85
Myrick, Andrew J. 36, 37

Nebraska **19**, 41, 74
Nevada 74
New Mexico **14**, 40, 51
New Ulm 38, 39
newspapers 75, 77
Nez Percé War 27, 73
North Dakota **19**, 39, 57, 85
Northern Plains Wars 7, 17–19, 31–2

Oglala tribe 46, 71
Oklahoma **14**, 46, 77
Oklahoma, Treaty of 85
Omaha Daily Herald 77
Omahas tribe 77
Oregon 18
Ouray, Chief of Utes tribe 85, 88
Owyhee Avalanche 75

'Panic of 1873' 75–6
Pao Duro Canyon 53
Parilla, Colonel Diego Ortiz 15, 16–17
Parker, Quanah, Chief of Comanche tribe 51, 54, 86, 88
Parker, Rev. James W. 29
Parker's Fort **30**
    raid 28–9
Parkman, Francis, Jr. 18
Pawnee Killer, Chief 43
Pawnee tribe 9
Peace Policy 10
Pierre, Fort 35
Pike, Brigadier General Albert 39
Pine Ridge 83, 86, 87
Plum Creek, battle of 29
Ponca tribe 77
Pope, Brevet Major General John 38
Powder River 55
Price, Major William R. 51

Quakers 49

railroads 57, 85, 86
Red Cloud, Chief of Oglaga tribe 56, 57, 65, 67, 86, 88
Red Cloud War (1866–68) 42, 56–7
    reactions to 74
Red Fork 67, 71
Red Leaf, Chief 65
Red River 48, 52
Red River War (1874–75) 7, **43**, 51–4
Ree or Arikara tribe 9, 17
Remington, Frank 69, 72
Reno, Fort 56, 57
Reno, Major Marcus A. 61, **61**, 63, 72, 73
reservations 44–5, 57–8, 65, 68, 77, 83, 85–6
Reynolds, Colonel Joseph J. 59, 70
Rice, Fort 39
Ridgley, Fort 38
Robinson, Fort 83
Rockefeller, John D. 74
Roman Nose, Chief of Cheyenne tribe 46
Rosebud, Montana, battle of 20, **35**, 71
Rubí, Marqués de 28

San Antonio, Texas 13, 16, 28

San Francisco Evening Bulletin 75
San Sabá project, Texas **15**, 15–17
Sand Creek valley massacre 41, 42, 79
Santa Cruz de San Sabá *see* San Sabá project, Texas
Santee Sioux tribe 36–9
Santiesteban, Fray José de 16
Satank, war leader of Kiowa tribe 20, **22**, 88
Satanta, war leader of Kiowa tribe 42, 49, 53, 86, 88
Schurz, Carl 77, 78, 85
Schuyler, Lieut. Walter S. 64–5
Seventh Cavalry Regiment 46, 61, 72, 81, 82
Shakopee, Chief of Santee tribe 83
Sheridan, Major General and Lieut. General Philip H. 45–6, 51, 59, 63, 83
Sherman, General William T. 10, 46–8, **57**, 63, 64, 80
Shoshone tribe 9, 18, 20, 60, 70
Sibley, Brigadier General Henry Hastings 39, 41
silver 85
Sioux tribe 42, 44 *see also* Lakota Sioux tribe; Santee Sioux tribe
Sioux Wars 32, 56–7 *see also* Red River War (1874–75)
Sitting Bull, Chief of Hunkpapa tribe **8**, 9, 58, 60, 68, 71, 86, 87, 88
slavery, abolition of 77
Smith, C.F., Fort 57
Smokey Hill river 41
South Dakota **19**, 39, 57, 77, 85
Southern Plains Wars 7, 9, 13–17, 28–31 *see also* Red River War 9
    defensive reorganisation (1767) 28
    early exploration 13
    Louisiana ceded from France 28
    occupation of Texas 13–14
Spotted Tail, Chief of Sioux tribe **64**, 67, 88
Standing Bear, Chief of Ponca tribe 77, **78**, 83, 88
'Starvation March' 64–5, **66**, **67**
Strahorn, Robert 75
Sully, Brigadier General Alfred 39, 41, 46

Tejas *see* Hasinai tribe
telegraph 86
Terreros, Fray Alonso Giraldo de 15, 16
Terry, Brigadier General Alfred H. **57**, 59, 60, 63, 64, 67, 72, 73
Texas **14**, 50, 51, 74
Texas Rangers 28, 29
Third Colorado Cavalry Regiment 41
Tibbles, Thomas Henry 77
Tonkawa tribe 16
treaty settlements 44–5, 57–8
Twain, Mark 74
Twiss, Thomas 35
Two Moon's camp 70

Ugalde, Colonel Juan de
    campaigns against Apaches 28
Union States 36, 39
United States Army 33
    bugle 27
    communications 81
    fighting methods 23–5
    housing conditions 81
    marksmanship 27
    soldiers life style 25
    weapons and equipment **25**, 25–7, **26**
United States ex. rel. Ma-chu-nah-zah (Standing Bear) vs. George Crook 77, 83
Utah 32, 85
Ute tribe 18, 85

Varnum, Lieut. Charles 61
Vergara, Fray Gabriel de 13
Victoria, Major General Guadalupe, President of Mexico 75

Warbonnet Creek, Nebraska 64
Warner, William 85
Warren Wagon Train massacre 47, **48**
Washakie, Chief of Shoshone tribe 20, 89
Washita, battle of **34**
Wasson, Joseph 75
Wessells, Captain Henry 83
Whipple, Bishop Henry 39
Whittaker, Frederick 62
Wichita, Kansas 42, 53
Wichita tribe 13
Windolph, Sergeant Charles 71–3
Wolf Mountain, battle of 68, **69**
Wood Lake, battle of 38
Wooden Leg, Cheyenne warrior 70–1, **71**, 89
Wounded Knee 86, **87**
Wyllyams, Sergeant Fred **52–3**
Wyoming **19**, 42, 55, 57, 59, 60, 83, 85

Yates, Captain George W. 63
Yellowstone and Bighorn Expedition 20
Young County raid 39
Yruegas, Sergeant Francisco 16

ABOUT HABITAT FOR HUMANITY INTERNATIONAL

Nearly two billion people around the world lack adequate shelter. The mission of Habitat for Humanity International is to help as many of these people as possible build simple, decent homes in which to live safely, healthfully, and affordably.

Habitat's two thousand affiliates work locally to organize building projects. Donations finance the supplies, and volunteers provide most of the labor. Even so, the homes are not free. The partner families contribute hundreds of hours of labor and also pay for the homes through nonprofit mortgages. Their monthly payments fund more Habitat homes.

"You can see the pride in the faces of the partner families on the day that they receive the keys to their new home," Habitat's most famous volunteer, former president Jimmy Carter, has observed. "They know that they aren't being given a handout but a hand up, because they have done their share of the work and they will be paying their share of the cost."

Just as building Habitat homes remakes the lives of these families, so does it transform the lives of volunteers. Many had long wanted to help people in need but didn't know how until Habitat gave them an opportunity. Now they return to build again and again because of the way that helping makes them feel. Most have found that no matter how hard they work, they always get more in return than they put in.

Habitat, an ecumenical Christian ministry, welcomes all people to volunteer. Since its founding in 1976, it has built more than 400,000 homes around the world—providing simple, decent, affordable housing for two million people.

To learn more about the work of Habitat for Humanity International, visit habitat.org.

Pilson Kipkirui of Kenya outside the simple home his family built with Habitat

ABOUT THE CHRISTMAS TREE AT ROCKEFELLER CENTER

Since 1933, countless New Yorkers—and countless visitors to the city—have come to Rockefeller Center to marvel at the world's most famous Christmas tree. Adults who visited the tree as youngsters now bring their children and grandchildren to share in the amazement.

The first tree was erected by construction workers digging the foundation for Rockefeller Center in 1931. They wanted to show their appreciation for having jobs at a time—the Great Depression—when so many others were out of work. The twenty-foot tree, which they pooled their money to buy, was decorated with garlands and other ornaments handmade by their families.

Today, the Christmas trees that grace Rockefeller Center are much grander, measuring seventy to one hundred feet tall and about forty feet wide. Each is decorated with thirty thousand multicolored LED lights strung on five miles of wire.

Tree selection begins with helicopter flights over New York, New Jersey, and New England. Using a laptop computer equipped with GPS, the chief gardener of Rockefeller Center records the locations of promising trees and then visits them on the ground.

Once the choice is made, a team of twenty arborists fells the tree and uses a 280-ton all-terrain crane to lower it onto a custom-built trailer. When the trailer and its police escort reach Midtown Manhattan, the crane lifts the tree onto a platform beside the Rockefeller Center skating rink.

The annual tree lighting is a spectacular event, attended by crowds of New Yorkers and tourists and watched on television by people around the world. It takes place the week following Thanksgiving. In 2007, a new tradition began when Tishman Speyer, the company that owns Rockefeller Center, began donating the wood from the tree to Habitat for Humanity. Habitat uses this lumber to help families in need build affordable homes.

To learn more about the Christmas tree and the history of Rockefeller Center, visit rockefellercenter.com.

Henry walked over to the girl, and they stood together, gazing at the glittering tree. Then Henry reached into his coat pocket and pulled out the old claw hammer. "Here you go, Sparky," Henry said. "You'll be needing this."

Just before Thanksgiving, Henry received an invitation to the tree lighting. On the special day, a car picked him up and drove him all the way to Rockefeller Center, where he met the family whose new home would be built with the tree's lumber. They hugged him and thanked him many times for his generosity.

Afterward, Henry stood off to the side and watched the family's young daughter. "It's so beautiful," the girl said softly as she stared up at the enormous tree.

Then something caught the child's eye. A pinecone had fallen to the ground. Picking it up, she turned it over and over in her hands before stuffing it into her pocket.

If ever there was a magic moment, Henry thought, *this is it.*

A family in need? Suddenly, Henry felt a shiver, and the calendar in his mind flipped back to 1931—driving to New York City with his father, meeting Frank and the other workers, building the house, planting the tree. He knew what he had to do.

"I've been given so much," Henry said. "I want to give something back. The tree is yours."

"I know that I'm asking a lot," the man said. "But if you agree, I can promise you that your tree will bring joy to millions of people."

Henry thought some more.

"And when the holiday season is over," the man continued, "we mill the tree and use the lumber to help a family in need build a new home."

To keep himself busy, Henry began working on the house, which was showing its age. He especially liked using the old claw hammer. Its polished handle, smooth and dark from wear, felt comfortable in his hand.

One day, as Henry worked on the front porch, a man drove up to see him. The man told Henry that he worked for Rockefeller Center and that it was his job to pick out the new Christmas tree each year.

"I just love your spruce!" the man said. "When I saw it from my helicopter yesterday, I knew that it had to be this year's tree."

Henry wasn't sure what to do. He knew that being asked was an honor. But he and the tree had been together a long time, and he was reluctant to let it go.

As he got even older, Henry sometimes wondered where the time went. One day,
he was a young boy, waking up with a shiver. The next, he was an old man, living
alone. Not needing a big place anymore, he decided to move back into the house
where he had grown up.

As Henry grew up, however, he became busy with other things. He got married, moved away, and had a family. Most summers, though, he returned to visit his parents. On lazy days, he sat beneath the tree with his son, teaching him how to build things with the old claw hammer.

Henry planted the pinecone beside the new house. In time, a seedling emerged. Henry watered and weeded it. As time passed, both he and the tree grew tall and strong. Henry especially liked to hammer away in its shade, and he became quite a good carpenter, building many projects with his skilled hands.

In the spring, Henry's parents celebrated with a potluck dinner. They invited everyone who had helped build the house. Henry was glad to see Frank again. He was ready to return the claw hammer, but Frank wouldn't take it. "You keep it, son," he said. "It may come in handy someday."

After dinner, Henry sat happily in his very own room. He thought about his Christmas wish and couldn't believe it had actually come true! He knew he should do something special to express how thankful he was, and he thought long and hard about what that might be. Finally, he decided to plant the pinecone. Maybe he could be Jack from the beanstalk story, and the pinecone could be his magic bean.

The sound of sawing and hammering traveled far enough that Christmas morning for Henry's neighbors to wonder what was going on. A few walked over, saw the new house going up, and spread the word. By midafternoon, a dozen more people were pitching in.

As the new house took shape, Frank called Henry over. "See those boards?" he said, pointing to a stack of cedar. "We're going to use them to trim the windows, but they've got nails in them. I need you to pull the nails out."

Henry moved to fetch the boards, but Frank called him back. Digging into his toolbox, he handed Henry an old claw hammer. "You'll be needing this," Frank said.

By nightfall, the frame of the new house was nearly done. By week's end, it had a roof. Soon enough, it was ready for Henry and his family to move in.

THE ENCYCLOPEDIA OF
SCULPTING
TECHNIQUES

THE ENCYCLOPEDIA OF
SCULPTING
TECHNIQUES

JOHN PLOWMAN

731.4
p

RUNNING PRESS
PHILADELPHIA • LONDON

A QUARTO BOOK

Copyright © 1995 Quarto Inc.

First published in the United States of America
in 1995 by Running Press Book Publishers.

9 8 7 6 5 4 3 2 1
Digit on the right indicates the number of this printing

Library of Congress Cataloging-in-Publication Number 94–73870
ISBN 1–56138–532–8

This book was designed and produced by
Quarto Inc.
The Old Brewery
6 Blundell Street
London N7 9BH

Senior art editor   Mark Stevens
Consultant editor   Joseph Wesner
Senior editor   Sally MacEachern
Designer   Geoff Manders
Editor   Anna Selby
Photographers   Paul Forrester; Colin Bowling
Picture researcher   Jo Carlill
Picture research manager   Giulia Hetherington
Art director   Moira Clinch
Editorial director   Sophie Collins

Typeset by Genesis Typesetting, Rochester, Kent
Manufactured in Singapore by Bright Arts Pte. Ltd.
Printed in Singapore by Star Standard Industries (Pte) Ltd.

This book may be ordered by mail from the publisher.
Please include $2.50 for postage and handling.
But try your bookstore first!
Running Press Book Publishers
125 South Twenty-second Street
Philadelphia, Pennsylvania 19103–4399

CONTENTS

INTRODUCTION

TECHNIQUES

MATERIALS   8   ARMATURE   26

EQUIPMENT   14   ASSEMBLAGE   32

GETTING STARTED   22   BASES   38

                          BRAZING   42

                          CARVING   46

                          CASTING   56

                          COLORING   68

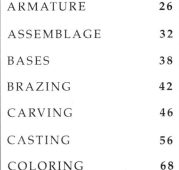

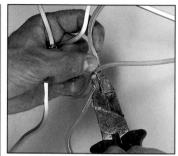

CONSTRUCTION   76

DIRECT MODELING   82

KILN FIRING   86

MODELING   90

MOLDMAKING   94

RELIEF   108

REPAIRS   112

RIVETING   116

WELDING   119

THEMES

HEADS   126

FIGURATIVE   132

RELIEF   140

WALLHANGING   144

ANIMALS   146

TOTEMIC   152

USE OF COLOR   156

ORGANIC   160

LANDSCAPE   162

CONSTRUCTION   164

OBJECTS   172

INDEX   174

CREDITS   176

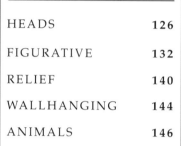

PUBLISHER'S NOTE

Some sculpting techniques can be dangerous, welding in particular. Always exercise caution when using power and hand tools or other equipment, read instruction manuals carefully, and wear appropriate protective and safety gear. Some of the chemicals are poisonous and/or corrosive. This means that you must take precautions when handling them. Always follow the manufacturer's instructions, always store chemicals securely in clearly marked non-food containers and keep them well out of the reach of children. Read the safety tips before undertaking any of the techniques. Some of the materials, equipment, and finished pieces will be heavy, so make sure that you lift correctly, minimizing the strain on your back.

As far as the techniques mentioned in this book are concerned, all statements, information, and advice given are believed to be true and accurate. However, neither the author, copyright holder, nor the publisher can accept any legal liability for errors or omissions.

INTRODUCTION

Making sculpture – the art of manipulating material to create three-dimensional form – is an extremely pleasurable, intense, and rewarding experience. It is an activity that is intrinsic to human nature, dating from prehistoric times when stone was first carved.

Carving and modeling are the traditional techniques used in sculpture. However, since the early years of this century, new techniques and materials have been introduced, greatly expanding the range of possibilities available to the sculptor.

The techniques described in this book are based on my experience of teaching them to students and provide a solid foundation on which to build your sculpture-making skills. If

you have never made a sculpture before, there will be a technique you can use that will start you on the road to making sculpture, while more experienced sculptors will discover the possibilities of other materials and techniques. The process of making a sculpture is both labor-intensive and time-consuming. You will find yourself engaged in tasks that are not creative. You may even ask yourself why you started in the first place. However, you won't feel overwhelmed if you plan out all the steps involved before you start and carry them out methodically. Certainly, you will find it well worth it in the end – as my experience of teaching these techniques to students has shown over the years.

MATERIALS

The materials you will require fall into five general categories: sculpting; moldmaking; joining and fixing; repair; coloring. A selection from each category is shown on pages 8–11.

Sculpting materials include: clay, papier-mâché, wood, stone, aerated concrete block, casting plaster, mild steel, and sheet steel. Constructed sculptures can be made from soft wood in a variety of shapes and sizes with either a prepared (planed) or rough (sawn) surface, split canes, and plywood. Assemblages use everyday material such as plastic coathangers, empty tin cans, and plastic bottles.

In addition to glue, you may need some of the following joining materials: wood dowel for joining pieces of wood; screws; a rawlplug inserted into a drilled hole in masonry keeps the screw firmly in place; heavy-duty bolts are good for joining large pieces of wood; washers, nuts, and threaded steel rod provide an adaptable method of joining diverse materials; netting staples anchor aluminum wire to a modeling board or a vertical wooden head armature support.

There are two recommended types of clay: a clay with added particles of fired clay (grog) suitable for large sculptures; **1** smooth clay suitable for modeling onto an armature where the sculpture will be cast in another material, fine detail and small-scale sculpture. **2** Clay slip is a mixture of clay and water. **3** Sandstone is easy to carve and shape. **4** Papier-mâché is made from newspaper strips and wallpaper paste.

5 Jelutong is an excellent choice of wood for the first-time carver as it is easy to carve and shape.

6 Laminating resin has to be mixed with **7** hardener to enable it to set hard (cure). To this mix, fine particles of **8** metal filler or a colored pigment can be added. This mix is used for the first coat of the cast and ensures that the surface is colored. Subsequent coats of ordinary resin mix are used with **9** fiberglass matting to reinforce the casting material.

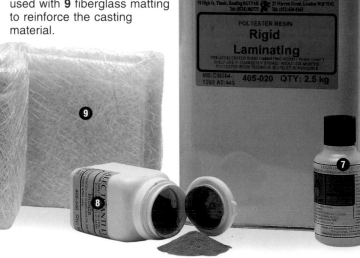

ALEC TIRANTI LTD
70 High St, Theale, Reading RG7 5AR 27 Warren Street, London W1P 5DG
Tel: (0734) 302775 Tel: (071) 636 8565

POLYESTER RESIN

Rigid Laminating

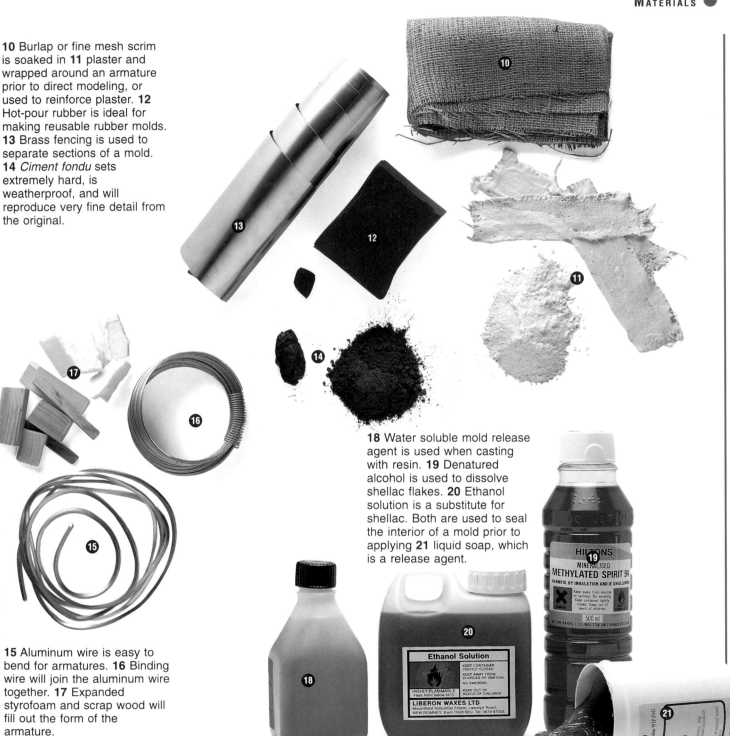

10 Burlap or fine mesh scrim is soaked in **11** plaster and wrapped around an armature prior to direct modeling, or used to reinforce plaster. **12** Hot-pour rubber is ideal for making reusable rubber molds. **13** Brass fencing is used to separate sections of a mold. **14** *Ciment fondu* sets extremely hard, is weatherproof, and will reproduce very fine detail from the original.

18 Water soluble mold release agent is used when casting with resin. **19** Denatured alcohol is used to dissolve shellac flakes. **20** Ethanol solution is a substitute for shellac. Both are used to seal the interior of a mold prior to applying **21** liquid soap, which is a release agent.

15 Aluminum wire is easy to bend for armatures. **16** Binding wire will join the aluminum wire together. **17** Expanded styrofoam and scrap wood will fill out the form of the armature.

5 Brass brazing rod is used with **6** flux during brazing. **7** Copper-coated steel welding rod is used in gas welding. The rods are available in different sizes.

1 Two-part wood putty can be used to fill gaps in a constructed wood sculpture. **2** Silicone sealant fills and joins plastic materials. **3** Sprackling compound fills gaps and cracks in a fired clay sculpture. **4** Car body filler (Bondo) is ideal for large gaps in the surface of a sculpture or for attaching and holding a sculpture in place or on a base.

8 Glue gun sticks are used with a glue gun for paper, cardboard and wood. 9 Wood glue. 10 Two-part epoxy resin glue will stick anything together, including steel and stone. 11 Pop rivets are used to attach sheet steel or tin.

12 Ferric nitrate and 13 hydrochloric acid are used to treat steel before coloring it. Handle with extreme care,

follow manufacturer's instructions, wear protective clothing, and check regulations for disposal.

14 Powder pigments can be obtained in a wide choice of colors. 15 Woodstain is absorbed by the wood and so enhances the grain. 16 Beeswax will enhance the

grain of a carving. 17 Varnish will seal and highlight any surface and is available in flat or gloss finish. 18 Oil paint can be used straight from the tube or thinned.

Materials and their uses

The beauty of making sculpture today is that you can choose from such a wide variety of materials, not all of them with a specifically sculptural use. Of course, some materials are used purely for a single sculptural technique and have no other function. Other materials cross the boundaries of several techniques. There are other indispensable items that could be regarded as the basic stock of a sculptor's studio. Similar to the contents of a kitchen cupboard, they may not be the main ingredient of a dish but, without them, the recipe would fail. These items include shellac, white craft glue, scrim, masking tape, liquid soap, clay slip, mineral spirits, binding wire, screws, and nails.

MATERIAL	TECHNIQUE	AVAILABILITY
Clay	Modeling	An economical fine clay and one with added grog are the two essential types
Plaster	Moldmaking, Direct modeling, Carving, Casting	Casting plasters are graded according to their strength when set and range from very hard, very white plaster through to a less hard, off-white and more economical plaster.
Wood	Carving, Construction	The two categories of hard and soft wood refer to the strength of the wood and the ease with which it can be cut and shaped. Sheet material is obtained from a lumber yard, as are lengths of wood which are either prepared with a planed smooth surface, or sawn, with a rough surface.
Stone	Carving	Types of stone vary in terms of their color, their surface texture, and the ease with which they can be carved. Like wood, stone is available in different grades of hard and soft and also in a variety of colors and surface textures.
Papier-mâché	Direct modeling	This is prepared using small pieces of newspaper or shredded paper and wallpaper adhesive or diluted white craft glue.
Polyester resin	Casting, Direct modeling	This is a synthetic liquid chemical product which sets hard with the addition of a catalyst.
Ciment fondu	Casting, Direct Modeling	A powdered cement that needs to be mixed with sand or an aggregate and water to set hard.
Every day objects	Assemblage	As the name suggests these are always available so keep your eyes open, and always be ready to pick up objects with potential.
Mild steel	Welding, Brazing, Riveting	Mild steel is available from a stockholder in a variety of forms – rod, bar, pipe, and sheet – all in different sizes to suit the job in hand. Hunting around scrapyards is also a fruitful way to locate interesting shaped pieces.
Aerated concrete block	Carving	Though this is a building material, it is extremely soft to cut and shape and ideal for making sculpture, leaving a very interesting surface finish.
Rubber	Moldmaking, Casting	Rubber is available both as a hot pour compound, which needs to be melted down, or in the now more popular form of room temperature vulcanizing rubber (RTV) which is used cold.

CONSIDERATIONS	TIPS
A clay with grog added is suitable for large kiln-fired sculptures. Fine clay is used for sculptures to be cast in another material and when fine detail is needed in the modeling.	Break dry clay into small pieces, put into a watertight container and completely immerse in water. After a while the dry clay will absorb the water to produce a sludge. Lay this on a flat surface to dry out a bit (but not too much), and you will be able to use it again.
The lowest grade is suitable for making molds. The higher grades will produce quality plaster casts and sculptures where structural strength is important.	Always store plaster in a dry place so it does not absorb moisture from the atmosphere. This will retard the rate at which it sets and affect its final strength.
Prepared and sawn timber is suitable for constructed sculptures, the latter for those jobs where the visual quality of the wood is not as important as the structural quality. The relative hardness or softness of a piece of wood is particularly important when carving.	Check your source to make sure that you are not using endangered or protected hardwood. Discarded wooden furniture is a good source of hardwood, especially if you need to prepare a base for a sculpture.
Granite is a very hard material to carve and should be left to experienced carvers. Sandstone is softer and suitable for those with less experience.	Demolition sites can be a good source of stone.
As papier-mâché takes a long time to dry, it is better to build it up in layers, especially for vertical and overhanging surfaces.	When it is dry, it is extremely hard and resistant and can be sanded and smoothed down.
Careful and exact measurement is essential.	Save old jars and tin cans to mix the resin in.
Ciment fondu is extremely strong and hard-wearing. You can use it for hollow cast sculpture suitable for siting out of doors.	A block of *ciment fondu* makes a good base for a sculpture.
Deciding how to fix disparate objects together can be a problem. You may need to make several trials before you hit on the best solution.	Aluminum drink cans which have been cut and flattened out make ideal sheet material to join with pop rivets.
Always use all safety precautions when working with steel.	The mild steel casing of domestic appliances, such as washing machines, are a very good source of sheet material.
Aerated concrete is a brittle material and care must be taken while carving to avoid breaking the block.	Ask on building sites for damaged blocks that will not be used.
Follow the manufacturers' recommendations carefully and make sure you use the right sort of rubber for the job.	Most rubber molds will keep for a long time so store them safely and securely until they are needed again.

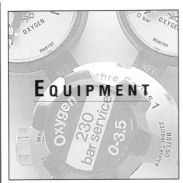

1 Clear goggles protect you from airborne pieces of material when carving, sanding, or grinding. **2** Welding goggles have darkened glass to allow you to look directly at the flame when brazing or welding. **3** An arc welding mask should be worn when electric arc welding. This protects both eyes and face from the intense light of the electric arc.

EQUIPMENT

In addition to the more specialized items shown on pages 14–21, you will find it useful to have the following general equipment: felt-tip pens, pencils and chalk for drawing and marking; steel tape measure, straight edge ruler, carpenter's square and square for measuring; masking tape; scissors; scales for weighing resin accurately; a food mixer for pulping papier-mâché mix; a blowtorch for welding and bending plastic; a selection of paint brushes; appropriate vises; a modeling board.

Jars and tin cans are always needed for mixing and storing. A toothbrush, sponge and scrubbing brush are good for cleaning out molds and casts. Plaster should be mixed in a plastic bowl or a bucket. Plastic wrap or plastic sheeting will prevent clay from drying out. A water sprayer will keep dust down and moisten clay. A sand-filled inner tube will support and protect awkward shapes. Strips of inner tube will hold pieces of a mold in place. A sheet of glass or formica is good for mixing epoxy resin glue or car body filler.

4 Barrier cream is useful for protecting your hands, particularly if you have sensitive skin. **5** Latex gloves are tight fitting and should be worn for intricate work. You can also use rubber gloves, but they are much looser fitting. **6** Leather gloves are essential for welding.

7 A dust mask will protect against the inhalation of dust particles and can be combined with **8** a respirator mask when working with toxic or irritating fumes. **9** Ear protectors or muffs should be used when operating loud power tools.

15

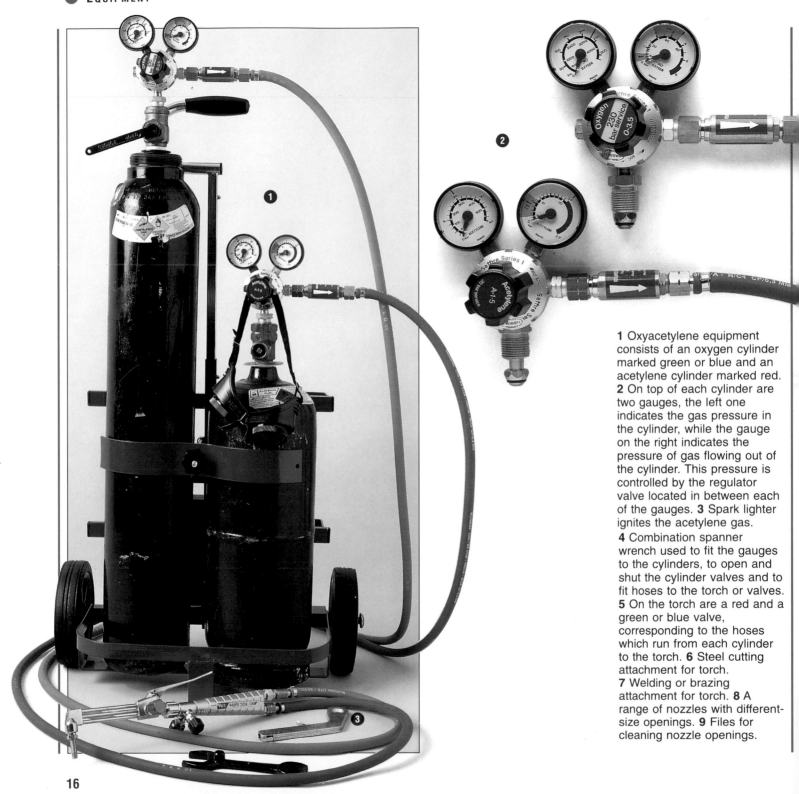

1 Oxyacetylene equipment consists of an oxygen cylinder marked green or blue and an acetylene cylinder marked red. 2 On top of each cylinder are two gauges, the left one indicates the gas pressure in the cylinder, while the gauge on the right indicates the pressure of gas flowing out of the cylinder. This pressure is controlled by the regulator valve located in between each of the gauges. 3 Spark lighter ignites the acetylene gas. 4 Combination spanner wrench used to fit the gauges to the cylinders, to open and shut the cylinder valves and to fit hoses to the torch or valves. 5 On the torch are a red and a green or blue valve, corresponding to the hoses which run from each cylinder to the torch. 6 Steel cutting attachment for torch. 7 Welding or brazing attachment for torch. 8 A range of nozzles with different-size openings. 9 Files for cleaning nozzle openings.

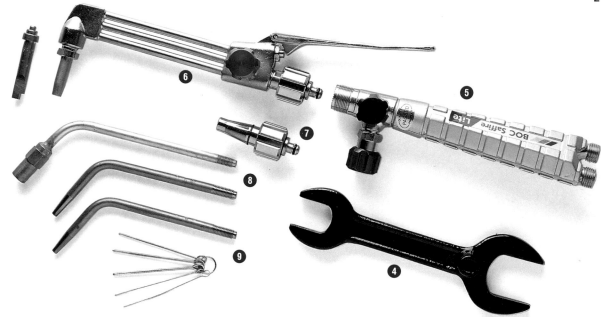

The electric arc-welding unit **10** is plugged directly into an outlet. The handle adjusts the strength of the electric current. Below this are two terminals. The lead of the electrode holder **11** is attached to one terminal and the ground clamp **12** to the other. You can use a Plasma-arc cutter instead of an electric arc-welding unit.

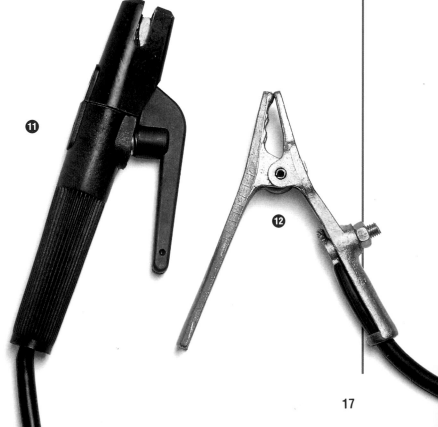

2 An awl is a hand-held tool for marking the position of holes to be drilled. It is especially effective on softwood and cardboard. **3** Drill bits for wood and thin gauge steel. **4** Zip bit or spade bit for large diameter holes in wood. **5** Counter sink bit to countersink a hole that has already been drilled in wood.

1 A modeling stand is very useful for modeling a portrait or life figure, as you can adjust the height.

6 Electric melting pot used for melting rubber to make a mold. A thermostat controls the temperature.

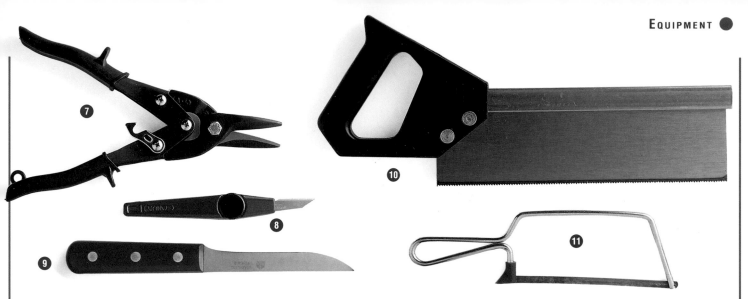

7 Tin snips cut steel wire, aluminum armature wire, sheets of tin and aluminum. **8** A craft knife serves as a general cutting implement. **9** An old kitchen knife has many uses, especially when working with plaster. **10** A tenon saw is useful for diagonal cuts or small-dimension work. **11** A junior hacksaw is suitable for found objects. You will also need a hacksaw for steel rod and pipe.

12 A C-clamp holds work securely to the work surface. **13** Pliers are useful for bending wire, pulling out nails, and holding material while you work. **14** An electric glue gun is used with glue sticks. **15** A rivet gun is used with pop rivets when joining sheet metal. **16** A sealant gun is used with a tube of silicon sealer.

19

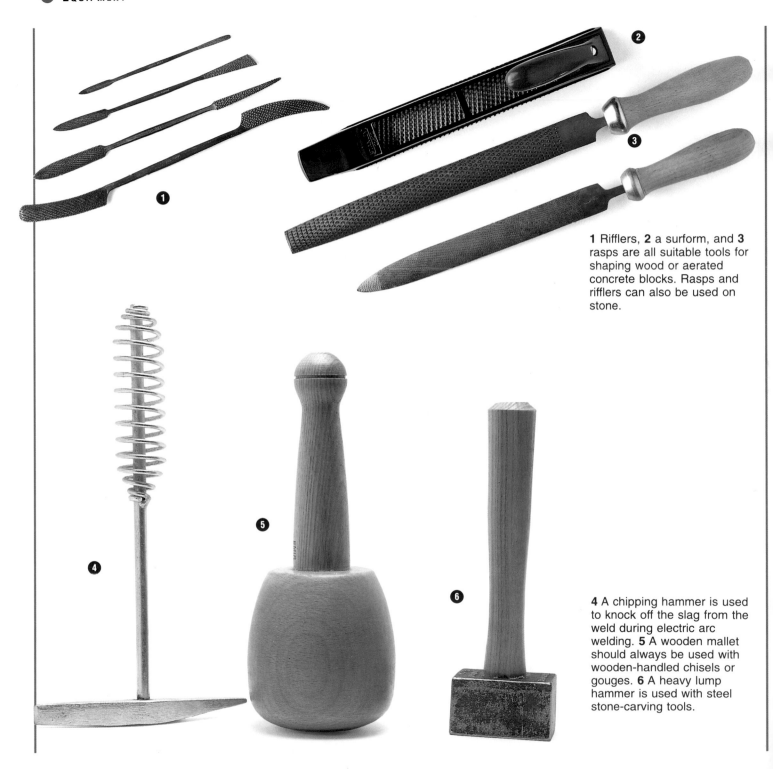

1 Rifflers, 2 a surform, and 3 rasps are all suitable tools for shaping wood or aerated concrete blocks. Rasps and rifflers can also be used on stone.

4 A chipping hammer is used to knock off the slag from the weld during electric arc welding. 5 A wooden mallet should always be used with wooden-handled chisels or gouges. 6 A heavy lump hammer is used with steel stone-carving tools.

7 Wooden-handled carving gouges with curved and shaped cutting edges are used for carving wood. **8** Stone-carving chisels come with a variety of cutting edges. Use a nylon mallet with round-handled tools and a lump hammer with the others.

9 Plaster and **10** clay wooden and wire-ended modeling tools come in a myriad of shapes and sizes and are absolutely essential when modeling, as they allow you to shape and define the sculpture in finer detail.

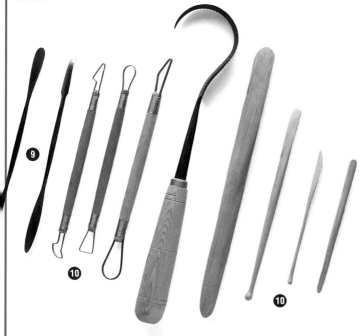

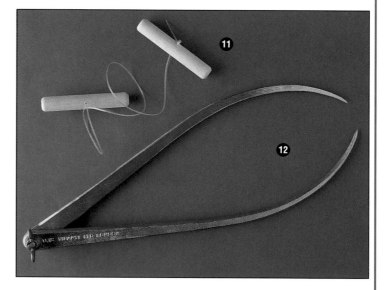

11 A clay-cutting wire is the most efficient way of cutting clay. The method is similar to cutting cheese. **12** Calipers are used to transfer measurements from a life model to your sculpture.

GETTING STARTED

When you have the material and equipment necessary to make a sculpture, you may find yourself wondering how to begin – this is a common problem, and sculpture can seem a mammoth undertaking. But there are ways to get started. Some decisions need to be pre-planned, while in some instances the technique itself determines the final form.

Drawings
Drawing has a role to play, but it is important to understand its limitations when making sculpture. Whether you are making a figurative or an abstract sculpture, drawing should be used only as a way to understand and develop the form you wish to sculpt. Being two-dimensional, it can never produce an equivalent of the sculpture that you wish to make, and it is far better that the important decisions regarding a sculpture's form are made in three dimensions.

For instance, when modeling a figure from life in clay, it is of enormous benefit to make drawings of the figure in order to gain a better knowledge of its forms and the way that they articulate

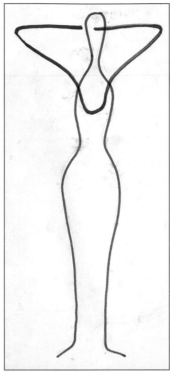

Armature design for the cast life figure (see pages 26–8 and 61–3).

one against another. This knowledge will help you when you start modeling the clay. However, it will be the successful making of the armature that allows you to start modeling in clay.

Drawing can play a part in the making of an abstract or stylized sculpture. A drawing from direct observation – a figure, a building, a landscape – can be used as the model for another drawing or drawings which would be abstractions of some or all of the forms in the original. Similarly, a photograph can form the original model to produce a similar set of drawings.

Drawing can be used in

constructed or assemblage sculpture to plan out the possible positions of the various parts and how they relate to one another.

Carving is, perhaps, the most problematic technique in terms of getting started. Because of the amount of time and energy expended in disposing of waste material, it is advisable to make a simple profile drawing on paper of the sculpture, which can then be transferred onto the face of the block by means of a grid.

This is not the only way to start a carving, however. Material can be carved

directly, without any decisions regarding the form of the sculpture being made before-hand. This type of carving is very dependent on the material itself being of such a configuration that it suggests a possible form or set of forms to be carved. This is far more likely to happen with oddly shaped branches, tree trunks or broken pieces of stone than with geometrically cut lumps of material. If you do decide to embark on a carving in this way, take care to avoid whittling the material away to nothing.

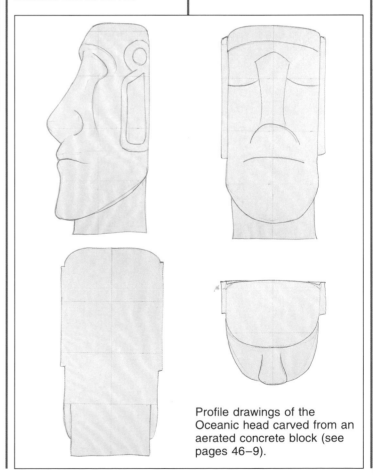

Profile drawings of the Oceanic head carved from an aerated concrete block (see pages 46–9).

Detailed drawing indicating the proposed shape and final coloring of the kiln-fired torso (see pages 86–9).

Maquettes
Making a maquette, or mock-up, of a sculpture is a very useful exercise and helps you to judge whether the form you have in mind for your sculpture will actually work three-dimensionally. A maquette is a small version of sculpture – though it is a rough-and-ready one, so don't spend too much time making it. Clay is a very useful material to use for maquettes, especially if your final sculpture is also to be modeled in clay.

A clay maquette is also another way to start a carving. You model a rough approximation of the sculpture to be carved and transfer the basic information regarding the location of forms onto the block of material to be carved.

Cardboard and wire are useful materials to use when making a maquette, too, especially for constructed sculpture. You can use wire to try out different configurations when making an armature, especially when it is a permanent one and will need to stay inside the sculpture. Cardboard cut to shape is useful as a template when you need to cut more than one shape of the same size from sheet material.

There are aspects of the construction and assemblage techniques which are totally reliant on the combination of the nature of the material and your own perceptions.

As you can see, there is no prescriptive method for starting a piece of sculpture. It is dependent on many things – the material, the technique being used, whether it is abstract or figurative. There are many variables involved, but I firmly believe that the best way to start a sculpture is by manipulating or "pushing" material around. This activity in itself acts as a catalyst and will help you generate ideas.

Clay maquette for the abstract plaster carving (see pages 50–2).

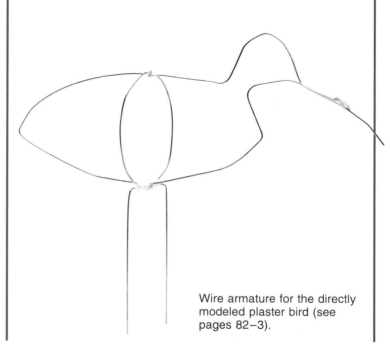

Wire armature for the directly modeled plaster bird (see pages 82–3).

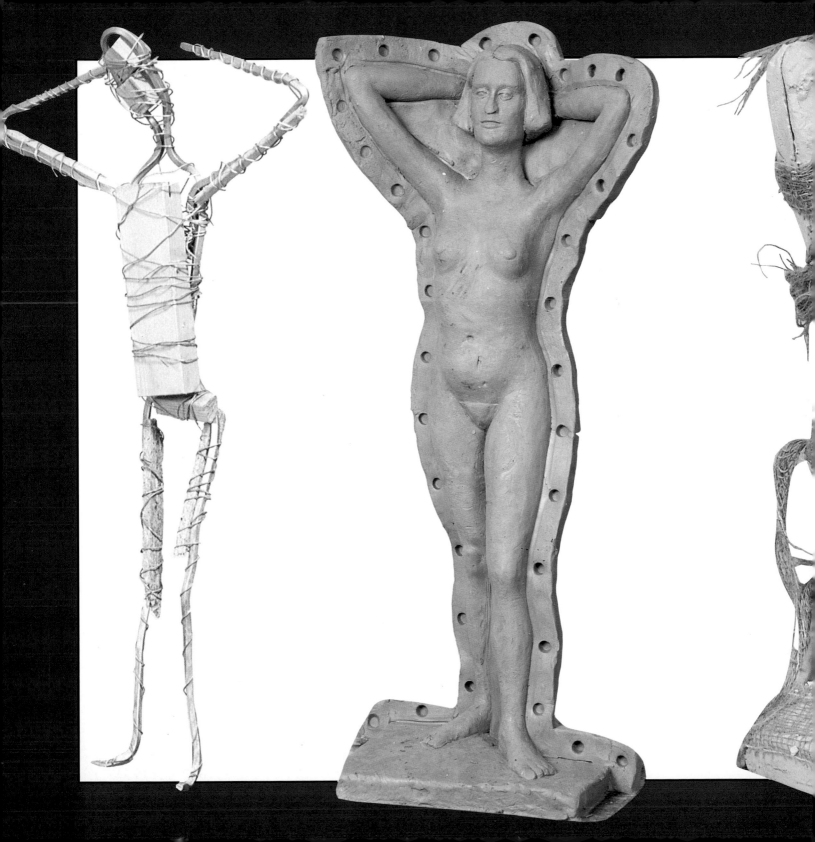

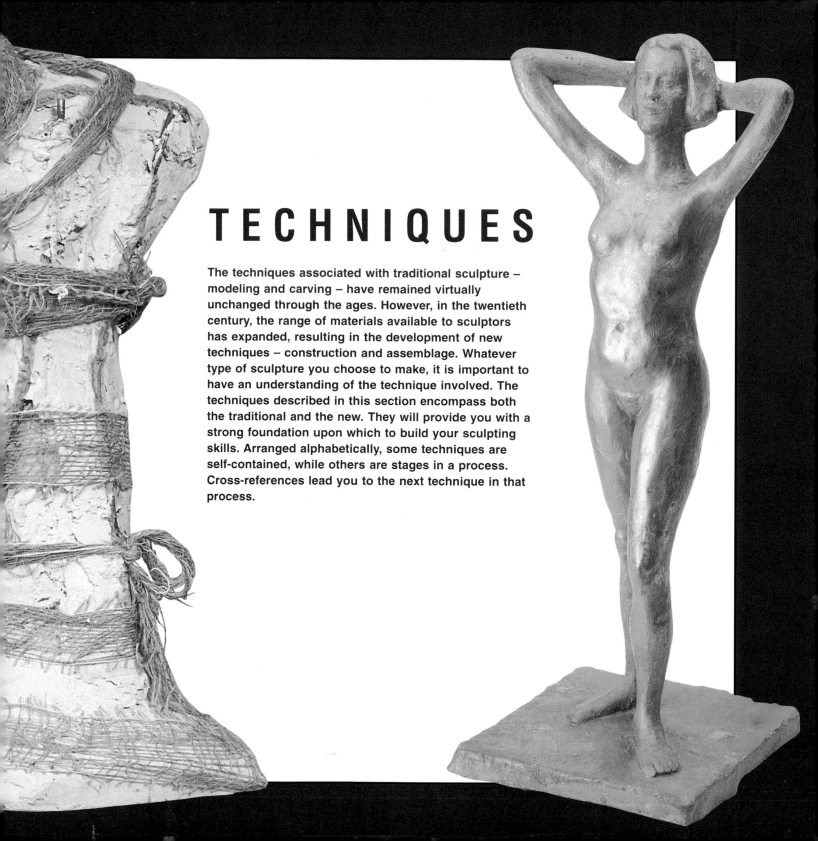

TECHNIQUES

The techniques associated with traditional sculpture –
modeling and carving – have remained virtually
unchanged through the ages. However, in the twentieth
century, the range of materials available to sculptors
has expanded, resulting in the development of new
techniques – construction and assemblage. Whatever
type of sculpture you choose to make, it is important to
have an understanding of the technique involved. The
techniques described in this section encompass both
the traditional and the new. They will provide you with a
strong foundation upon which to build your sculpting
skills. Arranged alphabetically, some techniques are
self-contained, while others are stages in a process.
Cross-references lead you to the next technique in that
process.

ARMATURE

In sculpture, the armature performs the same function as the skeleton of the body – it is the structure that supports an outer covering of material. It is used only in the modeling method of making sculpture, using materials such as clay, plaster, and papier-mâché. Because of the malleable nature of these media, they lack any inherent structural strength. Unless you use an armature, the size and form of your sculpture will be greatly limited.

Still thinking of the skeleton, it is important to realize the close relationship that exists between the armature and the final form of the sculpture. It is essential to plan the armature carefully. This will make it easier when you start to add material to it and develop the form of the sculpture itself. It is also difficult – and usually impossible – to make changes to the armature once you have started modeling.

Using an armature
An armature can be used in two ways. First, it can be permanent and remain inside the finished sculpture. The WELDING section will show you how to make a permanent

steel armature that is used in the DIRECT MODELING section. This section also has a sculpture that uses a ready-made permanent armature.

The other way an armature is used is as a temporary support structure for a modeling medium. This allows you to model a sculpture with clay prior to its being cast in another material (see the MODELING, MOLDMAKING, and CASTING sections). The example on page 31 shows a type of temporary armature for making a sculpture that will be fired in a kiln.

The following three techniques show the preparation of an armature for a life figure, a portrait head, and a simple armature suitable for a kiln-fired sculpture. Two sculptures will be cast in another material and use flexible aluminum armature wire, which can be bent easily when making the armature initially and also when it is time to remove the sculpture from the plaster mold.

Life figure
It is important to have the armature the right size from the start, as changes are difficult – if not impossible – to make later. This is especially true when making an armature for a figure, in this case one-third life size.

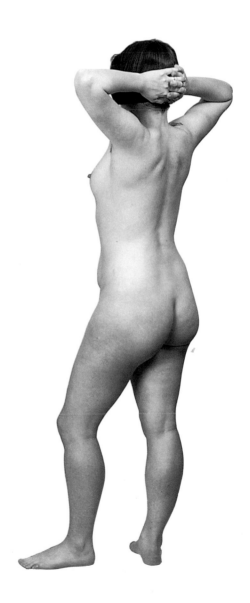

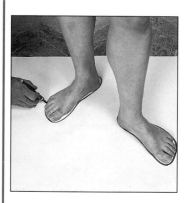

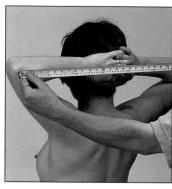

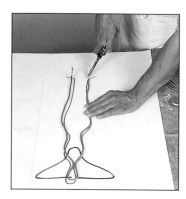

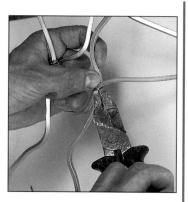

1 Once the pose has been established, mark the position of the model's feet on a sheet of heavy paper with a felt-tip pen. This will allow the model to resume the same position after rests and also help in taking accurate measurements.

2 Make as many measurements as you want, as they will all help when it comes to modeling the figure. At this stage, however, you are concerned with measurements that will help you construct the armature. These are the vertical measurements from the floor to the waist, the shoulders, the elbows, the top of the head, and the measurement across the arms from elbow to elbow.

3 Divide the measurements by three for the clay figure. The measurements for the armature will be slightly less to allow for the added layer of clay. Draw the design of the armature on paper, remembering to use the minimum number of lengths of wire possible. The fewer joins, the stronger the armature will be. For this pose two lengths are adequate. Using the drawing as a guide, bend the wire into the proposed design.

4 Attach the arms to the body with binding wire. Hold the pieces to be joined in position and wrap a short piece of binding wire around the two pieces of armature wire. Twist the binding wire around once with your fingers. Then, use pliers to hold the two ends of the binding wire and pull and twist both pieces of wire as tightly as possible. This produces a very secure attachment point which will be sufficient to hold the pieces of armature wire in place.

5 Paint the base board for the fixed iron armature support with three coats of shellac, allowing time to dry between coats. This prevents the board from drawing the water out of the clay, which can otherwise dry out and crack.

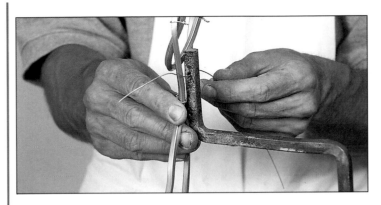

6 Attach the armature to its iron support, making sure that the feet of the armature are ½ inch above the base board. Use the binding wire and twisting technique to attach the armature, at the waist, firmly to the iron support.

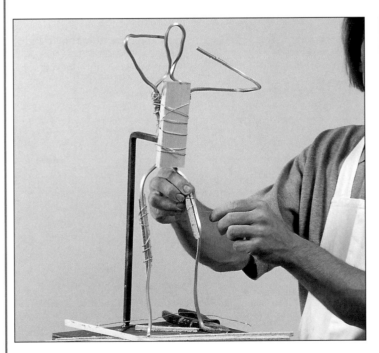

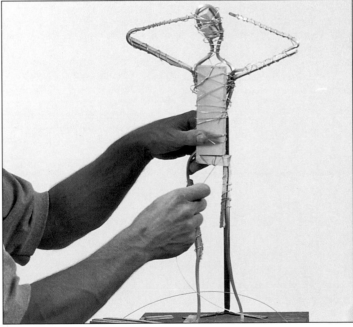

7 Pad out the torso area with a block of wood, holding it in place with binding wire wrapped tightly around the wood and the armature wire. Strips of wood can also be placed on the upper arms, upper legs, and a piece in the head section, bearing in mind the size of the form that is going to be modeled around it. This wood strengthens the figure, absorbs water from the clay, and expands, exerting an outward pressure on the clay that surrounds it.

8 Finally, wrap binding wire loosely around the entire armature to help the clay grip.

Head

This armature is for a life-size head and is designed so that you can model the head well above the surface of the base board.

1 Cut the plywood and softwood to size. Clamp the base board to the bench and countersink the drilled holes. Measure and mark the center of the board and drill a hole the same diameter as the shaft of the bolt.

2 Position the two small slats of wood underneath the board on opposite sides and screw them firmly into position. Raising the base board up in this way allows you to move the armature more easily when the clay head has been modeled onto it.

3 Taking a 12-inch length of aluminum armature wire, use netting staples to attach one end to the vertical shaft.

4 Bend the aluminum wire around in an even curve and use netting staples to attach the other end of the aluminum wire to the shaft.

5 Repeat this process, adding the aluminum wire to the other two sides. This configuration holds together the mass of clay that forms the basis of the head.

6 Position the shaft of the armature in the vise so that the aluminum wires are pointing down, and the square section at the other end of the shaft is level with the bench top. Drill a hole in the center of this section, slightly smaller than the smallest diameter of the bolt. Drill down 4 inches into the shaft. Place the inverted base board over the top, matching up the two holes, and use a wrench to screw the bolt tightly in place. The armature is now ready.

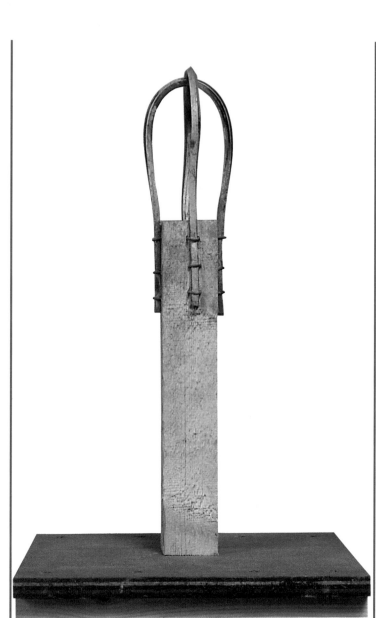

Simple armature

A simple armature for a large clay sculpture can be made using a broom handle. The one shown is suitable for the KILN FIRING technique. Construct a double modeling board by taking two boards 16 × 16 inches and drill a hole in the center of each, the diameter of the broom handle. Place two pieces of wood 2 × 2 × 16 inches in between the boards on opposite sides and screw in place. Cover the board with plastic wrap to stop the clay from sticking to it, and hold it in place with tape. Now, with a mallet, gently hammer the broom handle vertically right through the hole in the top board and down into the hole in the bottom board. This arrangement will hold the armature pole steady and stop it from moving from side to side under the weight of the clay. Make sure that the armature pole is not lodged too tightly in the hole. You should just be able to rotate it. Wrap the pole with plastic wrap.

ASSEMBLAGE

Assemblage was pioneered earlier this century and uses everyday objects, bringing them together to make a sculpture. A successful assemblage focuses our perception on what the sculpture represents or is doing and not on the identity or function of the original objects.

Inevitably with everyday objects, you will be dealing with a variety of shapes and materials, so it is helpful, when considering the format of the sculpture, to think carefully about the ways in which these disparate items are going to be joined and attached. It is also a good idea to keep to a minimum any cutting and shaping of the objects.

Creating the sculpture
By its very nature, assemblage requires that you use your imagination a great deal, identifying the sculptural potential that exists in the objects that surround you. The examples shown introduce you to this potential and to some attaching and joining methods, though the method you choose will always depend on the type of materials you are joining.

The first example is a representational assemblage of a bird. The main catalyst for this sculpture was the plastic container of household detergent. Other objects were then collected to provide the rest of the bird, and a drawing was made to plan how they all fit together.

The second example is a simple repetition of the same object – plastic coat hangers. Their shape makes them ideal for arranging in a spiral formation around a central axis – a threaded steel rod – to produce a sense of movement, a conventional theme of abstract sculpture.

Abstract sculpture
When making an abstract sculpture, you will need to pay attention to the shape of the individual parts and the relationship these parts have to one another within the form of the sculpture.

YOU WILL NEED

plastic coat hangers • C-clamp • junior hacksaw • electric drill • pencil • scrap wood • awl • blowtorch • leather gloves • felt-tip pen caps • threaded steel rod • vise • nuts • pliers

1 Cut off the metal hooks from all the coat hangers using a C-clamp to hold them steady. With a junior hacksaw, cut the metal shaft as close to the plastic coat hanger as possible.

3 Gently heat the hangers so they bend easily. You will need a controllable heat source with a gentle, slow flame, such as a blowtorch with the flame turned as low as possible. Plastic softens very quickly, so don't hold the hanger still. Wearing leather gloves and making sure that the flame is blowing away from you, gently wave the part to be bent in the flame. Do not breathe in the plastic fumes.

4 Once the plastic has softened, turn off the gas and bend the arms of the black hangers at 90 degrees in opposite directions.

2 Drill central holes of the same diameter in each of the hangers. The most efficient way to do this is to use one of each type of hanger as a template. Take one black and one yellow hanger and mark the central point of each with a pencil. Clamp the first hanger to the bench, using blocks of scrap wood to distribute the pressure of the clamp evenly. Then drill a ⅛-inch hole.

Repeat with the other hanger. Using a hanger as a template, place it on top of another of the same color, then push an awl through the drilled hole to mark the position of the hole to be drilled. Repeat with all of the black and yellow coat hangers, then drill a ⅜-inch hole in each one, making sure that the hanger is securely clamped to the bench as before.

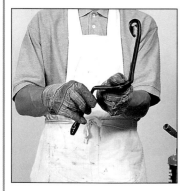

5 Hold the hanger in position until the plastic cools. Once cool, you will find the hanger will stay firmly in its new configuration.

6 The tips of the arms of the yellow hanger need to be bent into the most acute angle possible. Warm them as before, remembering not to hold the hanger motionless in the flame.

7 Felt-tip pen caps have an interior diameter slightly larger than that of the steel rod.

Place each in a vise and cut to the required length to use as a spacer between the hangers.

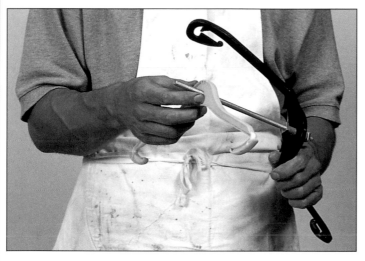

8 Thread a nut onto one end of the steel rod. Slot on a black coat hanger, then a pen cap. Thread on another nut, followed by a yellow hanger.

9 Repeat the sequence until the length of the steel rod is covered. End with a nut, screwed down tightly with pliers to hold all the components together.

Figurative sculpture

This figurative sculpture of a bird was inspired initially by the plastic container shape. Other everyday materials were then found to make the other parts of the bird.

1 Make a drawing of your planned sculpture. Then mark the parts of the plastic containers that you require and, using a craft knife, cut them away.

SAFETY

When using the craft knife, always hold the container firmly on the bench and draw the blade of the knife away from you. It is essential to work this way to avoid unpleasant accidents.

2 The neck is joined to the head by melting and blending the plastic together. Heat the tip of a knife in the flame of a blowtorch. Hold the two parts to be joined securely in position. Melt the plastic of the first container with the hot knife, then pull the knife across to the other container, so that the plastic melts and blends together. Repeat all the way around the points of contact. Once the head and neck have been joined together, they can be attached to the main body, using the same method. Parts that need to be joined in this way can be held in place with masking tape while you are working with the torch.

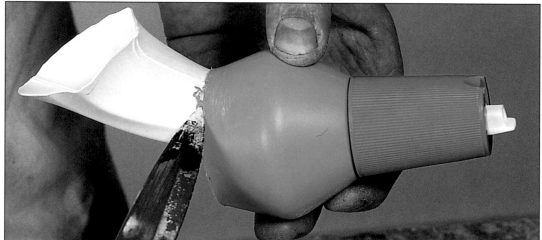

3 The legs of the bird are made from the ends of a coat hanger. Remove them with pliers.

4 Drill a hole ⅛ inch into the top of the leg. Use this hole as a template to make a corresponding hole in each side of the body with an awl. Measure the interior width of the body, saw a block of wood to this size, and insert it. Screw the legs to the body.

7 Using a riffler, roughen the surfaces of the body and wings where they are to be attached.

8 Wearing latex gloves, knead the epoxy resin putty to produce an even coloring (see REPAIRS). Press it firmly onto the roughened surface of the body.

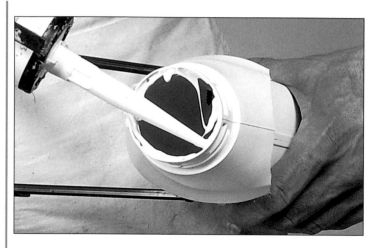

5 The cap of the container is inverted and placed into the top opening to make the bird's tail. Use the silicone gun to apply a bedding of silicone sealer around the top edge of the opening.

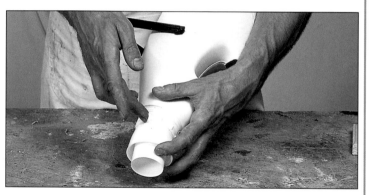

6 Push in the inverted top, wiping off any excess sealer with your finger. Hold the top in position with masking tape until the sealer has cured (set).

9 Now press the first wing down onto the putty, trimming and leveling the putty neatly all the way around with the modeling tool. Hold the wing in place with masking tape until the putty has set. Repeat the procedure with the other wing.

BASES

The main function of a base is to support a sculpture. Most sculptures require a base, although there are some exceptions. The welded steel construction, for instance, will, by virtue of the technique used to make it, provide its own support.

Sometimes, a base is an absolute necessity. Adding a base to sculptures like the cast of the portrait head and the carving of the fish allows them to be seen to their best advantage. The base of the figurative wooden construction is an integral functional part of the sculpture itself, and its weight keeps the sculpture in position. A base can, however, act as a purely compositional element. By using a base to define the space within which the cast plaster sculpture is seen, it produces a far greater sense of scale.

Traditionally, a base was made from stone or wood. Nowadays, ready-made materials such as the concrete paving stones are available. Alternatively, you can cast your own base in a casting jig, in materials such as *ciment fondu*, plaster, or resin.

Portrait head

YOU WILL NEED

car body filler and hardener • rubber gloves • sheet of glass or plastic-coated surface • filling knife • sand-filled inner tube • ½ × 5-inch metal pipe • riffler • cast-iron grate polish • toothbrush • soft cloth • wooden base • electric drill • ⅝-inch zip bit • two-part epoxy resin glue • palette knife • blocks of wood

1 Wearing rubber gloves throughout, put some car body filler on a sheet of glass. Squeeze out some hardener of roughly equal length. (Do not add too much hardener as this will speed up the setting time of the car body filler.)

2 Mix the two parts together so they have an even and consistent coloring.

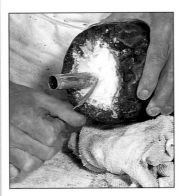

7 Even off the filler to the neck of the sculpture with a riffler.

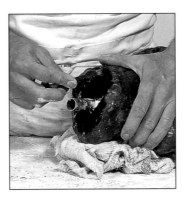

8 Apply the grate polish to the filler surface with a toothbrush, brushing it in well. When dry, buff with a soft cloth.

9 Position the head on the wooden base to mark the position of the pipe. Drill down 3 inches into the wooden base with the zip bit.

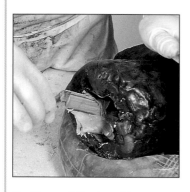

3 Support the head in a sand-filled inner tube. Add the body filler to the front wall of the neck cavity, working as quickly as you can.

4 Position the metal pipe centrally to the front of the neck and parallel to the front of the face before the mix sets. Press the pipe into the mix and hold it until it sets.

5 Take the metal pipe out. This leaves an impression of the pipe in the filler. Mix some more body filler.

6 Hold the metal pipe in its impression so that 2½ inches is left outside the neck. Apply more filler around the pipe in the neck cavity and allow it to set, holding the pipe in place. Make another mix of filler and fill the opening to the neck cavity. Leave it to set.

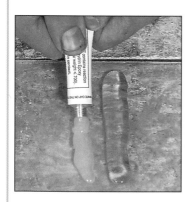

10 Squeeze out equal lengths of epoxy resin glue onto the glass sheet.

11 Using the plastic spatula that comes with the glue, mix the two parts together to obtain an even color. Put some glue in the hole with a palette knife, coating the interior surfaces well.

12 Put some more glue around the exposed pipe on the head, then place it in the hole on the base. This hole is slightly bigger than the pipe so you will be able to position the head easily. Keep the head supported with blocks of wood while the glue dries.

Fish carving

1 Lay your carving on the original drawing and mark the center point on the underside of the fish.

2 Place the carving in a vise, using a carpenter's level to check that it is level.

3 With the drill bit at a right angle to the underside of the carving, drill down 1½ inches, using masking tape on the drill bit as your depth guide.

Plaster cast

The residue of plaster that has set in the bottom of a bucket is used here as a base.

1 With a ruler, find and mark the center point of the plaster.

2 Clamp the base to your bench and drill a ⅜-inch diameter hole into both the base and the bottom of the sculpture at its approximate center point.

3 Fill the centre hole in the base with sprackling compound.

4 Mark the center point of the base, clamp it to the bench, and drill a hole. Gently tap the dowel down into it. Anchor the carving on the dowel and push it down as far as you can.

Wooden figurative construction

YOU WILL NEED

electric drill • ¼-inch drill bit • countersink bit • 6 × 18-inch concrete paving stone • square • awl • ¼-inch masonry bit • 2 rawlplugs • ½-inch No. 8 screws

1 Drill two holes in the foot section of the constructed sculpture with the drill bit. Countersink both holes. Place the sculpture on the base, using a square to make sure that the heel section lines up with the end edge of the base and the sculpture is centrally placed. With an awl, mark the position of the two drilled holes onto the base.

2 Using a masonry bit in your electric drill, drill two holes the depth of the base, and place a rawlplug in each of these holes. Once colored, the sculpture can be screwed in place. (See the COLORING and REPAIRS sections of this book.)

4 Cut the steel rod to length (it should be just shorter than the combined depths of the two holes). Fill the hole in the sculpture with sprackling compound and insert the steel rod. Pack the sprackle tightly around the steel rod.

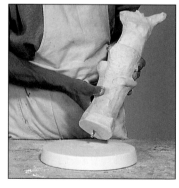

5 Before the sprackle sets hard, insert the rod into the hole in the base and set the sculpture vertically on the base. Adjust the sculpture so that it sits centrally on the base. Leave the sprackling compound to set.

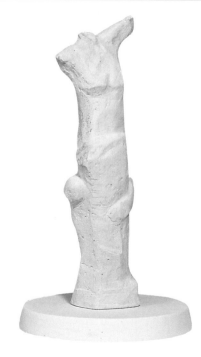

BRAZING

Brazing is a technique that uses molten brass to join two pieces of mild steel together at a low temperature. It is especially suitable for thin sheet and small-diameter steel rod and bar, which would be more likely to burn away, expand, and buckle under the higher temperature used in WELDING. Brazing makes a strong joint though not so strong as a welded joint.

For gas welding and brazing, the heat source used is the combination of two gases, oxygen, and acetylene (oxyacetylene), acetylene being the flammable gas. The gases are stored in cylinders, which have an on/off valve operated by a cylinder wrench. Mounted on the top of each cylinder are two gauges and a regulator valve. One gauge indicates the pressure of gas in the cylinder, the other indicates the pressure of the gas leaving the cylinder to the torch. Oxygen is denoted by the color green (or blue) and acetylene by red. Each cylinder is connected to the torch by a rubber hose. The torch itself has two valves – one red (acetylene) and the other green or blue (oxygen). With these you can control the mixture of gases for the correct flame. The size of the torch nozzle determines the size and intensity of the flame. As a guide, a nozzle with a small opening is suitable for brazing, while larger ones are suitable for welding. The gas pressures you require will depend on the nozzle size and the thickness of the mild steel being joined. Read the instruction manual carefully.

The sculpture being made in this section is a fish that forms part of a four-piece, wall-based sculpture. The flame of the torch is used to cut out shapes from a sheet of steel. The parts of the fish are then brazed together. Brass is used to form a decorative effect within the sculpture.

Obtaining correct flame

This flame is suitable for both brazing and welding. When using oxyacetylene equipment, always work in a well-ventilated area, away from flammable items. If possible, work above a concrete floor and always work on a steel surface. Always wear a boiler suit, leather gloves, a leather apron, welding goggles, and heavy-duty boots or shoes when using this equipment.

YOU WILL NEED

boiler suit • leather gloves • leather apron • welding goggles • heavy-duty boots/shoes • oxygen cylinder + regulator • acetylene cylinder + regulator • cylinder wrench • torch and hoses • welding nozzles • spark lighter • cutting attachment

1 The oxygen gauges and regulator. The right-hand gauge indicates the level of oxygen pressure in the cylinder, while the left-hand gauge shows the oxygen pressure flowing to the torch.

5 As you increase the amount of oxygen, the flame changes color to blue, and you will see it has three parts – a small cone near the tip of the welding nozzle, an area of flame around this, and a much larger area of flame that surrounds both of these.

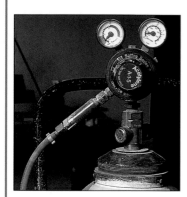  

2 The acetylene regulator and gauges. The right-hand gauge shows the acetylene pressure in the cylinder and the left-hand one the pressure flowing to the torch. Establish the correct pressure of each of the gases flowing through the torch, starting with the acetylene – being the flammable gas, it is the first one you turn on and the first you turn off.

3 Use the cylinder wrench to open the acetylene cylinder valve. Open the acetylene regulator at the cylinder, then open the (red) acetylene valve on the torch. Gas will now escape from the welding nozzle, cleaning the hoses and nozzle. Adjust the cylinder regulator to obtain the required pressure on the left-hand gauge (here 2 pounds per square inch) and close the acetylene valve on the torch.

Do the same with the oxygen, the pressure of which should be the same. Turn on the acetylene valve slightly and ignite the gas with a spark lighter, with the flame pointing away from you. Open the acetylene valve more and stop just at the point where the black smoke, given off by the burning gas, disappears.

4 Now open the oxygen valve. You will notice that the flame immediately becomes more powerful.

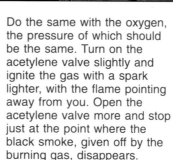

6 Keep increasing the amount of oxygen until the middle part of the flame is eliminated. You are now left with a flame in two parts, a small white cone at the tip of the nozzle and a blue area of flame that surrounds it. To shut off the flame, close the acetylene valve on the torch first, then close the oxygen valve.

7 The cutting attachment can be screwed onto the torch after the welding nozzle has been removed. Open the oxygen valve on the torch fully – there is an oxygen valve on the cutting attachment which is used to control the oxygen pressure. Increase the pressure to 30 pounds per square inch. Open the oxygen valve on the cutting

attachment and adjust the oxygen regulator at the cylinder until this pressure is shown on the gauge. The acetylene pressure remains the same. Light the torch and obtain the same acetylene flame as before. The resultant flame will be harsher as there are more outlets at the tip of the cutting torch.

8 Open the oxygen valve.

9 Increase the oxygen until you obtain a three-part flame.

10 Continue until you have a two-part flame, making sure that each of the cones of flame are consistent.

11 Finally, depress the lever on the cutting attachment to let oxygen out of the central opening, and adjust the oxygen valve to the correct type of flame. To turn off, close down the acetylene valve on the torch, followed by the oxygen valve on the cutting attachment. When you have finished working with the equipment, close both of the cylinder valves with a wrench. Then, one at a time, open each valve on the torch to expel any gas in the hoses; when the gauges register zero, close both of the regulators.

Wallhanging sculpture

The steel that is near the flame will be hot for some time after you have finished work, so don't touch or move it without leather gloves. Wear protective clothing throughout: leather apron, welding goggles, boiler suit and heavy boots or shoes.

YOU WILL NEED

leather gloves • leather apron • welding goggles • boiler suit • heavy-duty boots/shoes • chalk • sheet steel from a washing machine casing • oxy-acetylene equipment • wire brush or steel wool • ¼-inch steel rod • brass rod • flux • nuts • washers • clay • file

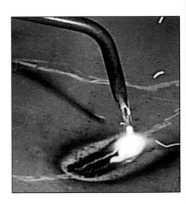

1 Using chalk, mark the profile of a fish tail on the sheet steel. Carefully follow the chalk outline with the flame until the shape is completely cut from the steel.

4 The central spine of the fish is a length of ¼-inch steel rod which is easily bent by hand. Thread on some nuts. Alternate curved sections of steel rod with the nuts. The curved sections are held in place with clay, the central curved rod touching all of the small curved sections. The curved sections have been made using small lengths of rod, heated and then bent to shape (see WELDING). When everything is in position, clean the areas to be brazed, then braze together.

2 A good brazed joint depends on both of the surfaces being clean, so clean the surfaces with a wire brush, steel wool or file beforehand.

3 The pieces of ¼-inch steel rod in the tail section are held in position by applying molten brass. Apply heat evenly to the area around the two pieces of steel to be joined (there should be a slight gap between them), until they reach red heat. At the same time, introduce a brass rod, which has previously been dipped into a powdered flux to stop oxidization, into the outer flame. When the steel reaches red heat (the melting point of brass), bring the brass rod into the area to be joined. The heat generated will enable the brass to melt and flow in and around this joint. Withdraw the rod, and turn off the gas. As the joint cools, the brass also cools, holding the two pieces of steel together.

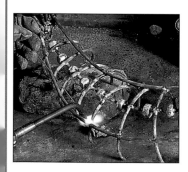

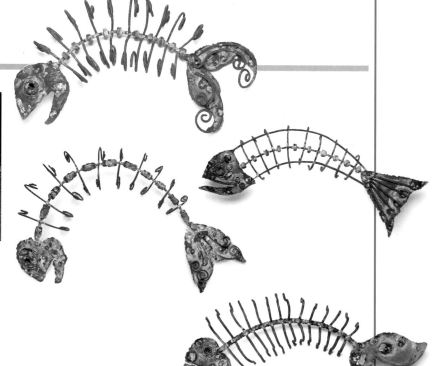

5 With the head and tail section brazed onto the central spine, add two more curved sections of steel rod on each side of the central spine. Braze into position where they come into contact with the small curved sections.

6 Finally, heat up an area of the face and brass rod. Drop molten brass onto the surface – this has a very pleasing decorative effect.

CARVING

Unlike modeling, which builds up a sculpture, carving is a reductive process, in which a sculpture is cut out of a block of stone, wood, or other material. This makes carving a very disciplined activity because, once material has been carved away, it cannot be replaced, so careful planning is essential.

Begin with a drawing or a small model of the proposed sculpture made from clay, called a maquette, and take this with you when you select your carving material. Try to match your material as closely as possible to the size and shape of your planned sculpture. Your first task will be to dispose of as much waste material as quickly and efficiently as possible, so you will want to keep this to a minimum, especially if you are working with a hard material.

Starting carving
In this section there are three examples of carving, each using a different material. The first is an aerated concrete building block. This is a very soft material that can be cut and shaped using basic tools. The sculpture is an Oceanic head, like those found on

Easter Island, which fits well within the geometry of the building block – so there will be a minimum of waste material to cut away.

The second exercise uses a block of plaster, another material that is easy to carve, especially in its wet state, using basic tools. This abstract sculpture is based on a clay maquette, and the result is very different from the geometry of the block from which it is carved. Variations in surface textures are also an important part of this sculpture.

The final carving is in wood. This is a more complex material to carve because of the grain. This stylized fish form is carved with particular attention to creating a smooth surface which highlights and accentuates the form of the sculpture. This exercise will also introduce the use of conventional woodcarving tools.

TIPS

A lot of dust is produced when working on one of these blocks, so work in a clear space where the dust will not be a problem. A water spray is essential to keep the dust levels in the air under control. You should also wear a dust mask, goggles, and protective clothing, such as an apron or coveralls.

Aerated concrete block
Concrete blocks are a readily available material that is ideal for those new to carving. The surface texture of the carving is well suited to this Oceanic head.

YOU WILL NEED

aerated concrete block • carpenter's square • water spray • goggles • dust mask • protective clothing • tape measure • chalk • wood saw • wooden mallet • carving gouge or flat chisel • rasp • surform with semicircular blade • long nail • riffler • sandpaper

1 Measure and mark a vertical center line on the front, back, and side faces of the block. On the top, mark two center lines from opposite sides of the block. Referring to your drawings for the sculpture, draw the side profile on each of the side faces of the block. Now draw the profile of the front on the front face of the block.

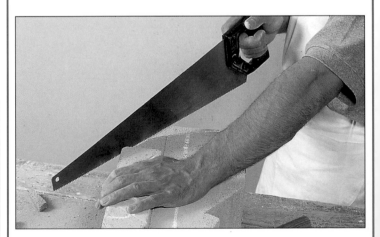

5 Cut away the material around the curved jaw using a series of straight cuts. The depth is shown by the profile drawn on the back of the block.

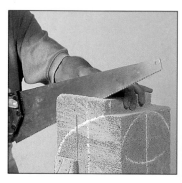

2 You are now ready to discard the first area of waste material by making a vertical cut with a saw across one of the corners of the block. This diagonal plane will form the basis of the forehead of the sculpture.

3 Next, saw off a section of material on the bottom and front faces of the block to form the basis of the chin and a recessed neck that will become the plinth on which the sculpture will stand. This means making two saw cuts, taking great care not to go over the guide marks, as this would result in a saw cut on the surface of the sculpture. However, if necessary, you can smooth down saw cuts later

with a rasp if they are not too deep. Staying on the side faces of the block, mark a rectangular section for the ear. Saw away the surrounding area in four saw cuts. The depth of the cut is determined by the drawn profile of the sculpture on the front of the block. There will now be, on each side, a raised area that will form the ears of the sculpture.

4 As areas of waste are cut away, it is important to redraw the center lines. Draw the profile of the face on both sides of the block and cut away the "v" section of eye sockets. Make a diagonal cut from the back of the block to prepare for the jaw area.

6 All the waste material that can be sawn has now been disposed of, and you are ready to start carving the sculpture. Initially, you will need a wooden or plastic mallet and either a flat chisel or a carving gouge. Do not hit the chisel too hard with the mallet or the material is liable to shatter and you could knock a large lump off the block! In fact, you should keep the use of the mallet to a minimum and you will find that you can

carve the material quite adequately just using the power of your hand to push the chisel. If you are using the chisel in this way, keep both hands behind the cutting blade. Remember that when you are carving, always cut away less rather than more, reducing the surface of the block in stages and not in one go. Begin by carving away the waste material around the nose and eyes.

7 Continue carving around the nose and deep into the eye cavities. You can now carve away the areas around the mouth and so start to form the chin. Remember that the tip of the nose is the highest point, the eye cavities are the deepest, and the raised mouth area is midway between the two.

8 The sculpture is really starting to take shape, and your most useful tools now are a surform or rasp, with a little help from a hand-held chisel. Because of the softness of the material, the surform or rasp are very efficient tools for shaping the broad areas of the back, top, forehead, cheeks, and chin. This is when a lot of dust is thrown up, so be ready with your water spray. A hand-held chisel can help further define the mouth, nose, and eye cavities.

10 Use an awl to define the stylized linear marks that form the ears.

11 Refine and shape the ears further with a hand-held chisel and a riffler, a very small rasp that comes in a variety of shapes which will allow you to get into hitherto inaccessible areas.

9 The surform quickly defines the rounded form of the top of the head.

12 The mouth, nose, and eye sockets can also be further refined using a riffler. Once these areas have been shaped and defined, finish by giving the whole sculpture a final rubdown with sandpaper.

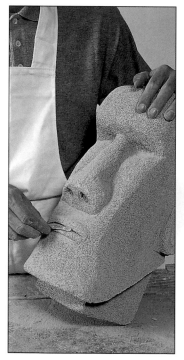

Abstract plaster form

This abstract plaster sculpture is based on a clay maquette. It is a very different shape from the original plaster block, so a great deal of waste material must be cut away.

YOU WILL NEED

casting jig • bucket • goggles • barrier cream • base board • nails • casting plaster • pencil • flat or carving gouge • chisel • wooden mallet • wood saw • knife with serrated edge • taping knife • tape measure

---

1 Set up your casting jig on a base board. Use a tape measure to determine the size of the jig, which in this case is 9 × 9 × 9 inches. Use a plastic-coated board, such as melamine, to ease the final removal of the casting jig. Alternatively, use soft soap or oil on all the surfaces of the boards that will come into contact with the plaster. Secure the boards where they meet the base board with nails, and pour the plaster in slowly – go too fast, and the pressure of the plaster may force the casting jig apart.

2 Once the plaster has set, gently pull the jig apart and away from the plaster block.

5 You now have a rough cylindrical shape. Referring to the clay maquette, draw the profile of the wedge shape that runs through the spiral on roughly opposite sides. These lines need to correspond with the rectangle already drawn on the top. Now, draw a spiral line around the cylinder from the top to the bottom. This will indicate the areas of waste material between the spiral form.

6 Using the saw, make a vertical cut to release the wedge shape. You are only able to go so far into the plaster before it gets very difficult. This is because of the high water content in the plaster.

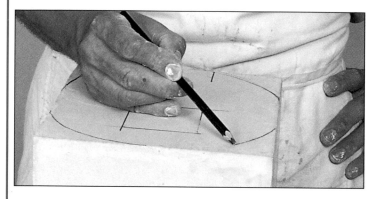

3 Look at the clay maquette to decide the areas of waste material on the plaster block. Mark a circle on the top of the block that touches all four sides. This corresponds to the widest point of the spiral. Next, mark the rectangular section corresponding to the one on the maquette on top of the plaster block.

4 Use a carving gouge and mallet to cut vertically down through the plaster to remove the four corners of the block. Plaster in its wet state is very easy to cut through and offers no resistance to the blade. Don't become too confident and hit the chisel too hard, though, as you may cut away more than you intended, or even fracture the block.

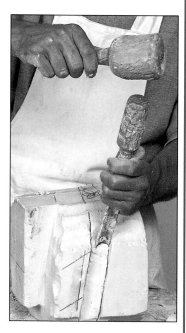

7 Carve away the plaster with the gouge to the depth of the saw cut. Then continue with the saw again. Alternate tools, in this way, until the top of the geometric form stands above the spiral form.

8 Use the same sawing and carving method to carve away the waste areas in between the spiral forms. This is best done initially by turning the sculpture on its side. However, parts of the sculpture will be sticking out, so be careful not to hit the chisel too hard. Just tap gently.

9 With the sculpture now the right way up, and the spiral forms now prominent, start to develop the form of the spiral, carving very gently through the plaster. Follow the spiral around the sculpture.

10 By this stage it will not be necessary to use the mallet, and the shaping of the spiral can be done with a hand-held chisel, always keeping both hands behind the cutting edge. Use the flat chisel to level the faces of the geometric form that runs up through the spiral, too. Other tools, such as a knife blade, can be used to shape the plaster. One of the advantages of plaster is the variety of tools that you can use to work it, but always remember to use them safely.

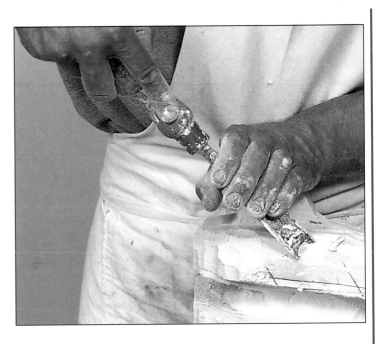

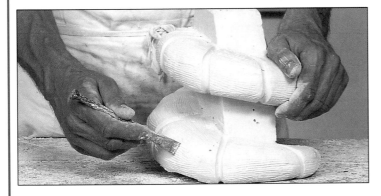

11 With the geometric and spiral forms well defined, attention can now be paid to the details. The jagged edge of a stone carving chisel is used to produce the indented lines that run around the spiral.

12 The deep indentations that fan out around the spiral are made with the round head of a large nail. The faces of the geometric shape are scraped flat with the blade of a taping knife.

Fish

The wood being carved in this section is called *jelutong*. It has a fine close grain and is very easy to cut and shape – an ideal carving wood.

YOU WILL NEED

jelutong wood • pencil • felt-tip marker • bandsaw • clear goggles • awl • tape measure • flexible ruler • vise • saw • C-clamp • wooden mallet • wood carving gouges • sand-filled inner tube • surform • riffler • sandpaper

1   Mark two grids, one on your plan of the sculpture, the other on the surface of the wood. Transfer the drawing to the grid on the wood, using a felt-tip marker.

2   Using the bandsaw, cut along the line of the fish. Wear clear goggles and keep both hands well away from the saw blade.

3   You will need to make a series of small cuts between the tail and the fins on the top and bottom of the fish to dispose of waste material.

4   Mark the center point on each side of the fish by placing your drawing over the cut-out fish and lining it up. Then use an awl to pierce the center point of the drawing, marking the center point of the wood.

5   Measure and mark the center of the side at equidistant points around the fish.

6   Using a flexible ruler, join these points and mark a line all the way around. On each side of this line, draw another, to give the width of the two fins and the tail, the position of which can now be marked.

7   Secure the fish in a vise and, with a saw, cut away the waste material on each side of the fins and tail. Make a vertical cut first, being careful not to cut into the body of the fish, but sawing down to the drawn profile.

8 Lay the fish down onto the bench and clamp it securely in position. Make a series of diagonal saw cuts at right angles to the existing ones, so that the waste areas of wood fall away to reveal the tail and fins.

9 Making sure not to carve too much wood away, use a mallet and gouge to carve from the center point on each side of the fish down to the center line. Keep the carving consistent to establish an even curvature from the center down to the edges. Start by carving away the edges down toward the center line and work slowly back to the center.

10 As the carving progresses, discard the wooden mallet and hold and push the gouge with your hands. Make sure that you keep both hands behind the cutting edge.

11 With one side of the fish carved, it now becomes difficult to clamp it safely to the bench. A sand-filled inner tube will hold it in place, while you use a wooden mallet and gouge to carve the curvature on this side.

15 Carefully carve away the waste material with a hand-held gouge to establish the curves in the fin.

16 Define and smooth out the surfaces of the fin with a riffler.

17 Use the riffler to shape and smooth the area between the fin and the tail. Mark a curve on the tail and the other fin, and shape each with a hand-held gouge and the riffler.

18 Use the riffler over the entire fish to eliminate all the gouge marks and undulations in the surface. Sand the surface, starting with a rough grade of sandpaper and moving through the grades to a fine one until you have a smooth surface over the whole fish.

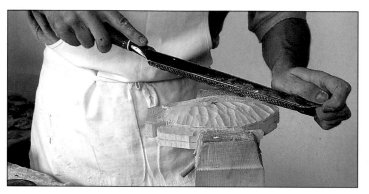

12 The inner tube is very useful for holding the sculpture when you need to carve the wood down to the base of the fins.

13 Place the fish in a vise and smooth out each of the carved sides with a surform. Keep a consistent curvature from the center of each side down to the center line all the way around the fish.

14 With the shape of each side now roughly defined, place the fish in the vise and mark a wavy configuration on the top of the fin.

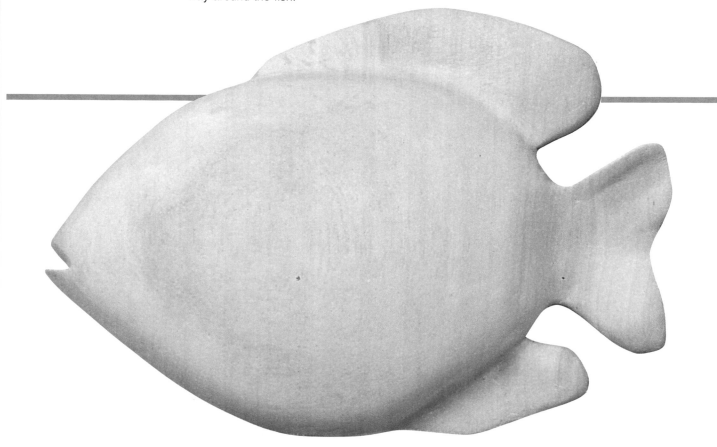

CASTING

With casting you can make copies of a sculpture. Usually, the sculpture will have been made using the modeling technique, although it is also possible to make casts of constructed sculpture. Casting produces sculpture in a variety of permanent and durable materials, and MOLDMAKING is the necessary preparation for it. Making a cast cannot be hurried – it is time-consuming, and labor-intensive, but well worth it in the end.

Traditionally, modeled sculpture was cast in bronze, a technique not dealt with in this book. However, casting in resin mixed with powdered bronze produces what is known as a cold-cast bronze. It has exactly the same surface as a bronze sculpture, but is a lot lighter than a traditional bronze cast. You should always identify the sculpture as a resin cast, because it is difficult to distinguish it from a traditional bronze cast.

Resin is a very adaptable material. If you add powdered substances, known as fillers, to it, you can reproduce the qualities of materials such as stone and slate. A number of metal fillers are also available – iron, copper, brass, aluminum, and bronze. A variety of pigments can be used with resin to produce colored and opaque surfaces.

Another casting material is *ciment fondu*, used here for a portrait head. Once set, it is extremely hard and durable. When used for a hollow cast, it is very light in weight. *Ciment fondu* is excellent at picking up fine detailing from the mold and so reproducing a very good cast of the original.

Ciment fondu

This is a hollow cast, made with a process known as lamination, in which the *ciment fondu* is built up in layers to a thickness of approximately ¼ inch. The *ciment fondu* is reinforced on the final layer with fiberglass matting.

YOU WILL NEED

liquid soap • paintbrushes • scrubbing brush • lubricating oil • steel rod • scrim • plaster • ciment fondu • rubber gloves • sponge • bucket • soft sand • jar or mug • rag • fiberglass matting • steel tool • modeling tool • riffler • chisel • wooden mallet • hammer • sand-filled inner tube/cushion • wire brush • scissors • palette knife

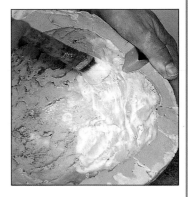

1 To prevent the cast from having a "bloom" on its surface (a white deposit from the plaster), soak the mold in water and paint on liquid soap, scrubbing it around to work up a lather. Let it dry, then repeat. Next, work a small amount of lubricating oil into a dry brush and coat the inside of the mold. When applying the liquid soap and the oil, do not let puddles form, as this will impair the quality of the cast.

6 Apply the mixture across the whole surface of the mold, to a thickness of ⅛ inch. Make sure that the sand and *ciment* mixture is flush with the seam. On vertical surfaces, there can be a tendency for the mixture to drop down, and if this is likely, leave these areas until after the initial application has cured (set).

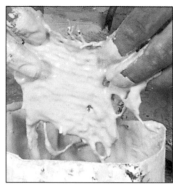

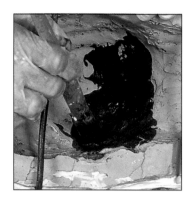

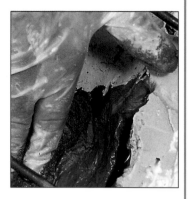

2 The mold needs to be kept wet while casting in *ciment fondu* as dry plaster will draw moisture from the *ciment fondu* and affect the setting time and its final strength. To prevent the wet mold from warping and distorting under its own weight, attach steel bracing across the top of the mold, using lengths of steel rod.

3 Push these "irons" tightly into position, making sure that they rise above the surface of the mold seam. Use scrim and plaster to anchor them to the exterior of the mold. Once the plaster has set, the irons will hold the mold firmly in position.

4 Working on one half of the mold at a time, mix some *ciment fondu* with water to the consistency of light cream. Paint this slurry onto the mold interior without it getting onto the seams of the mold. If any does, wipe it off immediately with a sponge.

5 Wearing gloves, mix together 3 parts sand to 1 part *ciment* in a bucket. Use an old cup or jar as a measure. Mix together well, then add water until the mixture has the consistency of soft cheese. Take a small amount of the mixture and place it gently on the slurry, tamping (compacting) it down with a patting motion. The slurry will be pushed out in front of the sand and *ciment* mixture.

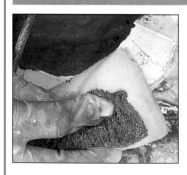

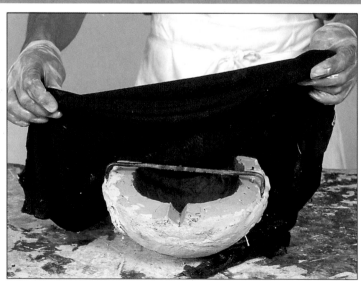

7 With the interior of the mold now fully compacted with sand and *ciment*, clean the mold seams thoroughly so that the two halves of the mold will fit together satisfactorily.

8 Leave the mold overnight, supporting it if necessary, and covering it with a damp rag. Repeat the whole process with the other half of the mold.

9 The next day, the first layer will have cured. Thoroughly soak both halves of the mold for about 30 minutes, removing any excess water with a sponge. Cut enough fiberglass matting into strips 1 × 2 inches to cover the interior surface of the mold twice. Mix some *ciment fondu* slurry and paint this on the inside of the mold. Take a piece of the fiberglass matting and dip it into the slurry. It should be fully impregnated, but any excess should be wiped off.

10 Lay the fiberglass onto the mold surface, going up to, but not above, the seam of the mouth. You need to keep the top edge of the cast level with the mold seam.

14 Once the two halves fit together satisfactorily, apply a beading of slurry along the seam of the cast using a modeling tool or palette knife.

15 Apply the slurry to both halves of the mold so it stands just above the seam. Keep the slurry contained to the seam of the cast and do not let it get onto the seam of the mold.

16 Join the two halves together, locking them into the correct position. With the bottom half of the mold supported on each side, gently tap the top half down so that the two halves are well and truly squeezed together.

17 To keep the two halves in position, join them together along the seam using scrim and plaster.

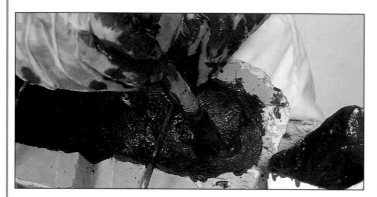  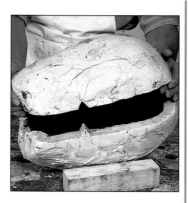

11 Overlay the pieces of fiberglass matting to cover the surface of the mold. Use a brush and a stippling action to push the fiberglass down into the slurry. Mix a sand and *ciment* mixture and tamp it down on to the surface as before, making sure that the cast seam remains level with the mold seam. This mixture need not be so wet, because as you tamp it down onto the surface, it will draw out moisture from the slurry and fiberglass matting. Clean the mold seams, cover with a damp cloth, and leave to stand overnight. Repeat the process with the other half of the mold.

12 On the third day, remove the irons from both halves of the mold and run your finger carefully along the seam edge to see whether there are any areas of the cast seam that rise above the level of the mold seam. Use a riffler to file these areas down.

13 The two halves of the mold should fit together snugly. If you can see daylight when looking through the neck opening, or you are able to rock the top half of the mold on the bottom half, you will know that there is still an area of the cast seam that rises above the level of the mold seam. Use the riffler to level it off.

18 Make sure that the scrim is soaked with plaster and leave it to set overnight. Alternatively, the seam of the cast can be traversed with slurry-impregnated fiberglass matting and backed up with a sand and *ciment* mixture, again left overnight to cure. This method is used for molds or parts of molds where you are able to reach inside them to the seam.

19 On the final day, soak the mold thoroughly for about 30 minutes. Then chip off the plaster, putting the mold onto an inner tube filled with sand for support. Start by knocking off plaster from around the neck area until you reach the layer of blue plaster. Once you reach this, you know that you are right next to the surface of the cast.

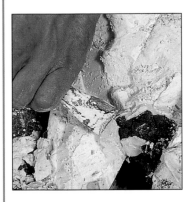

20 When you chip off this blue layer of plaster, tap the chisel very gently, or you may accidentally damage the surface of the cast.

21 With an area of the cast revealed, you will have some idea of where the cast lies within the mold, so you will be able to chip the plaster off accordingly. Because of *ciment fondu*'s aversion to plaster, large chunks of the mold will be displaced at a time.

22 With the mold of the back chipped off, turn the head over and chip the plaster from the side up to the highest point of the cast, the tip of the nose. Chip away around this area, with great caution.

23 As chunks of the mold come away from the cast, you will find that plaster is lodged behind and in the ears, so gently chip at these areas.

24 There will still be areas of the sculpture impregnated with plaster, especially the rough texture of the hair. There will also be a slight bloom on the surface. Place the head under running water and give it a good clean with a scrubbing brush. For stubborn areas, use a wire brush.

Life figure

The temperature of your work area will affect the length of time it takes for the resin to cure or set. Immediately before setting, it starts to gel (takes on the consistency of jelly), and it is essential that you finish working with it before it reaches this state. A higher-than-average room temperature will make the resin set quickly and, conversely, it will set more slowly in a low temperature. Try to avoid working in a draft or a damp atmosphere.

When making a cast with resin, the mold needs to be absolutely dry as water prevents the resin from curing properly. A liquid hardener or catalyst is added to enable it to cure, and accurate measurements of both resin and hardener are essential for the success of the mix. When the hardener and resin are mixed together, there is an exothermic chemical reaction and heat is generated. If too much hardener is added, the exothermic reaction increases, and the resin becomes dangerous, so the manufacturer's instructions should always be followed carefully.

The resin cast is built up in layers using a combination of resin and fiberglass matting, a technique known as laminating. The first layer of the cast is called the gel coat. In this cast, finely powdered bronze is added to the gel coat to produce a bronze finish.

You Will Need

respirator mask • clear goggles • barrier cream • latex gloves • skin cleansing cream • concentrated resin detergent • paintbrushes ¼–½ inch • scissors • mold release agent • polyester resin • bronze filler • jars and tin cans • weighing scales • catalyst or hardener • fiberglass matting • palette knife • scrim or string • old chisel • wooden mallet • pointed tool • sand-filled inner tube

1 Generously paint the surfaces of the whole mold with a release agent, without letting it collect in pools. Leave it to dry.

2 Meanwhile, prepare the gel coat which is a mix of resin and bronze filler. Place a mixing tin on the scales and put the indicator arrow to 0.

Safety

Polyester resin is highly flammable and excess exposure to its fumes is harmful, so take the following precautions:

• Always work in a well-ventilated area.

• With both resin and fiberglass matting, wear a respirator mask, protect your eyes with clear goggles, use barrier cream on your hands, wear disposable gloves, and when you have finished working, clean your hands with a heavy-duty cleansing cream.

• Containers that have been used for mixing should be discarded, as the residue of set resin is impossible to remove.

• Brushes should be cleaned with a resin detergent cleaner immediately after use – if the resin sets, they will also need to be discarded.

• Always store resins and hardeners in a cool, dark place.

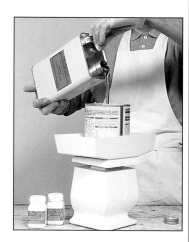

3 Weigh enough resin for all three pieces of the mold – in this case 8 ounces.

4 The bronze filler is now added and mixed with the resin, in the proportion of 7 parts of bronze filler to 1 part of resin (or as recommended by the manufacturer). Stir thoroughly. The bronze content of this gel coat, the weight of which is now 56 ounces, will now be consistent for each part of the mold.

5 Work on one piece of the mold at a time. Weigh half the amount of gel coat (28 ounces) and add 50 drops of hardener. Stir thoroughly.

6 Paint the gel coat onto the interior surface of the mold as quickly as you can. If any resin gets onto the seam, clean it off immediately before it has a chance to cure.

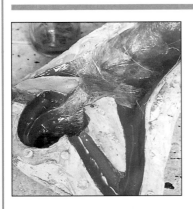

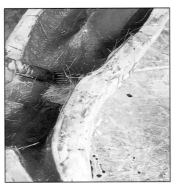

9 Lay down and overlap strips of fiberglass matting in the resin as soon as you have painted it in, allowing the matting to soak up the resin.

10 Apply more resin onto the matting with a stippling action (hard vertical strokes) to make sure that the resin is pushed well into the fiberglass matting and then repeat the process. Two layers of matting are enough for a sculpture of this size, and you can add the second layer before the first layer has cured.

11 The cast can now be joined together. Apply a thick beading of a resin and bronze mixture with a palette knife along the seam of the cast in the main part of the mold. Do not get any of this mixture on the seam of the mold.

12 Add the other two sections to the main mold, adding a beading of resin and bronze along the adjoining seam. When all three parts of the mold are positioned correctly, tie them in place with scrim or string and leave for at least 24 hours to allow the resin to cure.

7 Apply a thicker layer of gel coat to the face and breasts, to make sure that all of the detail in these areas is captured. Finish applying the gel coat before the resin starts to gel. Leave it to cure and repeat with the other parts of the mold.

8 Cut some fiberglass matting into 1 × 1½-inch strips – enough to cover the surfaces of each mold piece twice over. Weigh 4 ounces resin and add hardener. Don't weigh more or it may start to gel before you have had a chance to use it all; you can always mix up some more, if necessary. Coat an area of the mold with the resin, avoiding the seam.

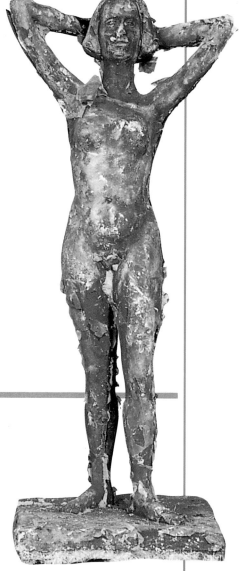

13 Soak the mold in water overnight to dissolve the release agent. You can now start to chip away the plaster from the cast with a chisel.

14 Chip off the plaster until you reach the blue layer, taking care not to damage the surface of the cast. Extreme care needs to be taken when you are removing the plaster from the features of the face.

15 Use a pointed tool to remove plaster from awkward cavities or areas that are too small to use a chisel.

16 When the figure is released from the mold, repairs may be needed to parts of the seam where the join was inadequate. This is an essential part of the finishing process, and any discrepancies are easily made good (see REPAIRS section).

Using a rubber mold

Rubber molds are very useful since they not only are excellent at picking up detail, they can be used over and over again.

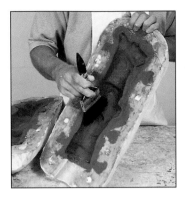

1 Clean the rubber mold with a brush, paying particular attention to areas of detail.

2 Apply three coats of shellac to the opening at the end of each plaster case, which is the pour hole for the plaster.

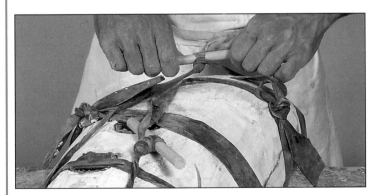

5 You will need to tighten the rubber ties further to prevent the mold from splitting open when plaster is poured into it. Insert short lengths of dowel under each of the ties and twist them around as many times as possible. Finally, hold the dowel in place by tucking it under the tie to produce a tourniquet.

6 Support the mold, with the pour hole uppermost, in a bucket. Pour plaster slowly into the mold as soon as it has been mixed. The plaster will start to harden if you leave it, and it will not pour smoothly and consistently. Let the plaster settle and gently tap the sides of the mold to make sure the plaster is evenly distributed and to force any air bubbles to the surface. Top up with plaster if necessary. Leave the mold undisturbed while the plaster sets.

3 Put the two parts of the mold together, making sure they fit snugly.

4 Hold the two halves firmly in place with rubber ties (strips of rubber cut from inner tubes). Put these on as tightly as possible.

7 Place the mold on the work surface and remove the rubber ties. Gently separate the two parts of the mold by placing a taping knife blade into the seam in two or three places.

8 Lift off the top of the mold to reveal the cast. You will notice a small amount of plaster left in the pour hole.

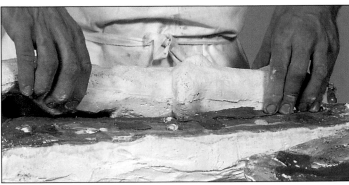

9 Chip away the plaster from the surface of the pour hole.

10 The cast of the sculpture can now be removed easily from the bottom of the mold. Lift it out gently and do not put undue pressure on delicate parts of the cast.

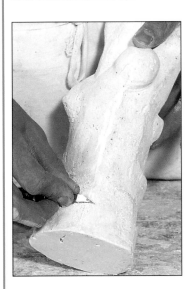

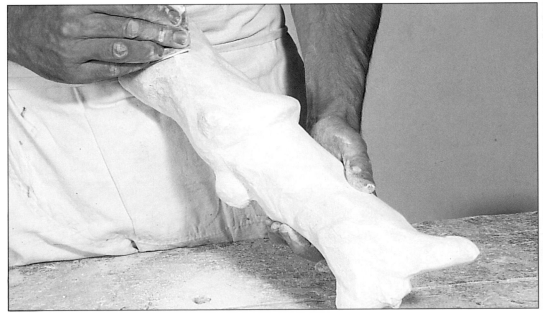

12 There will be a small amount of raised plaster from the mold seam. Using the blade of a modeling knife, cut this back, level with the surface of the sculpture.

13 Smooth the seam down with sandpaper to produce a consistent surface.

11 Saw off the remains of the pour hole from the base of the sculpture, leveling the surface so the sculpture will stand.

14 Rubber molds pick up all the details from the originals and produce excellent casts. You can repeat the technique to make as many casts as you want.

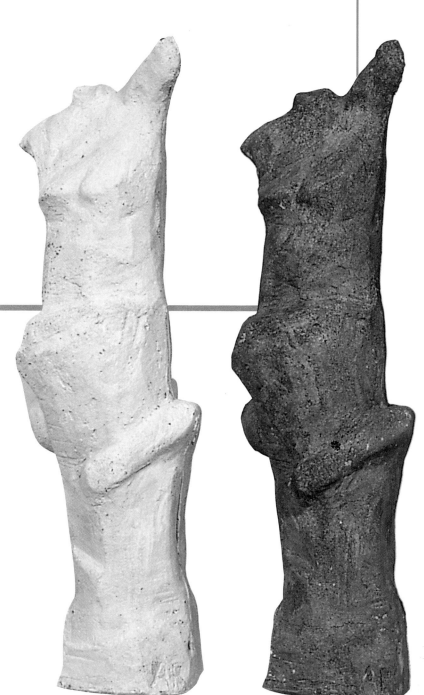

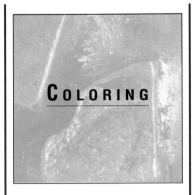

COLORING

Color can affect a sculpture in many ways. It can be an important compositional element; it can be purely functional; it can be an integral part of the technique; it can create the illusion that the sculpture is made from a different material, or it can be used to cover up mistakes and repairs.

The wooden figurative construction and the welded steel sculpture use color to unite their separate parts. The dark color of the spatial construction gives the impression that it is heavier than it is. Color accentuates different parts of the constructed mobile sculpture. The sealing of the plaster bird is purely functional, in that it helps keep it clean and enhance the integrity of the material – similar to the use of beeswax on the wooden carving. The plaster relief has a color disguise, giving the impression of patinated metal. The plaster cast, on the other hand, has been unashamedly painted to produce a powerful sculptural statement. Various colors have been added to the carved plaster sculpture to enhance the dynamics of its forms. The resin surface of the life figure sculpture is broken

to reveal the bronze – a necessary procedure in this type of casting technique. The stylized torso uses color as another element in the overall composition. The *ciment fondu* of the portrait head has been darkened to cover up repairs, as well as to give a more consistent surface.

All these examples prove that there are really no hard and fast rules. The important thing to remember is that color is a way to complement the form of the sculpture – it never takes precedence over it. Whatever your choice, it is always a good idea to experiment with color first on a piece of spare material.

Wooden construction

YOU WILL NEED

wood stain • rag

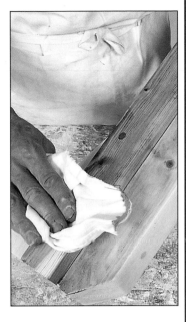

1 Rub the stain well into the wood with a rag, paying particular attention to all the corners. The wood will soak up the first coat quickly, so add another as soon as it is dry. The more coats you apply, the darker the color, will become.

Direct modeling

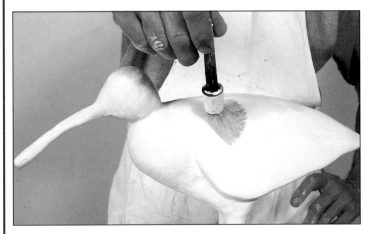

YOU WILL NEED

Craft glue (diluted 50:50 with water) • paintbrush

1 Seal the surface of the plaster by painting on diluted white glue. Apply a second coat when the first is dry. Clean your brush with water.

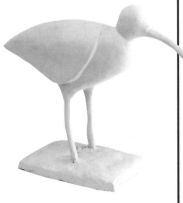

2 By not coloring this sculpture, attention is focused on its figurative form and the material and process by which it was made.

Spatial construction

Always work in a well-ventilated area, preferably outside, when using an aerosol spray can, and wear rubber gloves. Not all of the spray will hit the sculpture – it might land on the surrounding area – so protect nearby surfaces with newspaper.

YOU WILL NEED

aerosol spray paint • rubber gloves • newspaper

1 Hold the sculpture away from you and spray, turning continually to give an even covering of paint.

2 The gray paint, combined with the sculpture's form, suggests a heavy industrial structure which belies the size and lightweight material of the sculpture.

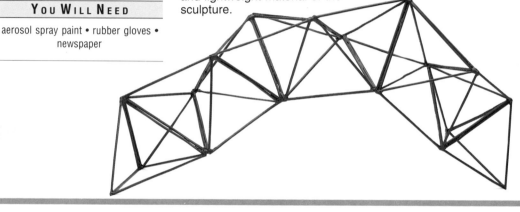

Plaster cast

YOU WILL NEED

paintbrush • shellac • silver enamel paint • mineral spirits

1 Paint on three coats of shellac to seal the surface, allowing each coat to dry before applying the next.

2 Paint the silver enamel paint evenly over the whole sculpture, taking care not to drip or splash. When dry, apply another coat. Clean your brush with mineral spirits.

Plaster carving

Craft glue (diluted 50:50 with water) •
paintbrush • a selection of oil colors –
burnt sienna, raw sienna, green,
cadmium red • rags • mineral spirits

1   Seal the surface of the
sculpture with diluted white
glue. This makes the color
stay on the surface so it is not
absorbed by the plaster.

2   Apply a color direct from
the tube with a rag onto the
sculpture. Rub it well into any
crevices.

3   Wipe off excess color with
a rag and mineral spirits.
Repeat, adding a different
color each time, until you have
an interesting combination.

Riveted sculpture

Always use aerosol spray cans
in a well-ventilated area and,
if necessary, protect adjacent
work surfaces.

masking tape • newspapers • aerosol
spray paints

1   Spray the top half of the
sculpture with yellow paint,
masking off the bottom half
with newspaper and masking
tape. When the yellow paint
has dried, remove the
newspaper and tape.

2   Mask the upper (yellow)
part of the sculpture, placing
masking tape precisely at the
meeting point of the two parts
of the sculpture. Hold the
sculpture at arm's length and
apply an even coat of red.

3   Spray the steel stand and
hanging wire with black paint.

4 The mixed color enlivens what was previously a bland material, enhances the forms, and focuses attention on the contrast between the textured and smooth surfaces.

Plaster relief

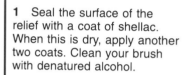

YOU WILL NEED

shellac • paintbrush • denatured alcohol • gold enamel paint • mineral spirits • flat blackboard paint • rags

1 Seal the surface of the relief with a coat of shellac. When this is dry, apply another two coats. Clean your brush with denatured alcohol.

2 Apply a coat of gold enamel paint and leave to dry. Repeat, avoiding drips or pools of paint. Clean your brush with mineral spirits.

4 Aerosol sprays provide very smooth flat areas of color, which blend in extremely well with the construction and joining techniques used in this sculpture.

3 When the gold paint is dry, completely coat the relief with flat black paint, making sure that you reach all the crevices. Clean your brush with mineral spirits.

4 Before the black paint has a chance to dry fully, start to rub it off, so that the gold starts to show through. The raised parts of the relief need to have the black paint rubbed off completely to reveal a shiny gold highlight. The crevices and undercuts should remain darker than the edges of the cubes.

5 This technique is an economical way to simulate the effect of patinated bronze and is especially effective, as in this case, on plaster or fired-clay sculpture.

Carved fish

YOU WILL NEED

beeswax • rag • soft cloth

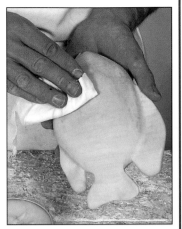

1 Rub beeswax well into the surface of the sculpture with a rag. Apply one or more coats of wax, depending on the porosity of the wood. Repeat with the wooden base.

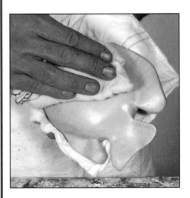

2 When the wood has absorbed the wax, polish the sculpture and base with a soft cloth to produce an even shine.

3 The close-grained nature of the wood and the highly polished surface emphasize the forms of the sculpture.

Stylized torso

For steps 1–4, clean your brush with denatured alcohol and use water to clean the brush used in step 5.

YOU WILL NEED

denatured alcohol • paintbrush • shellac • blue pigment • gold pigment • craft glue

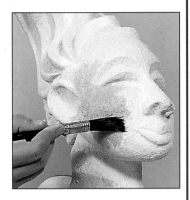

1 Cover the whole surface of the sculpture with three coats of shellac, leaving each coat to dry before adding another.

Papier-mâché

YOU WILL NEED

Craft glue (diluted 50:50 with water) • red oxide paint • paintbrushes • mineral spirits • yellow acrylic paint • paper • polyurethane gloss varnish

1 Seal the surface of the sculpture with diluted white craft glue.

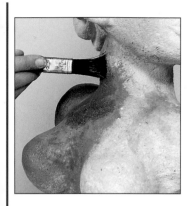

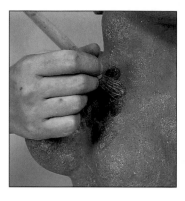

2 Mix the blue pigment with denatured alcohol, to produce an opaque mix of an even consistency. Paint onto the sculpture and leave to dry.

3 Apply gold pigment (mixed with denatured alcohol) to the surface with a stippling action – hold your brush at a right angle to the surface and gently dab the surface. Cover the whole surface of the sculpture using this stippling action.

4 Paint the sculpture with diluted craft glue to set the gold and blue pigments.

5 Although color is an important compositional element, it has been used very subtly. The result is a dramatic effect that does not detract from the forms.

2 Paint on one coat of red oxide paint and leave to dry. Clean the brush with mineral spirits.

3 Load the brush with yellow acrylic paint. On a piece of paper, brush the paint out until the brush is nearly dry, then slowly drag the brush over the surface of the whole sculpture. The uneven surface means that yellow paint will be deposited on its higher points. Clean the brush with water.

4 When the yellow paint has dried, apply one coat of polyurethane gloss varnish over the whole sculpture with a brush. Leave to dry and clean your brush with mineral spirits.

5 The final coat of polyurethane varnish has added more definition to the textured surface and really brought the sculpture alive.

Portrait head

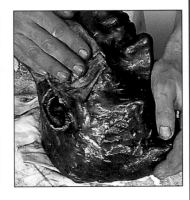

1   Rub the grate polish well into the surface of the head with a rag.

2   Use the polish on a toothbrush for any tricky areas and crevices on the head.

3   Once the polish is dry, buff the surface of the sculpture to produce a dull shine.

Welded steel

Before you start work, make sure you are adequately protected – wear clear goggles, a respirator mask, a long-sleeved coverall, and rubber gloves. Protect your work area with a plastic sheet. When applying chemicals to steel, use a lightly loaded brush and make gentle strokes to avoid splashing. Clean the brushes with water immediately after use and dispose of the plastic sheet, having first rinsed it thoroughly under running water. Chemicals should be stored in containers which are specifically for their use and correctly labeled. Clean the brush used for the lacquer with the manufacturer's recommended solvent.

1   Carefully brush on the diluted hydrochloric acid to clean all the dirt and grime off the steel. Rinse the acid off with water. **Note** Check regulations for safe disposal of chemicals.

2   Paint on the ferric nitrate and leave the sculpture to rust – the longer you leave it, the rustier it will get. If necessary – if the ferric nitrate evaporates or the first coat did not get into all parts of the sculpture – apply more ferric nitrate.

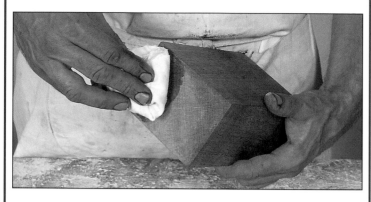

4 Apply beeswax to the wooden base, working it well into the grain of the wood, especially the end grain. When the wax has been absorbed, buff the whole surface with a soft cloth (see pages 38–9 for finished head.).

Resin cast

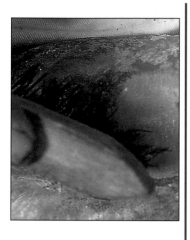

1 Gently rub the surface of the sculpture with a wire brush to break through the resin and reveal the bronze.

3 Once the sculpture has reached a suitably rusty state, brush on a coat of clear lacquer to seal the surface.

4 By speeding up and controlling the rusting of the mild steel, you are able to produce a consistent surface.

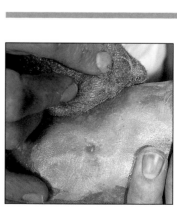

2 Rub the whole sculpture with steel wool to buff the bronze. Finally, apply some metal polish to the whole of the sculpture and polish it with a soft cloth.

A constructed sculpture is one whose parts have been joined together using everyday methods – such as gluing, screwing, doweling, welding, riveting. What sets this type of sculpture apart from the everyday objects that surround us and which are made in a similar way is that the sculpture is nonfunctional or, more precisely, its function is purely visual. It is made to be looked at.

As a generalization, it can be said that this now-established form of sculpture has a particular feel or look to it – most notably, that it is geometric and would tend toward an abstract sculptural format. The making of sculpture is not the primary function of the techniques and tools used in constructed sculpture.

The two sculptures made in this section use different construction techniques. The first is a spatial construction with an architectural form and a mass-production method of construction. The sculpture uses a repeated unit of the same size and form. The component parts are joined together with a glue gun – an extremely useful tool for joining lightweight materials.

The other sculpture is the calf and foot of a leg. Whereas in the first example, the form is determined by the process of fabrication, in this sculpture the form is derived from drawings from life. Knowing that a constructed sculpture was to be made using standard sizes of wood, the drawing was modified to take this into account. This sculpture is made using a wood-dowel and glue joining technique.

Figurative sculpture

Although this is a constructed sculpture, it is taken from a life drawing. The drawing was modified to take into account the standard-sized wood.

YOU WILL NEED

prepared softwood: 2 × 3 inches, 2 × 2 inches, 1 × 2 inches, 1 × 4 inches • pencil • ruler • C-clamp • tenon saw • carpenter's square • vise • plane • sandpaper • masking tape • wood glue • ⅜-inch dowel • electric drill • wooden mallet • wood putty • wood stain • taping knife

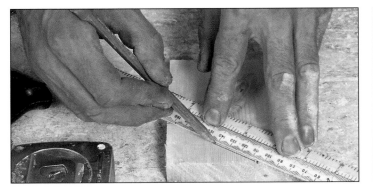

1   A piece of wood 2 × 3 × 4 inches forms the toe section. With a pencil and ruler, draw lines to indicate the profile of the front of the foot.

2   Clamp the wood securely to the bench and saw down the lines with a tenon saw.

3 Cut a wedge shape from a piece of 2 × 2-inch wood for part of the length of the foot. Measure 7 inches, then draw a line with a carpenter's square.

4 Mark a diagonal line on the face of the wood from a point ½ inch in from opposite sides. Then, on opposite ends of the block, draw a line at a right angle to the diagonal line on the face of the wood.

5 Clamp this block of wood to your workbench and use a tenon saw to make the cut.

6 The heel section, a block of wood 2 × 3 × 4 inches, needs to have a wedge section cut from it. Mark a line at right angles to the longest sides and 1½ inches in from one end, "A." On this line mark a point "B" 1 inch down. Then mark another point "C" ¾ inch in from "A." Using a carpenter's square, place the point of the right angle on "B" and the short length of the square on "C." Draw a line along both of the edges of the square where they are in contact with the block of wood. Repeat on the other side of the block.

7 Place the block in a vise so that one of the drawn lines is vertical. Saw down to the apex. Reposition the block in the vise and again saw down to the apex so the wedge of wood is released from the block and falls away.

8 After each cut, you may find the surface rough and not quite square. Place the block in a vise with the cut surface uppermost and level it off with a wood plane.

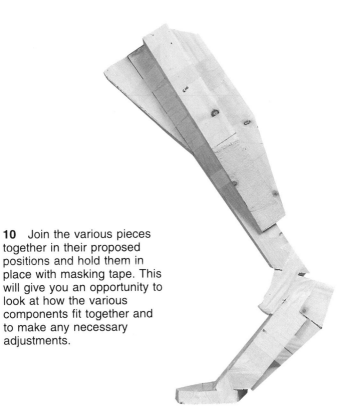

9 Sand it down so that all the surfaces are consistently smooth.

10 Join the various pieces together in their proposed positions and hold them in place with masking tape. This will give you an opportunity to look at how the various components fit together and to make any necessary adjustments.

11 Join the parts together using wood glue and dowel. On one of the surfaces to be joined, spread a thin layer of wood glue, applying it evenly and consistently.

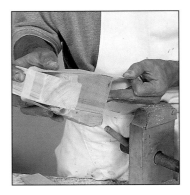

14 Gently tap a length of dowel into each hole. The length of each should be slightly longer than the depth of the hole.

15 Cut off the protruding ends of the dowel with a tenon saw.

16 Masking tape is one way to hold awkward shapes together securely. Apply the glue first and then bind the parts together with the masking tape.

17 With the heel section taped to the foot (which is held in the vise), drill the holes and insert the dowel to join the two sections.

12 Position the two pieces together, and apply as much pressure as you are able with your hands. Then secure the two pieces in a vise.

13 Drill two holes the diameter of the dowel in both of the pieces to be joined. Put some masking tape around the drill bit to indicate the depth of the hole to be drilled.

Spatial construction

This spatial construction with an architectural form can use as many of the triangular units as you choose. Use the jig to hold them in place while they are joined to make a sculpture that gets longer with each addition.

YOU WILL NEED
masking tape • piece of wood • pencil • tape measure • split bamboo canes • tin snips • scissors • carpenter's square • Blu-tack • glue gun • modeling knife

SAFETY
When using the glue gun, take great care not to spill any of the hot glue on yourself.

1 Place a strip of masking tape on the board. Draw a line 24 inches long, along the tape and mark each end. Divide the line into three 8-inch segments. Now place each bamboo cane against the line and use it as a marker to divide the cane into three equal parts.

18 Fill any gaps with wood putty, first adding some wood stain to it. When you stain the whole sculpture, the filled areas will have more chance of blending in.

19 Once the putty has set, sand the whole sculpture down to a smooth and consistent finish.

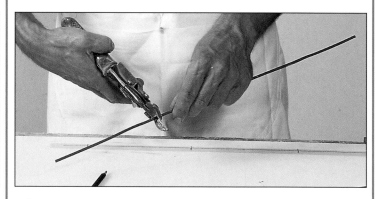

2 Cut each cane into thirds with tin snips. These three canes are used to produce one triangular unit of the sculpture.

3 Using scissors, cut a diagonal of approximately 30° as near to the end of each cane as possible.

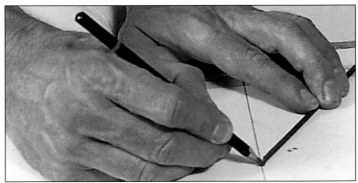

4 As you are making a number of similar units, you will need a jig. Take the center 8-inch section of the drawn line on the masking tape and mark the halfway point. This is your base line. With a square, draw a vertical line from this point at right angles to the base. Align one end of a piece of cane with the mark at one end of the base line. Align the other end of the cane with the vertical line and mark it.

7 Take another piece of cane and apply glue to both ends. Insert this cane into the jig and hold it in place until the glue has set. Gently lift the triangle out of the jig, turn it over, holding it in one hand. Apply more glue to each corner of the triangle.

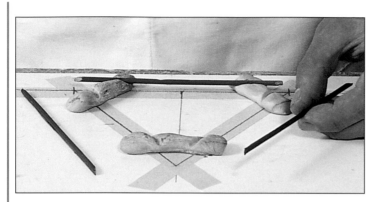

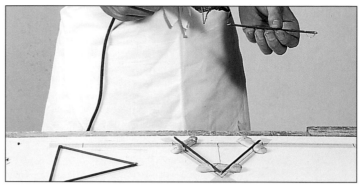

5 Position two lengths of masking tape from the marks on the base line to the new mark on the vertical. Join the marks with a pencil to produce a triangle. Put a lump of Blutack on each corner of the triangle. Firmly embed a piece of cane into each lump of the reuseable adhesive, making sure that the canes meet to form a triangle that matches the one drawn on the masking tape. Carefully remove the canes. You will be left with an indentation in each piece of adhesive.

6 Apply glue to one end of the cane. Put the glue gun down, and quickly take another piece of cane. Place the two pieces in the jig to form the apex of the triangle. Hold the pieces in place for a few seconds until the glue sets.

8 To join two units, put one side of each in adjacent positions in the jig so that they are vertical. Bring the tops together and glue the two lengths that touch. Glue each end of another length of cane and place it in the jig to join the bottom corners of the pyramid that is now created. Continue using the jig to add one triangle at a time.

9 Trim off any excess glue on the construction with a modeling knife.

DIRECT MODELING

There are two important factors that set direct modeling apart from the traditional sculptural practice of MODELING. Primarily, the material that you choose to model with is also the final material of the sculpture. Second, the ARMATURE to which this material is added is a permanent structure and remains within the sculpture, unlike a temporary armature.

Making the armature
The armature must be strong enough to support the modeling material, and the materials used to construct it must remain stable. Wood or strong cardboard (if used with plaster), *ciment fondu*, or papier-mâché, whose surfaces have not been sealed, will have a tendency to disintegrate because they will soak up the water in these materials. As with any armature, it is very important to plan its configuration fully, because once you have started to model, it will not be possible to make any alterations to it.

The modeling material itself needs to be resilient and strong enough to last in its final state, while being malleable and plastic enough to model. The two materials used in this section are plaster and papier-mâché. *Ciment fondu*, polyester resin, and car-body filler are also suitable.

The armatures in the plaster and papier-mâché sculptures both have strong, rigid constructions and will not deteriorate. The shape of the armature for the plaster sculpture is based on a series of drawings of a wading bird. The major decisions regarding the final form of the sculpture have, therefore, already been made. The armature for the papier-mâché sculpture is a found object, chosen for its stability inside the sculpture. However, this does not mean that the sculpture has a pre-determined final form. It can be developed further during the modeling process.

Plaster
Plaster is a very messy material to work with, so bear this in mind when choosing your workplace. Plaster is best removed from tools and work surfaces by letting it dry and then scraping it off. It will lift up easily. Never pour plaster down drains as this will clog them up.

YOU WILL NEED

steel armature (see WELDING) • electric drill • base board • paintbrush • shellac • expanded styrofoam • wire brush • barrier cream • gauze bandage (fine mesh scrim) • plaster • plaster modeling tool • small kitchen knife • taping knife • scissors

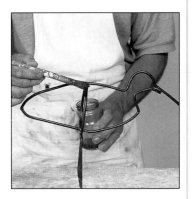

1 The steel armature comes from the WELDING section. Drill a hole into the base the same diameter as the steel rod and push in the vertical leg of the armature. Paint three coats of shellac onto the base and the armature, letting the shellac dry between coats to seal the surface. If wet plaster comes into contact with untreated steel, rust will form and bleed through to the surface of the plaster, eventually weakening and rotting the plaster.

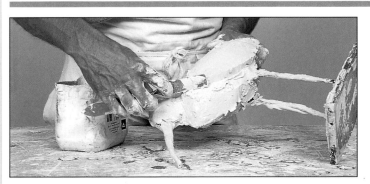

6 Next, gradually build up and develop the wings, head, and body areas of the sculpture, making sure that the sculpture remains symmetrical.

It can be very easy to lose sight of this, so continually check from all angles and make adjustments where necessary.

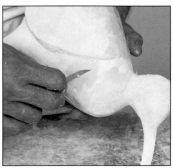

7 The body of the bird is shaped with the serrated edge of a kitchen knife.

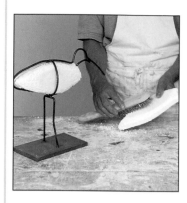

2 Pack out the armature so that it starts to resemble the sculpture you intend to make. This reduces the amount of plaster you need and makes the sculpture lighter. The best material to use is expanded styrofoam. This is easily shaped with a wire brush and can be jammed inside the armature. Once inside, the styrofoam can be shaped further, if necessary, with the wire brush.

3 Before using plaster, apply barrier cream to your hands. Mix the plaster (see MOLDMAKING). Using scissors, cut the bandage into small strips, mixing up small quantities of plaster at a time. Each strip is then dipped into the plaster, so that it becomes fully impregnated, then pulled out taut and quickly laid flat on to the sculpture. Be careful pulling the bandage out of the plaster, as it can very easily wrinkle and stick to itself.

4 Cover the whole sculpture with the plaster-impregnated bandage, taking special care when you wrap it around the legs as it will tend to bunch up. Keep the bandage smoothed out, working on top of the sculpture first and then, when the plaster has set, turn it upside down and lay the plaster bandage flat on the underside of the sculpture – this way, it does not have to defy gravity! Carry on until you have covered the whole surface of the sculpture, including the base.

5 Mix a very small quantity of plaster and wait for it to set to the consistency of cream cheese. Using a plaster modeling tool, apply this plaster to the sculpture quickly until it is completely covered. You only have a short time to work with the plaster before it becomes too stodgy. Now go back quickly over the surface you have just worked, cutting back and shaping the plaster where necessary. Once set, plaster is difficult to remove, so the golden rule is to keep the surface of the sculpture under control.

8 The wings are given a smoother finish with the flat edge of a taping knife. Any undulations or imperfections in the surface can be corrected by applying a small quantity of plaster and letting it set before scraping it back to the required shape.

Papier-mâché

This abstract papier-mâché sculpture uses the shape of its armature as an inspiration for developing forms on it.

YOU WILL NEED

newspapers • scissors • wallpaper paste • bucket • food mixer • found object/bicycle frame • electric drill • aerated building block • wooden mallet • dowel • sandpaper • paintbrush • white craft glue

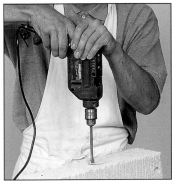

1 A good strong papier-mâché is made by leaving small pieces of newspaper to soak in a mix of wallpaper paste in a bucket. Leave the paper until it is well soaked and starting to disintegrate. This will take at least 48 hours. Then use a food mixer to mix and break it up thoroughly to produce a pulp. It is then a very good modeling medium, with the feel of clay and used in much the same way.

2 The armature, a bicycle frame, is now mounted on its base which also becomes part of the sculpture. Drill a hole the same diameter as the seat opening into an aerated concrete block, which willl have enough weight and stability to support the bicycle frame.

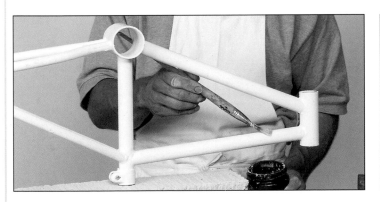

5 Lightly abrade the surface of the armature with sandpaper and coat it with diluted craft glue. This will help the papier-mâché adhere to the armature.

6 Apply a thin layer of papier-mâché, compressing it firmly onto the armature. Use the configuration of the armature as inspiration to model forms while applying the papier-mâché.

7 Papier-mâché will not defy gravity, so parts of the sculpture, especially built-up overhanging areas, will have to be modeled in layers, leaving the papier-mâché to dry out overnight. Apply a coat of diluted craft glue to the dry papier-mâché to help the new layer adhere to the surface.

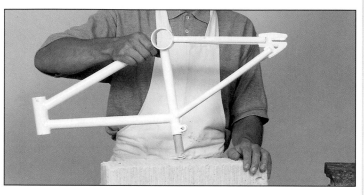

3 Hammer a piece of dowel firmly into the seat opening of the frame, leaving a length sticking out.

4 Place the dowel in the hole in the aerated concrete block and push down firmly. You now have a permanent armature derived from a found object.

8 Seal the aerated concrete block thoroughly – otherwise, it will act like a sponge and soon draw out the moisture from the papier-mâché, rendering the wallpaper paste ineffective. Paint a few coats of diluted craft glue onto the surfaces of the block, allowing time to dry between coats.

9 Apply papier-mâché to the block, packing it down firmly. If any areas of the sculpture need to be made good, now is the time to do it. Leave the sculpture to dry out completely – it is very wet at this stage, and vulnerable to breakages. It will then dry to a very hard and compact finish.

KILN FIRING

Kiln firing is a process similar to cooking something in an oven – except that the temperatures reached in a kiln are much higher. The sculpture is fired only when the clay has dried out completely. After firing, the clay is hard and permanent.

Kiln firing restricts you somewhat in the type of forms you are able to make. An armature cannot be left inside the clay during firing, so you need to use an armature system that is easy to remove. A system of single straight poles will support the clay during modeling and can be pulled out easily before the clay has fully dried out. The sculpture can then be hollowed out, in preparation for the sculpture being fired in the kiln.

The size of the kiln also determines the maximum size of the sculpture you can make. You can make a sculpture larger than the kiln, but you will need to model the parts separately and reassemble them after firing with an epoxy resin glue.

Selecting a pole
Whatever size of sculpture you choose to make, there will be a type and size of straight pole for it – broom handles, wood dowel of various diameters, and for small sculptures, particularly figures, wooden skewers are very suitable. Whatever the size, the principle remains the same. The poles can be vertical, diagonal, or even horizontal, depending on the configuration of the sculpture, but they must always be used in such a way so that removal is easy.

Wrap poles with sheets of plastic or plastic wrap to prevent the dry wood from absorbing moisture from the clay and thus drying out and cracking the sculpture. If you are using wooden skewers, soak them thoroughly in water before you start instead of wrapping them in plastic. They will then have the same moisture content as the clay. If you are modeling a small sculpture, such as a figure up to a foot high that will not need to be hollowed out prior to firing, you can leave these sticks inside to burn out during the firing process. Turn them gently from time to time when modeling and while the sculpture is drying out. Otherwise the clay may contract around them and fracture as it dries out.

When using this type of armature, the best clay is one with "grog" (small particles of fired clay) already added. It has a greater structural strength than fine clay. Although kiln firing involves certain restrictions, you will still be able to make an exciting piece of sculpture.

Stylized torso
This stylized torso is worked in clay, based on a drawing taken from a photograph. It is modeled on a large ARMATURE and hollowed out before firing.

YOU WILL NEED

broom handle • prepared modeling board • plastic wrap • tape • clay (with added grog) • water spray • plastic sheet • modeling tools • visegrips/ pliers • clay-cutting wire • clay slip • awl

---

1 Pack the clay tightly around the armature pole. Following your drawing, build up the clay to develop the basic shape of the torso. The combination of the armature and the grogged clay produces a very stable foundation for the sculpture, allowing you to concentrate wholly on modeling.

5 Get help to move the sculpture onto a lower level. Fix the visegrips tightly around the exposed part of the armature pole, then gently rotate the pole, clockwise and counterclockwise. After a while, the pole will turn freely in its hole. Continue to rotate it, at the same time starting to lift it up. You will find that it will lift out remarkably easily, but take great care not to damage the sculpture.

  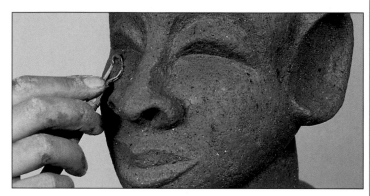

2 Work the clay up, developing the form of the sculpture as much as possible as you proceed. Don't let the clay dry out – keep it sprayed with water, especially in hot weather. Turn the armature pole gently from time to time. When you are not working on the sculpture, spray it all over with water and cover it tightly with plastic to retain the moisture content.

3 Two inches of armature needs to be left exposed above the top of the sculpture so you can pull it out at the end. You will need to take special care when modeling the hair because it goes off at a diagonal from the vertical armature and has no internal support. The grogged clay has enough inherent strength to support itself in this case.

4 By now the modeling of the sculpture is complete, save for any fine-tuning needed on the surface. Let the clay dry out slightly by leaving the sculpture uncovered overnight. Be careful not to let it dry out too much – it just needs to lose enough moisture to make the clay structurally sound and able to stand without the aid of the armature pole. While the clay is in a leather-hard state it is a good time to develop a consistent surface over the whole sculpture. Use a wire modeling tool to break the surface and reveal the bits of grog which are in the clay.

6 Now that the clay has dried out slightly, the sculpture is able to stand by itself. The next task is to hollow it out, which means slicing the sculpture into three sections. Using a clay cutting wire, slice horizontally through the clay. Don't pull the wire too hard and take care that the uppermost section does not topple over. Before you separate the two sections, make a couple of marks, which cross the cut line, on each side of the sculpture. These are location marks to help join the sections back together. This dismembering of the sculpture may seem rather alarming after all the time and effort that has gone into the modeling – but don't worry, everything will be put back in its place.

7 The inside of each section of the sculpture is now hollowed out to clay walls ½–¾ inch thick. The thickness of each clay wall is determined by its structural function. The walls at the bottom of the sculpture will need to be thicker than the walls at the top of the sculpture. The clay walls of the neck need to be thicker still, because they have to support the weight of the head and hair, which have the thinnest walls. Make sure you take out the base area inside the bottom section of the sculpture to create an escape passage for the expanded hot air during firing.

8 Once all the sections have been hollowed out, you can join them together using a clay slip. This is clay that has had an excess of water added to obtain a consistency of heavy cream. Score straight lines on both of the surfaces to be joined and brush on the slip.

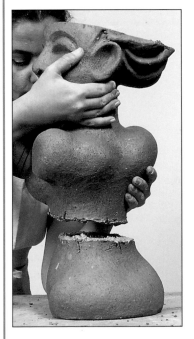

10 Line up the location marks and push the top section down into place, firmly bedding the two parts together.

11 Clean the excess slip from the joint with your finger and remodel the surface so there is no evidence of the seam. Join the top section to the main section in the same way, filling in the hole on the top of the head that was left by the removal of the armature pole.

9 Work the slip well into the surface to produce an even consistency. Be careful not to make these areas too wet as this will weaken the sculpture at the joint.

12 Using a small tool such as an awl, make air escape holes in the sculpture, especially around enclosed areas, such as the head, and the thicker walls of clay, such as the neck. This establishes an unobstructed flow of air through the whole of the sculpture. Push the tool through gently and slowly. Withdraw, taking care not to damage the surface. The sculpture now needs to be left to dry out. Don't be surprised if this takes three or four weeks. When it is completely dry, the sculpture can be fired. Take care when placing it in the kiln, as air-dried clay is very brittle.

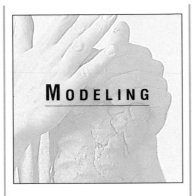

MODELING

Modeling is an additive process in which the form of the sculpture is developed by adding material – the opposite of the other basic method of making sculpture, CARVING, where material is removed.

With all sculpture the material itself, to a certain extent, determines the form that the sculpture contains. A modeled sculpture is no exception. Modeling depends on the use of an inert and malleable material, usually clay. Wax, plaster, and papier-mâché can also be used (the latter two are used in DIRECT MODELING). When modeling, the material itself has no form and is totally dependent on your manipulation of it to give it form. Modeling material has limited structural qualities and needs an armature, unless you are making a very small sculpture or maquette (see ARMATURE).

The golden rule in modeling is always to add material in small amounts. This keeps the development of the form under control.

Modeling is most suitable for making sculptures of the human form. There is a close affinity between clay and the substance of human flesh itself. In this section, two sculptures are made. One is of a standing figure, one-third life size, and the other a life-size portrait head.

The armatures for both were made in the ARMATURE section. For the standing figure, measurements are taken from the model and reduced to a third to make the armature. For the portrait head, a standard head armature is used, and measurements are taken from the model and transferred to the sculpture during the modeling.

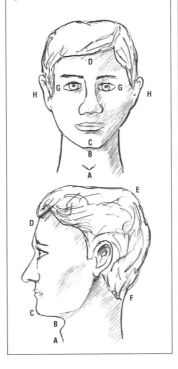

Portrait head

When transferring measurements from model to sculpture, always use the same corresponding points on each. Have your armature on a modeling stand at the same height as the model's head. Have the model sit on a swivel chair so that he or she can turn when you need to look at another part of the head – this saves you having to move the modeling stand and sculpture.

1   Pack clay tightly onto the aluminum wire of the armature, until you are able to cup both of your hands comfortably around it. Add some clay around the wood at the bottom of the clay.

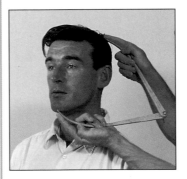

6   Measure the model from C to E. Transfer to your sculpture and mark the position of E with a matchstick. Push it in so that only the tip is showing.

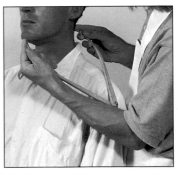

7   Take another measurement from C to F. Mark F on the sculpture with a matchstick. Now that the side profile is indicated, add enough clay to realize the shape of the head. Spend some time on the modeling so that you have a consistent curvature all over. From now on, don't depend on the measurements alone.

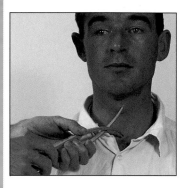

2 Decide which is to be the front and back of the sculpture – each should correspond with the flat planes of the vertical support. On the front, the midway point on the bottom edge of the clay corresponds to a point on the model's neck just below the Adam's apple. Cross your calipers so that the ends point away from each other. Position one end at A and adjust to measure to B.

3 Without adjusting the calipers, move to your sculpture and place one end on the bottom edge of the neck at its midway point and hold it in position. Where the other end of the calipers rests at the top of the neck, push a matchstick into the clay. Pack some clay on the front of the head above this point to begin establishing the chin.

4 Using calipers, measure from B to C on the model. Take the calipers over to the sculpture and place one end at the top of the neck. Add some clay to establish the depth of the chin. Next add more clay to the front of the head to establish a vertical plane from the tip of the chin to the top. Now add clay to the neck to produce a slight diagonal from the top to the base.

5 Measure from C to D on the model. Transfer this measurement to the sculpture and mark the top of the sculpture with the calipers. Using a modeling tool, mark a line in the clay that divides the face in half from top to bottom.

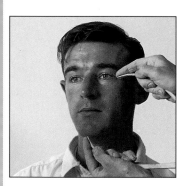

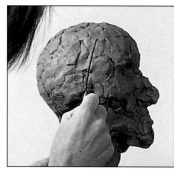

8 Measure the distance from C to G, placing your fingers over the sharp point of the calipers to avoid hurting the model. Check that the measurements are the same from the chin to the corner of each eye.

9 Being careful not to move the calipers, place one end of the calipers on the chin of the sculpture. Hold this point securely in position and draw an arc onto the front of the face.

10 Gouge out an area of clay with a wire modeling tool on each side of the dividing line, but just below the arc. This establishes the eye sockets and leaves a raised area of clay in the center, to which more needs to be added for the nose.

11 On each side of the head, mark a center line running from the top to the bottom to help you position the ears. As a general rule, they lie at some point on this center line.

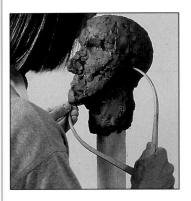

Life figure
In modeling this figure, clay will be added to the armature made in the ARMATURE section, so the major decisions regarding the size and relative proportions of the figure have already been made. The final sculpture, however, depends very much on using your eyes to look at the configuration of the pose and transferring this information to the clay.

YOU WILL NEED

clay • armature • pliers • tape measure • water spray • small modeling tool • plastic wrap or sheet

12 Take a measurement from C to H. Double-check this measurement on the other side. On the sculpture, hold one end of the calipers on the tip of the chin and make a mark with the other end on the vertical line on each side of the head. Place matchsticks in these marks.

13 Measure the distance between the two points marked H on the model. Position the tips of the calipers just above the tops of the matchsticks and adjust the position of the ends of the matchsticks so that they just touch the ends of the calipers. You must now rely solely on your eyes to complete the modeling.

1 Build up a base of clay on which the sculpture will stand. Once it has been built up to the level of the feet, they can be put in the position that corresponds with the pose of the model, whose left knee is bent slightly. Using pliers, hold the armature wire at the knee and bend the lower part back until you have a bend that relates to the pose of the model.

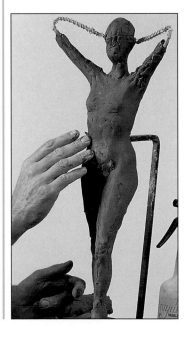

14 For the final modeling, line up your sculpture so that it is in the same position as the head of the model.

15 The hair is always a tricky part to model and should be the last part of the head to be completed. Identify a significant form within the hair of the model and develop this form in clay. Use a modeling tool to finalize fine details.

5 Make sure that the clay does not start to dry out. Keep a water spray handy and spray the sculpture from time to time as you are modeling, keeping the clay moist and workable. Do not overspray the sculpture, or the clay will become too wet to work with.

2 Measure the distance between the feet of the model and divide this measurement by three (remembering that you are making a one-third lifesize sculpture). Distance the feet on your sculpture accordingly, holding the legs in position by packing clay around (not over) and under the feet.

3 Working from the bottom, start to add small quantities of clay to the armature.

4 Constantly check the model to make sure that the forms you are developing are kept in proportion and do not grow too large.

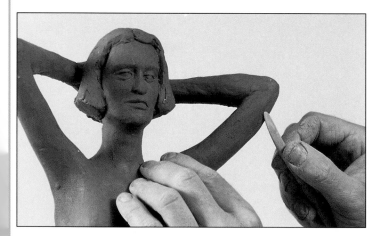

6 Use a wooden modeling tool to shape those forms that are too small to be adequately modeled with your fingers.

7 With the modeling complete and all the forms and features of the sculpture now finalized, use the modeling tool to level off the top and side edges of the base. Spray the whole sculpture with water and cover tightly with plastic wrap or a plastic sheet. This will keep the clay moist until you are ready to make a mold of the sculpture.

MOLDMAKING

Clay, when left to dry out, quickly deteriorates and disintegrates. So when modeling a sculpture in clay, there are two options: either to reproduce or cast it in a more permanent material, or to fire it in a kiln (see KILN FIRING).

The first step in making a cast is to make a mold of the original sculpture. A mold is a negative impression of the original sculpture. Using the mold, you are able to produce a positive – the cast of the original sculpture in another material (also see CASTING). Making a mold is a time-consuming and messy operation. However, it is also a vital one, as the quality of the mold determines the quality of the casts taken.

The first consideration when making a mold is whether you will want more than one cast. If you require only one, you make a waste mold which, as its name implies, is a mold that is used only once. It is subsequently destroyed during the casting process. If, however, you want more than one cast, you will need a mold that can be re-used. This means that the mold must be easy to remove from the original sculpture and subsequent casts in one piece without being damaged. A flexible rubber mold is best for this purpose.

Casting plaster is a basic sculpting material with a variety of applications when making sculpture, including moldmaking. This plaster is available in various grades, reflecting the whiteness and hardness of the plaster when set and, of course, its cost. The type of plaster you choose will depend on the type of sculpture you are making. As a general rule, the basic grade casting plaster will be suitable for the majority of your needs. If, however, you are casting in plaster and want a hard and durable cast, you would choose a higher grade.

Waste molds

Making a good mix of plaster is an important sculptural technique. This mixing technique will apply to any grade of plaster you choose. Two types of waste mold are shown being made in this section, each taken from sculptures modeled in clay. The first is a straightforward two-piece waste mold of a portrait head. The second is one taken from a life figure. Because an iron has been used to support the armature of the figure, it is a slightly more complex mold in three pieces.

The third is a flexible rubber mold. This mold is not damaged when separated from the original sculpture or its subsequent casts, so you are able to re-use it again and again. It is also worth remembering that, because of its flexible nature, this type of mold should be used when working with a sculpture which has undercuts. An undercut is the term given to concave parts of a sculpture or parts that protrude or overhang. When completely embedded in another moldmaking material, such as plaster, these parts are difficult or impossible to separate from the mold without damage. Undercuts are very likely to occur in sculptures whose forms articulate against one another.

As making a mold is such a messy business, you need to work in an area separated from your main workspace, preferably with a wall surface behind the sculpture and with easy access to running water. If this is not possible, make sure that the area you choose to work in is adequately protected with plastic sheets. Finally, whenever you are working in plaster, don't forget to clean up as you go along, for the sake of your working area and your piece of work.

Mixing plaster

Plaster comes in a powdered form. When it is mixed with water, a chemical reaction takes place so the plaster hardens and sets. This reaction is exothermic – which means it gives off heat. As the plaster starts to harden, it becomes warm to the touch; when it has cooled down, you know that the reaction has finished and the plaster has set.

The chosen method of mixing determines the correct proportion of plaster to water, with the plaster always added to the water and not vice versa. However, the amount of water you start with always depends on the job at hand, and naturally, the level of water rises as plaster is added

---

SAFETY

- Work in a well-ventilated area where it doesn't matter if you make a mess. Alternatively, protect your working area with a plastic sheet or other suitable material as much as possible.

- Always use barrier cream on your hands when working with plaster and wear a dust mask when mixing it.

to it. The final mixture will be about half as much again as the amount of water you started with. Plaster sets very quickly, so never mix too much at once. It is always better to mix less than more. When the plaster residue left inside your mixing container has set, you can break it free simply by tapping the sides and bottom of the plastic container. Any remaining small amounts of plaster are easily dislodged with a scraper. Never dispose of plaster by pouring it down a sink or drain, because it will set and block the pipework. It is useful to have a bucket of water near you when mixing, so you can clean your hands and tools.

YOU WILL NEED

casting plaster • plastic sheet • barrier cream • dust mask • plastic bowl or bucket • scraper

1   Sprinkle plaster gently and evenly onto the surface of the water.

2   As you add the plaster, it will sink slowly to the bottom. Do not let it drop down in one place as this will impede its ability to break up and disperse in the water.

3   When the plaster starts to rise above the level of the water (or peak), enough plaster has been added to the water. A useful analogy to use is that of an iceberg, where the majority of its mass is underwater and only a small amount shows above the surface.

4   Allow the plaster to settle, to be certain the peaks will not sink into the water. While in this state, no reaction is taking place between the plaster and the water. When you are satisfied that the peaks have formed, mix the plaster well in with the water, making sure that any lumps are broken up.

5   You should now have achieved a smooth and creamy mixture. A simple test can be carried out to make sure that you have a proper mixture. Dip your fingers into the plaster and bring them up above the surface. The plaster should move slowly down your fingers but stop short of falling back into the container.

6   This test shows a weak mixture of plaster, where too little plaster has been added. This mixture is very transparent and falls quickly off the fingers. However, it is pointless to add more plaster – this will not rectify the problem. The weak mix will set in time and can be discarded. Make another mixture of plaster.

Head

This portrait head uses the most straightforward kind of two-piece waste mold.

YOU WILL NEED

shims (brass fencing) • scissors • plaster • powder paint • bucket • knife • plaster modeling tool • pliers • toothbrush

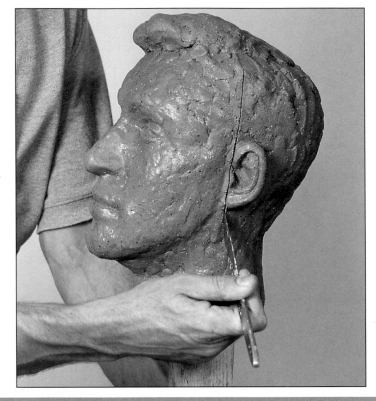

1 Mark a dividing line on the surface of the clay, bringing it down in front of the ears.

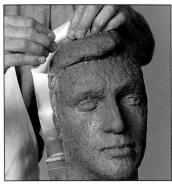

2 Using this line as your guide, insert brass fencing or shims, about 1 × 2 inches long into the clay so that they protrude ¾ inch above the surface of the sculpture. Alternatively, you can use the aluminum from soft-drink cans. Follow the line around the head, making sure that the tops of the shims remain level and overlap slightly so there are no gaps between them.

5 Sometimes you will have shims that do not fit neatly together. This is because the shims have not been pushed vertically into the clay. Any gaps that do occur can be rectified by bending over a small slither of shim as a clip to join the two offending shims.

6 Trim the shims with scissors to establish a consistent height all around the sculpture, ¾ inch above the surface.

7 Mix a small quantity of plaster adding some powder paint to make colored plaster. This first coat of the mold, immediately adjacent to the surface of the cast, will prove a useful indicator during the casting process. You need to flick this colored plaster mix onto the sculpture quickly before it starts to set. Scoop up some plaster with your index and middle fingers and flick it as hard as possible onto the surface of the sculpture to prevent air pockets, which have the potential to weaken the mold.

4 Continue all the way around the head. There will inevitably be a discrepancy in the height of adjoining shims, especially when going around the top – use smaller lengths of shim cut into a wedge shape at this point.

3 Place three shims, bent into "v" shapes on top of and on each side of the head. These will provide positive and negative registration shapes along the seams of the mold and ensure that the two halves can be fitted back together correctly.

8 Cover one whole side of the sculpture with the colored plaster. In any areas inaccessible for flicking, the plaster can be patted on tightly. Alternatively, let the first plaster mix set, then reposition the sculpture for easy flicking. For difficult areas – inside the ears and nostrils, for instance – blow the plaster into and around them.

9 Now apply a first coat of plaster to the other side of the head, again making sure that no air is trapped between clay and plaster. Clean off any plaster from the tops of the shims before it has had a chance to set.

10 Using an ordinary mixture of plaster, start to build up the thickness of the mold case. This thickness is determined by the height of the shims and must be consistent throughout, including high points such as the nose.

11 While the plaster is in this wet state, go over the details of the face. There is still a danger that air will be trapped and weaken the mold, so do not let any plaster drip down and set.

12 As the plaster starts to set, its state will change. As it starts to harden, you can apply larger amounts, building up the thickness of plaster more quickly.

17 When both sides of the mold are complete, scrape along the seam which separates the two halves to reveal the top edge of the shims.

18 Pull the shims out of the mold with pliers. To get a grip, cut a bevel in the plaster on each side of the shims all the way around the mold.

19 Take your pliers and grip the shims firmly, pulling at the same time. You should be able to extract the shims relatively easily.

13 Compact the plaster tightly onto the surface to prevent air traps. Push plaster up to the shims without covering the tops. Then quickly add more plaster, compacting it tightly and moving away from the shims, continuing around the sculpture and maintaining an even thickness.

14 With one half of the mold made, the plaster needs to be cleared away from the shims, especially from the top. Scrape carefully along the top of the shims and mold case so that the top edges of the shims are revealed. It is much easier to do this while the plaster is in its semisoft pre-set state – it is extremely difficult to cut back hardened excess plaster.

15 An even thickness of the mold case gives it a consistency of strength. Any variation in the thickness of these walls will be a source of weakness.

16 Add the plaster to the back of the mold. Make sure that the plaster is compacted well in behind the ear.

20 Unscrew the baseboard from the armature stand and place the mold under running water. Direct the water so it runs down into the slight gap left by the extracted shims. Turn the mold occasionally so that water runs evenly around the mold. After a while, the water will find its way in between the clay and the interior surface of the mold so that the mold starts to separate from the sculpture.

21 As the two halves start to separate, gently pry them apart. Take care not to apply too much pressure in case you break the mold.

22 Clean out the clay from inside the molds and wash them out under a faucet. Use a toothbrush, where necessary, to remove pieces of clay lodged in awkward crevices. The mold is now ready for casting.

Life figure

The mold for this life figure is in three parts. The mold for the front is made first and becomes the main part of the mold, to which the two back pieces are attached. The clay-wall technique can be used to separate the parts of the mold or you can use the previous technique of a mold for a portrait head. The mold for the life figure is made in the same way as the head, the main difference being that the life figure has far more detail in a much smaller area and so needs greater care when applying the plaster.

| YOU WILL NEED |

clay • rolling pin • knife • modeling tool • paintbrush • plastic wrap • clay slip • plaster • powder paint • steel rod • screwdriver • barrier cream

1 Roll out the clay to an even thickness. Cut the clay into strips ¾ inch wide.

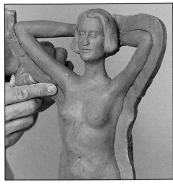

2 Place the strips of clay along the outside edge of the figure. The bottom front edge of the clay wall should separate the figure in half with no gaps between the bottom edge of the strip and the sculpture.

5 Using the end of a paintbrush, make a series of indentations in the clay wall at regular intervals. These are the location marks for fitting the mold back together satisfactorily.

6 Cover the back of the sculpture in plastic wrap to protect it from plaster.

3 Fill in the openings between the arms and legs with clay. Roll out a slab of clay, and hold it up behind the opening. With a modeling tool, mark the interior profile of the opening onto the surface of the clay.

4 Cut the shape of the opening from the clay slab, then fit it inside the hole, squarely in the center, making good and filling in any gaps.

7 Paint a border of clay slip onto the base board around the base of the sculpture to prevent the mold from sticking to the base board.

8 Coloring the water with powder paint, mix a small quantity of plaster. Flick the plaster onto the front of the sculpture. Make sure it gets into all the small crevices around the head and arms, blowing it in them, if necessary.

9 Cover the front of the sculpture with plaster. As it starts to set, build up the mold to the height of the clay walls all across the front of the sculpture. Do not cover the top of the wall with plaster – if you do, clean it off before it sets.

10 Once the plaster on the front of the figure has gone off, you can make the two pieces of mold for the back. Start by peeling off the clay wall and remove the plastic wrap from the back of the sculpture.

11 Gently remove the infills of clay from between the arms and legs. Dig the tip of a modeling tool into the clay slab near one of the edges and carefully lift it up and away without damaging any of the modeling on the figure.

12 Next, split the back of the sculpture in two, using the point where the armature iron enters the back of the sculpture as a dividing line. Roll out a slab of clay to the thickness of the armature iron and cut it into a ¾ inch wide strip. Wrap some of the clay around the armature iron at its point of entry – this allows for a gap in the mold case. Place a strip of clay horizontally from the mold seam to the armature iron, either side of the sculpture.

15 Cut back the plaster before it has set hard to reveal the seam all the way around the sculpture and the tops of the clay wedges. Take out these pieces of clay, together with the clay that was wrapped around the armature iron, using a screwdriver.

16 Place the mold, still attached to the armature iron and base board, under running water and direct the water into the holes and seam around the top half of the back of the mold. Turn the mold occasionally so that there is an even penetration of water. As the back piece of the mold becomes looser, gently help it on its way – but don't pull too hard or you may break the mold.

17 Scoop out as much of the clay from the top of the sculpture as possible and pull the aluminum armature wire free from the mold. Place the mold under running water again, directing the water down between the two remaining parts of the mold.

13 Paint clay slip onto the mold seams, including the areas between the arms and legs. Cut some clay wedge shapes ¾ inch high and place three along each side of the plaster seam of the main mold and one along the top. Cover the top half of the back with plastic wrap and make the bottom half of the mold, as in steps 8 and 9. When the plaster has set, remove the horizontal clay wall and the plastic wrap. Make the last part of the mold, and paint some clay slip onto the horizontal plaster mold seam of the bottom mold piece.

14 Because of the delicate configuration of the pose, the main part of the mold needs to be strengthened, using steel rod held in place by scrim and plaster. This also reduces the likelihood of the mold warping and distorting as it dries out. Place a steel rod horizontally across the arms and anchor in place with scrim and plaster. Attach two lengths of steel rod vertically onto the front of the main mold.

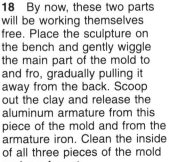

18 By now, these two parts will be working themselves free. Place the sculpture on the bench and gently wiggle the main part of the mold to and fro, gradually pulling it away from the back. Scoop out the clay and release the aluminum armature from this piece of the mold and from the armature iron. Clean the inside of all three pieces of the mold under a faucet.

19 Finally, because this mold is going to be used for a fiberglass cast, it must be completely dried out. To prevent warpage and distortion, piece it together and tie it securely to hold the three parts in place.

Flexible rubber mold

Rubber molds are very useful: they are excellent at picking up details and can be used over and over again. In this section a hot pour rubber has been used. This comes in solid blocks and needs to be cut into cubes approximately 1 inch square, which are then melted in a thermostatically-controlled electric melting pot. Depending on the grade of rubber, it melts at between 300° and 340° and should be poured at around 280°.

You can also use a pourable Room Temperature Vulcanising (RTV) Silicone Rubber for this technique. The rubber cures when you add a catalyst to it. The advantage of this type of rubber is that you need no specialized equipment to make it pourable. When using RTV silicone rubber, follow the manufacturer's guidelines on safe handling and usage.

1 Thoroughly clean the original fired-clay sculpture and soak it in water to displace any air trapped in its slightly porous surface.

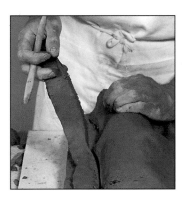

6 Trim off the excess clay where the top slab meets the clay bed.

7 Work around the sculpture with a modeling tool, closing any seams between the clay slab and the clay bed and making it neat as you go, so that you are left with a clay form that resembles the original sculpture.

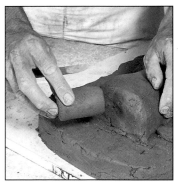

8 Cut some wedges of clay and space them evenly along the clay bed. Roll some more clay into a conical shape and place it on the clay bed at the bottom of the sculpture.

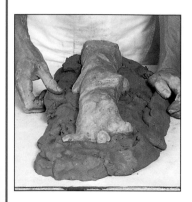

2 Lay the sculpture down on a modeling board and submerge it halfway in a bed of clay.

3 Develop this clay bed until it is 2 inches wide all the way around the sculpture. Level off and smooth the surface of the clay bed.

4 Roll out a slab of clay about ½ inch thick, and cover the exposed part of the sculpture with it.

5 Gently mold the clay around the sculpture.

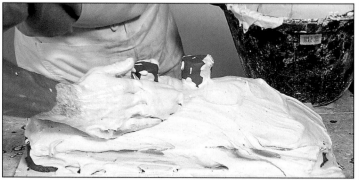

9 Roll two more conical shapes in clay about 2 inches high and place them on top of the clay, one at the highest point – these will be the pouring holes for the rubber.

Finally, make some indentations on the surface of the clay bed with the end of a paintbrush. These are the location marks for the two halves of the mold.

10 Mix some plaster and cover the mold, gradually building up the thickness. Use the height of the clay cones as your guide, to produce a mold case that is 2 inches thick all over. Be careful not to go over the edges of the clay bed at the sides.

11 Wait until the plaster is in a semisoft state and quickly trim off any excess from the sides so you have a straight seam between the clay bed and the plaster case. Trim off the plaster from the area around the top of the clay cones.

12 Once the plaster has set, turn the mold case over and peel off the clay bed.

13 Clean up the surface of the original. Then, with a modeling tool, smooth the surface of the embedded clay up to the surface of the original.

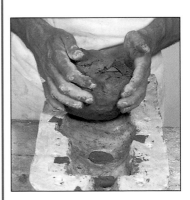

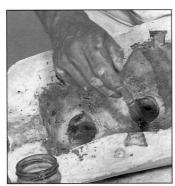

18 Place this half of the mold on top of the other, using the location points along the seams to position it correctly. Melt the rubber in an electric melting pot and gradually pour the hot rubber into the pour hole. The rubber will rise up to the brim of the hole. Gently tap the sides of the mold to dislodge any trapped air. Leave the rubber to cure (set) completely overnight.

16 Take the mold section without the original and remove all the clay from its interior, including the pour holes.

17 Apply three coats of shellac to the inside of the mold. This will allow you to keep the rubber mold in the plaster case, as there is a danger that the dry plaster of the mold could in time draw some of the constituent oils out of the rubber. Finally, block up the pour hole at the base of the figure with clay.

14 Paint the plaster seam of the mold case with three coats of shellac and smear on a layer of petroleum jelly. Repeat steps 4–11 for this side of the exposed original.

15 When the plaster of the second mold case has set, gently insert a knife blade into the seam. You will be able to separate the two halves of the mold, with the original staying in one half of the mold.

19 The next day, turn the mold over and lift off the top, making sure that the original stays in the rubber. Repeat steps 16–18.

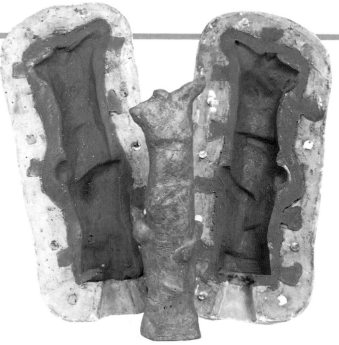

20 After leaving the rubber to cure, the mold can be separated and the original removed.

RELIEF

A sculpture in relief is not totally "in the round" – it exists somewhere in between two and three dimensions. In relief, forms come out of and recede into a common ground, exploring aspects of real and illusory form and space. Relief can be *bas* (low) or *haute* (high), depending on the distance between the highest point of the sculpture and the ground from which it rises. Relief is as old as sculpture's history itself. Its earliest use, by the ancient Greeks and Egyptians, was in architecture, where the interior and exterior surfaces of buildings would be carved with images. The introduction of coinage is an early example of modeling being used to make a relief.

Whether a relief is carved or modeled, a drawing is essential to enable you to plan the highest and lowest points. You then need to consider not only the restrictions of the relief format, but also those of the technique involved, whether carving or modeling. Relief does not involve only carving and modeling and is now frequently associated with a construction technique – which, interestingly enough, also has architectural associations, particularly where the sculpture is hung on a wall. In the BRAZING section, you will see an example of a constructed metal relief.

Two types of relief are shown here. The first, a stone carving, develops further the exercise in the CARVING section, using a harder and more resistant material, as well as examining the discipline of working within a relief format.

Another type of relief is made combining a molding and casting technique. By referring to the MOLDMAKING and CASTING sections, you will be able to find out more regarding these two techniques.

Plaster

In this abstract plaster relief, the impressions are made on the clay base using simple geometric shapes.

4 When you are happy with your impressions, you are ready to pour on the plaster. It can, however, be quite difficult to imagine what the resultant plaster cast will look like, because the plaster cast will, of course, be a negative impression of the clay bed.

5 Make good any imperfections in the clay bed and then pour the plaster out of the bucket and slowly onto the clay, aiming for the center and letting it flow out toward the sides.

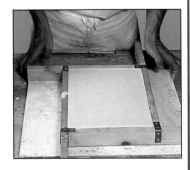

6 Gently shake the base board from side to side to disperse the plaster evenly. This will also get rid of any pockets of air that have been trapped. Do not shake the base board too much or the casting jig may become dislodged and the plaster will spill out.

1 Roll out a bed of clay to a consistent thickness of at least 1 inch. Use a plastic-coated board or one that has been lined with a plastic sheet or plastic wrap on which to roll it out and place two strips of wood of the right depth on each side of the clay to measure the thickness. Roll out the clay with a rolling pin to the required width with each end of the rolling pin resting on the strips of wood.

2 Using a tape measure and a carpenter's square, cut the clay bed to shape with a knife. You now need to make an adjustable casting jig for the plaster. The height of the sides of the jig above the clay determines the thickness of the plaster. Screw a right-angle corner bracket onto one end of four pieces of wood.

Slot a fixed bracket over another piece of wood at a right angle to it to construct a square box. You can adjust the size to fit the cast you require. Paint the interior surfaces of the wood with liquid soap, so it will be easy to release. Position the casting jig around the clay bed.

3 Press a wooden block into the surface of the clay, taking care not to push it in too far or the block will touch the base board. You will not be able to make an impression of any undercuts (see MOLDMAKING) with this technique. However, parts of most objects can be pressed into the clay, and even a basic geometric shape produces a variety of impressions.

7 When the plaster has set, gently remove the casting jig. Then slide the clay and plaster to and fro until both are free from the base board. Turn them over so that the plaster is now on the bench, and peel off the clay. The plaster can be washed with water to get rid of any clay residue left on the surface.

Stone carving

This relief is a stone carving and uses the techniques found in the CARVING section, as well as incorporating the special considerations of relief work.

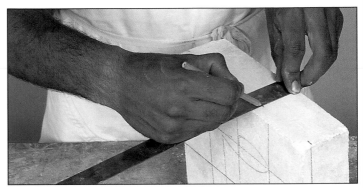

1 Make a drawing, the same size as the relief design. Measure and mark a grid on the drawing and on the stone. Transfer the design onto the face of the stone.

2 Work out the highest and lowest points of the design. The highest point is the mid-point of the scroll, while the lowest will be the background out of which the scroll emerges. Use a tape measure to mark the background depth on the four sides of the slab of stone.

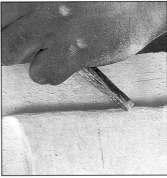

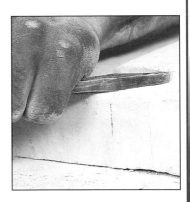

5 Begin carving the scroll, starting with the receding interior part. The straight edge of this area is just higher than the level of the background. The surface then rises gradually to a point just below the lower level of the exterior of the scroll. Take particular care when carving the undercut that runs under the edge of the scroll.

6 Carve both the straight edges of the scroll, gently rounding them off to a level just above the background.

7 The other side of the scroll is also an undercut and needs to be carved out very carefully. Tilt the chisel at the required angle and tap it gently with the mallet.

3 Wear goggles and a dust mask and keep a water spray to hand to keep the dust level down while carving. Start by disposing of areas of waste material, the biggest of which will be the background area. Using the mark made on each side of the stone, start cutting away the stone. Position the chisel horizontally and parallel to the bench and hit it with the dummy mallet with firm and consistent taps. It is good stone carving practice to keep up a rhythmic tapping of the mallet on the chisel. With this line cut away around the block, the depth of the background is established.

4 Start carving on the waste side of the drawn line which describes the scroll form and follow this line all the way around. This releases the scroll from the waste material. Make the surface of the background level with a flat chisel. Redraw the grid on this surface as a point of reference.

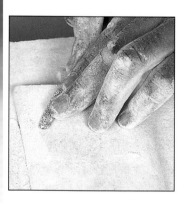

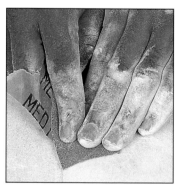

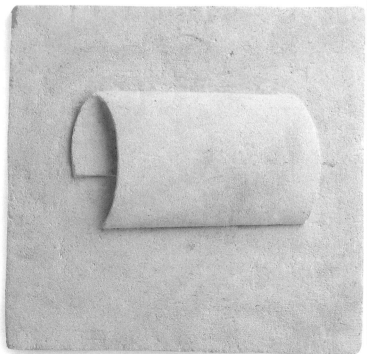

8 Use rifflers of various sizes for the final shaping. These tools will also be useful for leveling off any undulations on the surface of the background after smoothing with a rasp.

9 Finally, use sandpaper to smooth off and establish the sharp edges that run along the bottom and sides of the scroll.

REPAIRS

However meticulously you follow a particular technique, inevitably you will need to repair or "make good" parts that have been damaged. Learning by one's own mistakes, though – and we all make them – is by far the best way. Never abandon a sculpture because of damage – you will find that everything is repairable and well worth the effort in the end.

Sculptures can be damaged in a variety of ways. Some are totally beyond your control – such as the cracks that occurred in the stylized torso during kiln firing. Others, such as the broken corner of the plaster carving, occur while working on the sculpture. The broken ear and nose tip on the *ciment fondu* cast happened as the plaster mold was chipped off the cast – a common accident. Parts of the seam in the resin cast figure have not joined together properly, and part of the wrist needs to be repaired. When taking a cast from a mold of this size, you will inevitably have to do some making good. The countersunk holes in the figurative wooden construction have to be filled as part of making it.

Portrait head

Epoxy resin putty behaves in the same way as clay, so it is a very useful material to use for repairing modeled sculpture. Wear rubber gloves when handling it.

YOU WILL NEED

epoxy resin putty • rubber gloves • sharp pointed tool • sand-filled inner tube • angle grinder • clear goggles • dust mask • craft knife • riffler • water • modeling tool

1 Pick out as much as you can of the plaster in the crevices of the sculpture. A sharp-pointed tool will be useful for this.

2 Position the head securely in a sand-filled inner tube and use an angle grinder to level out the edge of the opening to the neck. Always wear clear goggles and a dust mask.

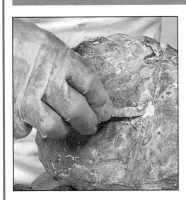

6 Fill in any holes with the putty and use a modeling tool to shape it to the sculpture.

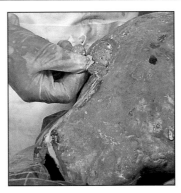

7 Use putty to model the section of ear that broke off.

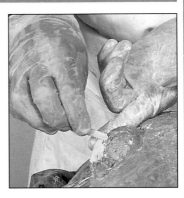

8 Finally, use the modeling tool to shape the putty so that it matches the rest of the ear.

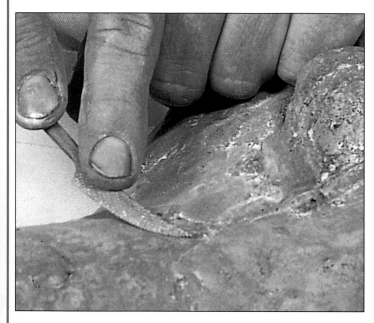

4 Cut equal lengths of the two parts of the epoxy resin putty with a craft knife.

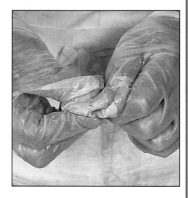

5 Knead them together until you have an evenly colored mixture. Add a little water to the mixture to make it more malleable and easier to knead.

3 There will be raised pieces of *ciment fondu* around the seam of the two halves of the cast. File these down level with the surface with a riffler.

Figurative construction

YOU WILL NEED

screwdriver • 2 1½-inch screws • wood stopper/putty • taping knife • sandpaper

1 When the sculpture has been colored, screw it down onto the base.

2 The countersunk drill holes will need to be filled with wood putty. Once it is dry, sand it and restain.

Stylized torso

YOU WILL NEED

spackling compound • sandpaper

1 After firing, you can see that there are some small cracks on the surface of the torso.

2 Mix some spackling compound and work it into the cracks with your fingers.

Resin cast

YOU WILL NEED

scissors • riffler • epoxy resin putty • bronze/resin gel coat mix • modeling knife • palette knife • rubber gloves • modeling tool

1 Trim off the excess fiberglass matting around the edge of the base with scissors.

2 Use a riffler to level off the raised areas of resin, where the two halves of the mold were joined.

3 Use epoxy resin putty to fill any damaged parts of the cast or open seams. Leave to set.

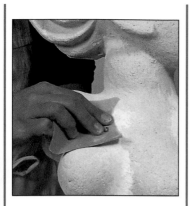

3 When the spackle has set hard, level off the filled areas with sandpaper down the surface of the sculpture.

Abstract plaster carving
White craft glue helps the spackling compound adhere well to the plaster carving.

1 Add water to a small quantity of spackling compound and mix to the consistency of soft cheese.

2 Paint some diluted white craft glue onto the areas to be repaired.

4 Apply a layer of bronze/ resin gel coat mixture over the putty. (Refer to the CASTING section for instructions on how to prepare a mixture.) When the resin has the consistency of jelly, trim it back into shape with a modeling knife. Leave to cure fully.

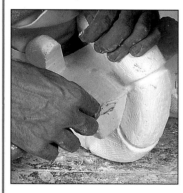

3 Load a taping knife with spackling compound and fill the holes. Pull the knife back over the holes to produce a level surface.

4 For a sharp edge along the corner section, hold the blade of a taping knife hard up against the face of the sculpture. Fill the corner area using another knife, then drag the blade back up the surface of the sculpture using the edge of the first knife as your guide.

5 Fill any holes on the surface of the sculpture. When the spackle has set, gently smooth it level with sandpaper.

RIVETING

Rivets are an extremely efficient and permanent joining method for thin-gauge sheets of steel or tin. Although it is an industrial technique, riveting is very suitable for constructed sculpture – either big or small – and a minimum of nonspecialized tools and equipment is needed (see CONSTRUCTION). You can create voluminous geometric forms using flat sheets of steel or tin joined with rivets. Rivets are available in various lengths depending on the thickness of the material.

Plan out beforehand the form of the sculpture and figure out how you are going to join its various parts together. The sculpture in this example is composed of two volumes of four sides each. The sheet tin has been cut to size using cardboard templates.

Mobile sculpture

Wear leather gloves throughout to protect your hands from any sharp edges on the cans.

YOU WILL NEED

leather gloves • empty tin cans • can opener • scissors • heavy weight (such as books) • soft lead pencil • ruler • cardboard • hole punch • hammer • electric drill • C-clamp • wood • metal working vise • wooden mallet • 1/8-inch pop rivets • rivet gun • 1/16-inch diameter steel welding rod • pliers

1 Remove the bottom of the can with a can opener, and make a straight cut down the side using scissors. Flatten out the can by placing a heavy weight on it – such as books – and leave overnight. It will retain its new flatter form and will not curl up at the ends.

2 Draw around the cardboard templates with a pencil to create the end panels for the top shape.

7 Clamp the tin sheet securely to your bench and drill a 1/8-inch hole in each of the punched marks.

8 Cut diagonally across the corners of the tin where the inner lines of the margin meet. On one of the long edges of the bottom panel, mark the width of the top shape, equidistant from the ends. Cut out a wedge shape, so that the apex is on the inner margin line.

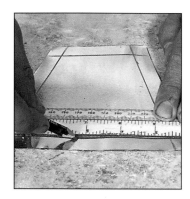

3 Use the diagonal edge of the template to mark the edge of the long panels for the bottom shape.

4 Cut out the shapes that have been marked with scissors.

5 Draw a line parallel to each of the edges, to make a ½-inch margin.

6 Mark points about 1½ inches apart in the center of the margin and, with the hole punch and hammer, indent the surface of the tin.

9 Position the tin between two pieces of wood, lining up the inner margin on the tin with the top edges of the wood. Place the whole thing in a vise and secure tightly. Bend the tin back at right angles to the wood.

10 Place a piece of wood on top of the bend and tap with a wooden mallet to reinforce the right-angle bend.

11 Clamp the top shape to the bench and place the bottom section on top of it. Make a mark on the underside of the top shape using the holes drilled in the bottom as your guide. Indent the tin with the hole punch, and drill the holes. Join the two parts together using pop rivets.

12 With the two sides of the bottom now joined to the top, slide a strip of tin underneath the flanges of the bottom shape. Mark corresponding holes on this strip to those on the flanges. Clamp the strip of tin, with a piece of board underneath it, to the bench and drill holes.

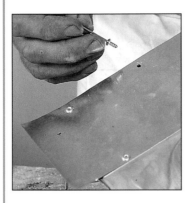

13 Place the strip on top of the flanges and line up the holes. Insert a pop rivet through both of the holes to attach it to the underside of the bottom.

14 Insert the wire length from the rivet into the hole in the rivet gun. Pump the gun a couple of times until the wire snaps. The underside of the rivet has been pulled up, and the two pieces of tin are now joined together.

15 Riveting is an extremely efficient technique for producing geometric sculptural forms. Note how the positioning of the rivets can play an important compositional role.

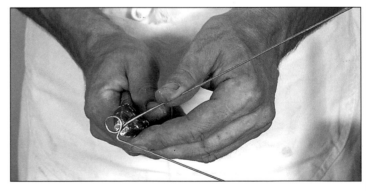

16 Place a length of steel rod into a vise, position a length of welding rod around it, and bend it toward you.

17 Bend it around to form a circle, then lift it off.

18 With pliers, bend the rod back at right angles to the circle. Cut the two ends off 6 inches from the right angle. At the ends, bend 1½ inches up at right angles. This wire will be used to hang the sculpture (see COLOR).

WELDING

Welding is the technique of fusing together two pieces of metal by the application of heat. There are different welding processes for different metals and working conditions, and this section deals with the welding of mild steel using the oxyacetylene and electric arc-welding techniques. The oxyacetylene safety precautions in the BRAZING section also apply to oxy-acetylene welding and further precautions are given below.

The other technique uses an electric arc-welding unit. The unit has a grounded clamp cable and an electrode holder cable, as well as a dial to set the appropriate current. This will depend on the thickness of the steel to be joined. Consult the instruction manual.

To make a weld, clip the ground terminal onto your piece of work, or the steel bench upon which it is placed. Select the required current and switch on the electricity supply to the arc-welding unit. You will not be able to see anything through the welding mask, so position the welding rod just above and at a 70° angle to the area to be welded, before bringing the mask up to your face. Hit this area with the welding rod using one swift action, and raise it immediately $\frac{1}{8}$ inch above the surface of the steel to create an arc, which will light this area up. Move the rod slowly back and forth, keeping it above the surface of the steel, between the two points to be joined to make the weld. Knock off any slag that has built up on the weld with a chipping hammer. Wear eye protection. It takes a bit of practice to perfect the arc, but once you have acquired the technique, it will never be forgotten. You may find at first that the welding rod sticks to the surface of the steel. In this case, you have not raised the rod quickly enough. If this happens, release the jaws of the electrode holder, turn off the arc-welding unit, and remove the stuck electrode.

The steel armature made here is used in the DIRECT MODELING section. The steel rod is heated up, bent into shape, and the parts are then welded together using the oxyacetylene technique.

An abstract sculpture, made of pieces of steel of various gauges and sizes, is shown being cut, heated, bent, ground, and welded to produce a homogenous composition. Arc-welding is a quick and efficient method of joining steel, allowing you to juxtapose different elements at quirky angles.

SAFETY

• When welding, wear heavy-duty boots or shoes, coveralls, leather gloves, and a leather apron. Avoid loose clothing and jewelry. Tie hair back.

• The intense light produced by the arc welder is harmful to eyes and exposed skin, so your whole body should be covered, and an arc-welding mask should cover your whole face and have an area of darkened glass for the eyes. When looking through this glass under normal circumstances, you will not be able to see a thing. It is only when the electric arc is produced that the area you are working on is illuminated. **NEVER ON ANY ACCOUNT LOOK AT THIS ARC WITH THE NAKED EYE**. Any other people watching also need to be adequately protected.

• When using the oxy-acetylene equipment, wear welding goggles. These have darkened glass so you can look directly at the flame without harming your eyes.
• After making a weld, the area around the seam is hot, so always wear leather gloves. Let the grounded clamp cool before moving it, and let the electrode holder cool before inserting a new welding rod.

• Beware of the potential risk of trailing cords and hoses, and do not let arc-welding cords come into direct contact with heat or water.

• Never weld on a wooden surface – a steel bench or a sheet of thick steel placed on top of a bench is preferable.

• See BRAZING for other oxyacetylene welding precautions.

arc welding mask

strong coverall

leather gloves

leather apron

heavy work boots

Gas welding

YOU WILL NEED

¼-inch steel rod • oxyacetylene
equipment • visegrips • metal vise

1 Make a same size model
from thin wire. Refer to this
when using ¼-inch steel rod to
make the three parts of the
armature. Weld the legs and
body sections together,
applying heat at the point of
contact. Remember that the
hottest part of the flame is at
the tip of the cone. Apply the
flame in an even, circular
motion. The steel welding rod
should be held in the outer
edge of the flame until it starts
to heat up. After a while, the
area being heated by the

flame will start to puddle (i.e.
the steel melts). Move the
welding rod through the flame
and dip it in the puddle. It will
now be the same temperature
as the other two pieces of
steel and so will also melt into
the puddle. When all three
pieces of steel are fused
together, withdraw the welding
rod, turn off the torch, and let
the weld cool down.

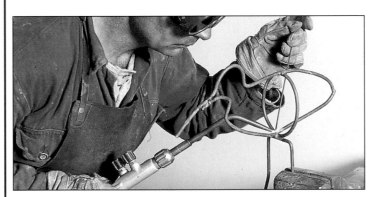

4 Remove the visegrips and
weld the lower part of the body
to the bird profile.

5 By using the minimum
number of lengths of steel rod
and welds, you can make an
extremely strong and durable
armature. This is an essential
requirement for the DIRECT
MODELING technique.

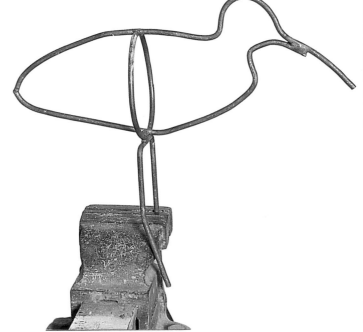

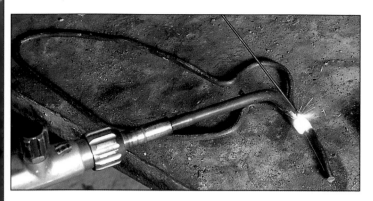

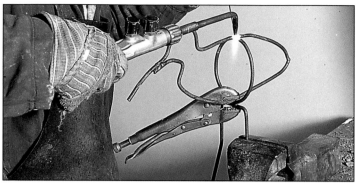

2 Weld the back section of the bird together.

3 Clamp the leg and body section in a metal vise. Use visegrips to hold the bird profile in place at right angles to the body section and make a weld to join this section to the bird profile.

Gas cutting and bending

The cutting torch of the oxy-acetylene equipment produces a very powerful flame which will bring mild steel to red heat very quickly. Once the steel has reached this state, add extra oxygen to the flame to cut the steel. The cutting torch can also be used to heat the steel until it becomes pliable and easy to bend. You must use suitable tools and equipment for this operation.

YOU WILL NEED

mild steel offcuts • steel rod • cutting torch • oxyacetylene equipment • metal vise • angle grinder • heavy hammer

1 Cut a circle from the flat section of steel with the cutting torch. Always hold the torch at a right angle to the surface you are cutting, so that the tips of the flame cones just touch the surface. Keep the torch in this position, directing the flame downward. When the steel becomes red, depress the oxygen lever on the cutting torch to release a stream of oxygen to blow away the molten steel. Slowly move the cutting torch around the circle, still with the oxygen lever depressed. When the circle has been cut out, release the oxygen lever and turn off the acetylene first and then the oxygen.

2 Place the tip of the steel plate in the metal vise, and heat up the steel with the cutting torch on each side of the circle at a point just above the jaws of the vise.

3 When the steel is red hot, turn off the gas, put the torch down, and bend the steel at a right angle to the piece held in the vise.

4 An angle grinder can be used to grind down the welded seams or to grind down part of the surface of the steel sculpture, but beware of the density and velocity of the sparks that occur. Always wear clear goggles and never work near anything flammable.

7 Continue hammering the end back. As it cools, you will need to put it back in the vise and apply more heat.

8 When it is again red hot, hammer the end of the rod back on itself and start to hammer the tip of the rod flat.

9 Place the rod in the vise and heat up the middle section. When red hot, push the rod away from you to produce another bend.

5 Hold a piece of steel rod in the vise and heat up the end until it is red hot.

6 Hold the rod on top of the vise and then hammer the end of the rod at a right angle to the main length.

Electric arc-welding
A Plasma-arc cutter is quicker and more efficient than an arc-welding unit, but more expensive to buy.

YOU WILL NEED
bent steel rod • electric arc-welding unit • visegrips • chipping hammer

2 Knock the slag off the weld with a chipping hammer.

1 This bent rod is held in place with visegrips on top of the sculpture. Using the technique described in the introduction, weld it into position.

123

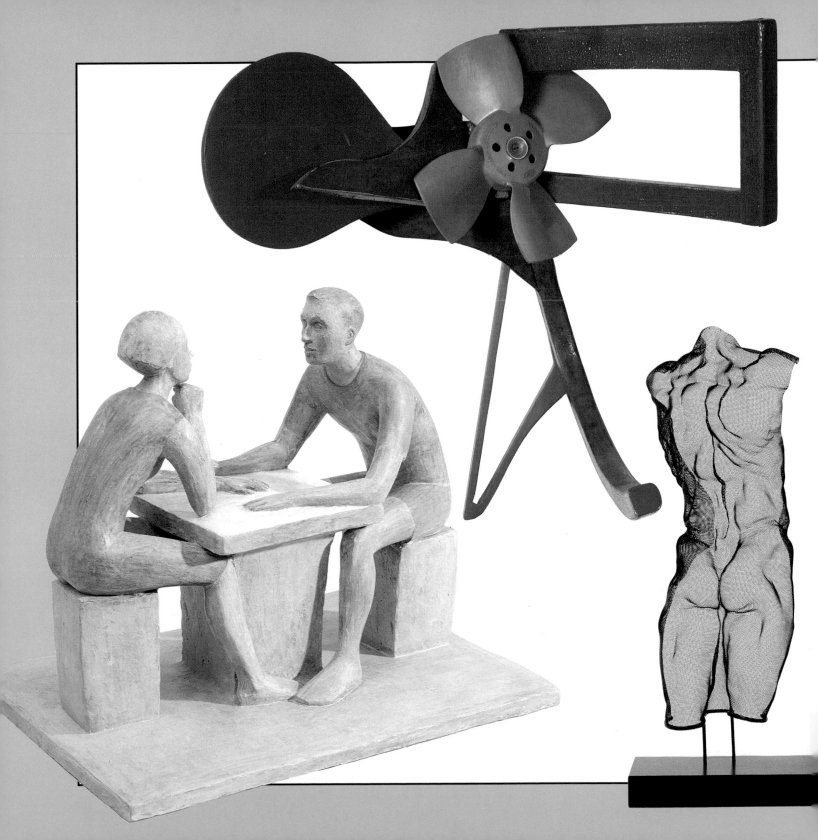

THEMES

Understanding technique does not in itself guarantee a
successful sculpture. Your own ideas are equally
important. Looking at the work of other sculptors is
extremely useful as it will help you develop your own
ideas about materials and techniques. The sculptures
shown in this section are designed to give you an
indication of the diversity of modern sculpture – its
themes, materials, techniques, and even, in some cases,
its location. You will notice that working within a
particular theme does not limit you to a particular
technique or material, and that sometimes materials and
techniques are combined. Bear this in mind as you
develop your own ways of making sculpture.

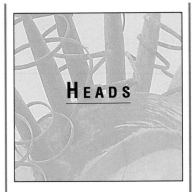

HEADS

There is a tradition in western sculpture of producing portrait busts of prominent people, the antecedents of which can be traced back to classical Greek sculpture. Originally, they would have been carved in stone, but now they are more likely to be modeled in clay and then cast in bronze, sometimes in small editions. Portrait sculpture has always existed in other cultures, too. Egyptian, African, and Mexican sculpture spring to mind, and as these have all become accessible through museums and publications, they have had an enormous influence on twentieth-century western sculpture by introducing new and different forms. Equally new and different materials are now available to sculptors. However, portrait busts still and will always continue to be sculpted within the classical convention, too.

▲ PATRICIA FINCH • **Sam Wanamaker**
This cold cast bronze sculpture has all the attributes of bronze, but the advantage of being much lighter in weight. It was modeled from life in clay, and a plaster mold was made of the clay original. The mold was used to produce a resin and bronze cast, which has been mounted onto a block of wood.
Life size

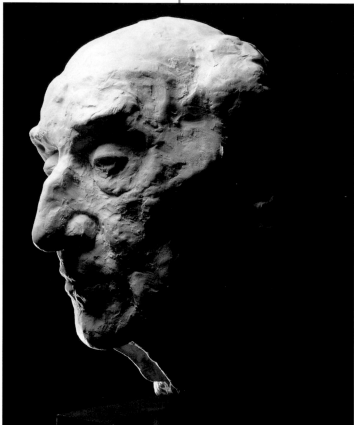

◀ **GERALD LAING • Portrait of Luciano Pavarotti**
This portrait of the opera singer has been modeled from life in clay. The clay original has subsequently been cast in bronze, a traditional sculpture material. The oversized head and the way it has been mounted give the sculpture a magisterial quality, in keeping with the subject and the classical tradition of sculpture. *1½ life size*

▲ **MARTIN YEOMAN • Sir Brinsley Ford**
A portrait of the sitter, was originally modeled in clay, from which a rubber mold was made, and is shown here as a plaster cast of the original. It was later cast in bronze. Note how the surface of the sculpture highlights the depth of feeling and intensity which went into the clay modeling. *13 inches high*

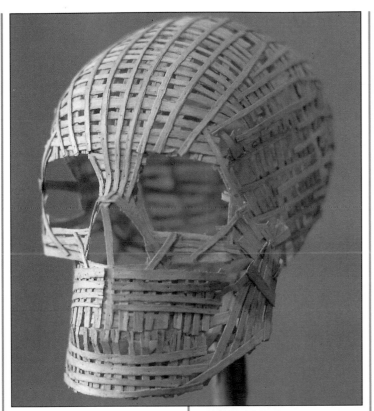

◀ CHRIS DUNSEATH • **Veneer skull**

Concentrating on the structure of the head, this sculpture is made from laminated ash veneer. Strips of the veneer were laid over a plaster skull, coated with wood glue, and then covered with more strips, and held in place with pins until the glue had set. This process was repeated over the whole sculpture. After removing the pins, the laminated sections were removed from the skull and reassembled.
5¾ × 8 × 13 inches

▶ PAUL BARTLETT • **Janus Variation from Metamorphosis Series**

A rubber mold was made of an imaginary head modeled in clay. This mold was used to produce plaster casts. Each of the cast heads has been given individuality by carving into the plaster surface. The heads have been arranged to produce a sculpture that takes its inspiration from Janus, the character in Greek mythology.
Each head 15 inches high

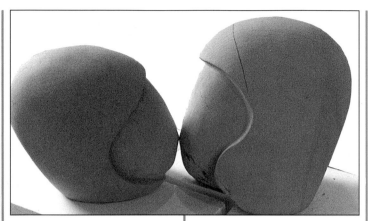

▲ MAX BARRETT • **The Kiss**
This sculpture relies on the positioning of the two forms for maximum effect. The stylized forms, which have been carved from sandstone, show the influence of art from other cultures, notably the Oceanic. *8½ × 16 × 27 inches*

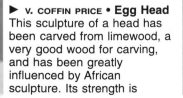

▶ V. COFFIN PRICE • **Egg Head**
This sculpture of a head has been carved from limewood, a very good wood for carving, and has been greatly influenced by African sculpture. Its strength is enhanced by the addition of wooden spikes wrapped in pieces of cane. Ink has been used to color the surface. *6 × 11 × 13 inches*

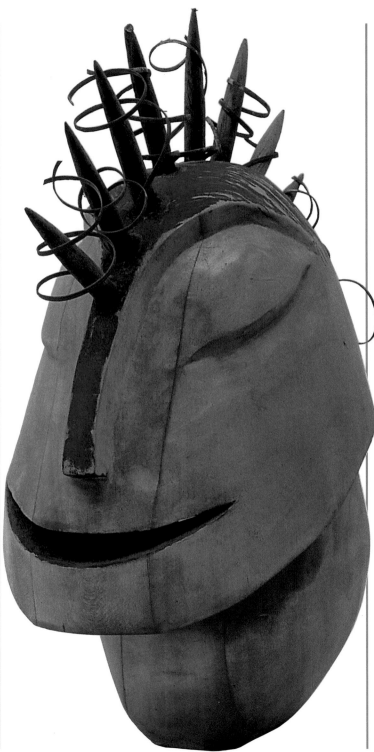

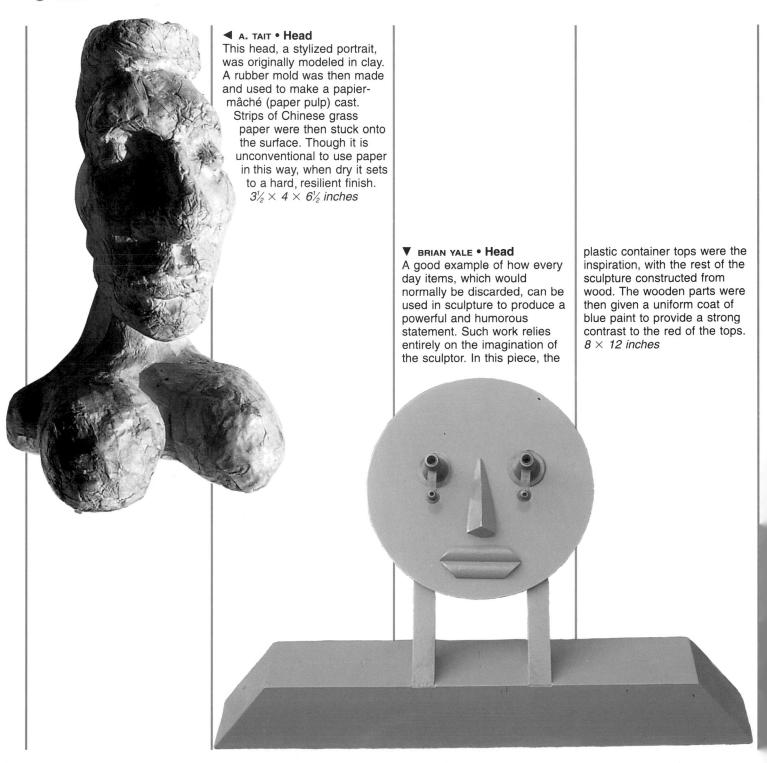

◀ **A. TAIT • Head**
This head, a stylized portrait, was originally modeled in clay. A rubber mold was then made and used to make a papier-mâché (paper pulp) cast.
Strips of Chinese grass paper were then stuck onto the surface. Though it is unconventional to use paper in this way, when dry it sets to a hard, resilient finish.
3½ × 4 × 6½ inches

▼ **BRIAN YALE • Head**
A good example of how every day items, which would normally be discarded, can be used in sculpture to produce a powerful and humorous statement. Such work relies entirely on the imagination of the sculptor. In this piece, the plastic container tops were the inspiration, with the rest of the sculpture constructed from wood. The wooden parts were then given a uniform coat of blue paint to provide a strong contrast to the red of the tops.
8 × 12 inches

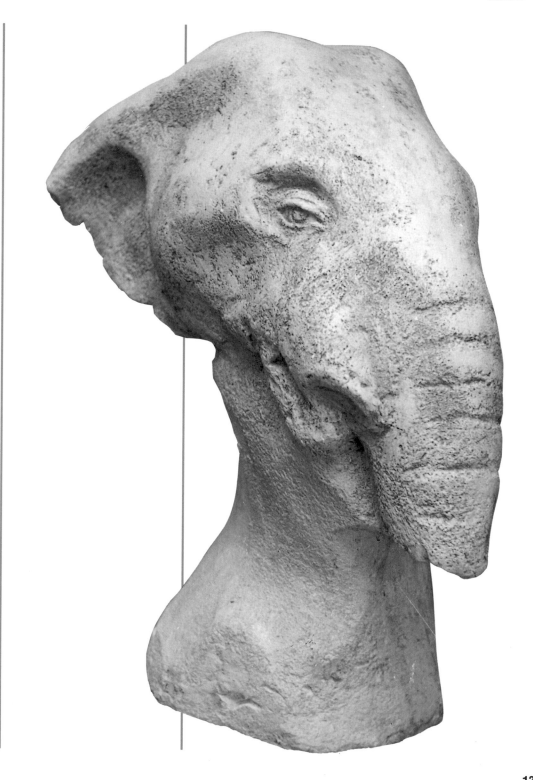

► DEBORAH SCALDWELL ●
Elephant Fossil
A sculpture whose inspiration came from the skull of an elephant, it was modeled in a coarse clay. A plaster waste mold was made to produce this plaster cast. Once the plaster had dried, the sculpture was sealed with shellac and colored with oil paints to simulate the appearance of bronze. Although it is a small sculpture, its subject gives it a real sense of monumentality.
21 inches high

FIGURATIVE

The human form has been the basis of art since the beginning of time, and across all cultures. The first figures were carved in stone, and the tradition of figurative sculpture continues to this day. A diverse range of sculpture is made nowadays, ranging from the classically inspired to figures fostered by new materials and technology, as well as by contemporary issues the artist wishes to address. There is still a tradition of figurative sculpture being made for public spaces, carved in stone or cast in bronze. Some contemporary sculpture incorporates casts taken directly from the figure. Much can be learned from direct observation of the human form, and there is a vital correlation between the structure of a figure and sculpture, whether abstract or figurative. This is particularly relevant when using an armature and a modeling technique, where you place the materials used under the same stresses and strains as occur in the figure itself.

◄ JON BUCK • **Looking to the Future**
This sculpture is sited in a public space. Its figures were originally modeled in clay, then cast in resin. Each figure is reinforced with a concrete core and has been colored to produce a very naturalistic appearance; this, coupled with natural relaxed positions, gives a sculpture which is the antithesis of the more common formal bronze or stone public figurative sculptures.
Over-life size

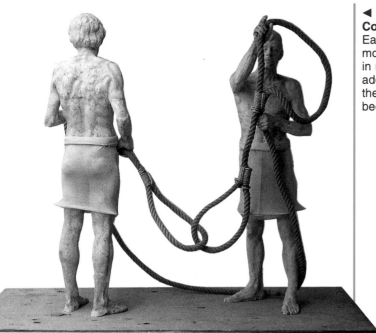

◄ **CHARLES HAZZARD** •
Connections
Each of these realistically modeled figures has been cast in resin with white pigment added to the first (gel) coat of the cast. Further color has been added to the cast to emphasize the muscularity of the figures. This sculpture demonstrates the role that a base can play, defining an area within which sculptural elements can operate.
Life size

► JULIE WESTERMAN • **Bringing Home the Bacon**
Cast in *ciment fondu*, this sculpture makes a striking contrast to the many sculptures of generals riding on horseback. The bodice of the tutu has been modeled with resin and bronze powder, the skirt is made from bronze mesh, and the whole tutu has been patinated. An unusual surface has been obtained by coating the rest of the sculpture with a mixture of resin and iron filings. Exposure to the elements has caused the iron filings to rust.
Life size

▲ JOHN SKELTON • **Winter Dreams**

This sculpture was inspired by the ballet of the same name to music by Tchaikovsky. From photographs and a life model, a full-size drawing was made of the sculpture and transferred to the block of Portland stone before carving commenced. Notice how the drapery has been used not only as a compositional device, but also as a very important structural support for the sculpture.

12 × 27 × 80 inches

▲ PHILIP COX • **The Green Children**
Papier-mâché, made from recycled cardboard boxes, has been applied directly onto a cardboard armature in this work. The vivid colors of this dramatic sculpture are produced by adding small pieces of torn-up paper to the papier-mâché mixture.
Life size

▼ ELIZABETH WATSON • **Figures at a Table**
This sculpture invokes that sense of intensity that can occur between two people seated at a table. The sculpture was modeled in clay and a waste piece mold was used to make a cast in *ciment fondu*. The sculpture was then lightly colored with pigments fixed with polyurethane varnish thinned with mineral spirits. The base is an integral part of the sculpture.
13 × 15 × 17½ inches

135

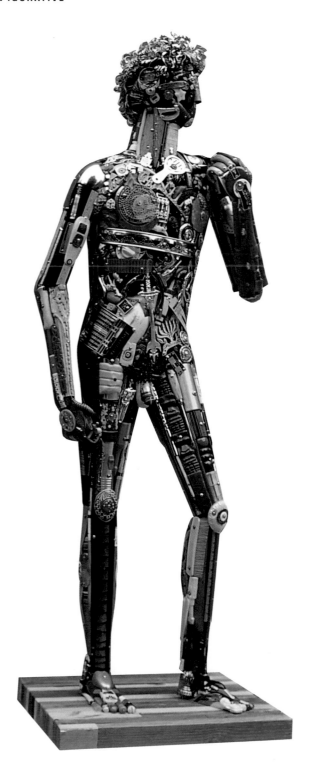

◄ LEO SEWELL • **Man**
Inspired by the stone carving of David by Michaelangelo, this assemblage uses found objects which have been screwed onto a wooden armature. All of the objects have been chosen and positioned with care to relate to a particular part of the anatomy.
Life size

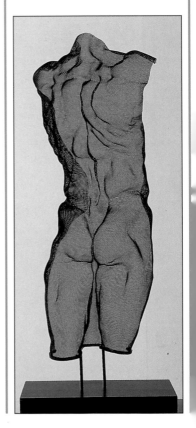

► DAVID BEGBIE • **Tight Truncus**
This torso of a figure is very much in the classical tradition. The subject matter, the figure, is solid and heavy, though the material used, steel mesh, is light and airy. The mesh has been worked to produce the undulating surface of the human form.
8½ × 13 × 33 inches

◀ LAURA DIMEO • **Remnants of Time**

A plaster cast was taken directly from the figure and used as a mold to make a concrete cast. The arm of the figure has been smashed to reveal the steel reinforcing rod, and the resultant debris becomes part of the final piece, suggesting the remains of some lost ancient culture one might encounter on an archeological dig.

17 × 39 × 62 inches

◀ KATE STEPHENS • **Strawberry Flesh**

Using plaster-impregnated bandage, this sculpture (which is an element of an installation) was cast in two halves directly from a figure. The two parts were reassembled, then plaster, scrim, and more plaster bandage were added crudely to the fine surface of the life cast. Part of this rough surface has been pulled back to reveal the smooth surface of the cast underneath.

Life size

▶ CORNELIUS GUISTE DE'JERSEY ●
Hands on Earth
This sculpture was carved
from a block of limestone, and
great care was given to
producing a naturalistic form
for the two hands. The central
stone column is used not only
as a support, but as a
compositional device as well,
conveying a flowing movement
through the hands. Fragments
of stone are scattered around
the base of the sculpture to
reinforce this sense of
movement. These are all
pieces cut away from the
original block.
25½ inches high

▶ SHAUN WILLIAMSON •
Medieval Knight
This large block of Ellel sandstone was carved directly, without any prior planning of the final form of the sculpture. This can be seen in the definite references to the original geometry of the block of stone. The sculpture takes as its inspiration the crusader knights of eleventh century England.
2 × 3 × 6 feet

◀ JON BUCK • **Bird Embrace**
This composition of stylized animal forms was modeled in clay and a mold made for a cast in plaster. This was worked further to develop the forms. Note how the relationship of the two forms draws the eye around the sculpture.
28 inches high

RELIEF

Relief has its roots in architecture, where it was used as a way to incorporate sculpture into the fabric of a building. Because stone and wood were the construction materials of buildings, relief sculpture is tied historically to the technique of carving, although modeling has also been used. Relief has only one viewpoint but uses three-dimensional form to give the illusion of a two-dimensional art form.

► **DAVID HEATHCOTE** •
Tribhanga
This relief makes good use of real and illusory space. It was initially modeled in clay, and a mold was then made to produce a plaster cast. This was carved to refine and further define the forms and surface in an interesting combination of modeling and carving techniques.
14 × 28 inches high

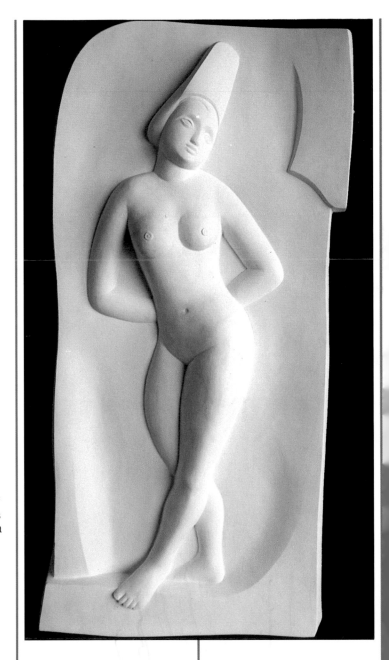

► PATRICIA COX • **Family Traces**

This mixed-media relief sculpture explores aspects of the sculptor's family history. It is reminiscent of the niches one might find in an old church. Noses have been cast from life, using plaster bandage, and placed in some of the openings. In the other openings are cast plaster slabs, which have had photocopies of family photographs applied to them. Each piece is backlit by a small light.

22 × 26½ inches

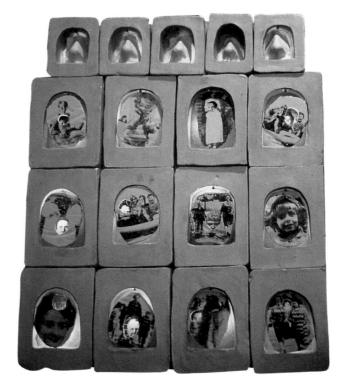

▼ SASHA CONSTABLE • **Bath Piece**

This stone-carved relief shows good use of the high relief technique, some of the forms rising well above the surface of the background. The profile of the bathtub has been used as a framing device that is an integral part of this sculpture's composition.

3 × 14 × 28½ inches

◄ ROBERT KOENIG • **Portal No. 5**
This relief, carved in wood, establishes a narrative within the overall composition, seen in the position of the figure at the base, the use of color, and the roughly carved motifs. This type of relief relies less on the relationship between real and illusory space and more on images and meanings.
56 × 110 inches

► ROBERT KOENIG • **Portal No. 7**
This relief alludes to a specific architectural function and relies for its overall impact on the symmetrical arrangement of a repeated motif carved into the wood. The use of color is very skillful and, together with the marks left by the carving gouge, enhances and brings together the whole composition.
61 × 124 inches

WALLHANGING

▶ BRIAN ORD • **Ikebena**
The success of this type of sculpture – an assemblage of found objects, made from diverse materials – depends a great deal on the choice of objects and the relationship they have with one another in the sculpture.
12 × 24 × 24 inches

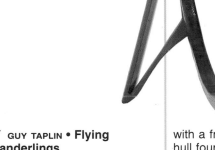

Wallhanging sculpture is a comparatively recent development using construction or assemblage techniques. A wallhanging does not have the same emphasis as a relief on the relationship between three-dimensional form and illusory two-dimensional form. Its main concern is to focus attention on the relationships between parts that comprise the sculpture, and this is facilitated by the limited number of positions from which to view it. A trend that is becoming more prevalent nowadays is to use the wall as an integral part of the composition.

▼ GUY TAPLIN • **Flying Sanderlings**
The seabirds have been carved from driftwood, which has been colored and waxed. These have been combined with a fragment from a boat's hull found on the shore to produce a sculpture with a form which is in harmony with its material.
40 × 55 inches

▶ ROSEMARIE McGOLDRICK • **In Memoriam: Kathleen**
A profile is painted onto a wall with graphite and, within this shape, are placed various forms made from welded mild steel sheet, derived from dress patterns, memorial stones, and English church interiors. Each form has been sandblasted to produce a rough pitted surface, as can be seen in the detail.
10 × 17 feet

◀ DEAN WHATMUFF • **30 Years in the Bathroom**
This sculpture shows effective use of a ready-made object. It relies on the recognition of the identity of the basket and fabric and at the same time the contrast of their differing surfaces and textures. Notice how the direction of the dominant grain of the basket is used within the composition of the sculpture.
17½ × 21 × 34 inches

ANIMALS

Closely aligned with the figurative tradition, animal sculpture has always been popular, allowing for more freedom of expression, both in terms of materials and techniques and styles, whether representational, stylizations, or abstract. Using an animal theme within sculpture means a greater variety of forms is available – from animals kept as pets, like cats and dogs, semi-domesticated animals such as horses and birds, or wild animals.

◀ PHILIP COX • **Elephant and Calf**

The success of this sculpture, directly modeled using laminated paper glued together, rests on the construction of a strong armature made from cardboard which delineates the main forms of the sculpture. Notice how the paper has been ruffled to mimic the texture of an elephant's skin. The tusks of the larger elephant have been painted white.
Life size

◀ DAWN BERESFORD • **Elephant**

This elephant sculpture is an assemblage of found objects. The strength of the elephant form over the objects is such that it is only on close inspection that you detect the beaten and bent trash cans, car hubcaps, car exhausts, and so on. As with all assembled sculpture, joining the disparate elements together is a problem, and in this sculpture a variety of techniques have been used – welding, riveting, brazing, and wire.
36 × 60 × 72 inches

▶ DAVID KEMP • **Fire Chariot**

This welded steel constructed sculpture makes clever use of scrap metal and old agricultural machinery to produce a chariot and animal form with the appearance of a relic from the late Iron Age. The fire relates to those ancient mythologies where "chariots pulled the sun across the heavens."
63 × 83 × 91 inches

▶ BEN JAKOBER **and** YANNICK VU • **Il Cavallo di Leonardo**
This dramatic piece of public sculpture in the form of a horse's head makes a direct reference to a drawing by Leonardo da Vinci and was the emblem of the 1993 Venice Biennale. It has been constructed in a regular grid-like format from steel tubing, very reminiscent of builder's scaffolding.
25 × 29 × 46 feet

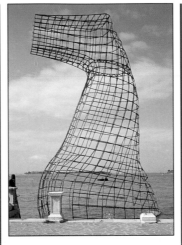

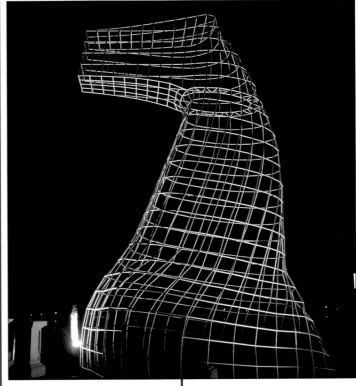

◀ SOPHIE RYDER • **Blue Horse**
This truly animated sculpture gives a real sense of a horse rolling in grass. The piece has been made from bed springs and wire, which have been manipulated to focus attention on the naturalistic forms of the sculpture. Once made, the sculpture was galvanized – an industrial process whereby a zinc coat is applied to metal objects – then painted.
Life size

▲ MARTIN RAYNER • **St. Sebastian's Fish**
Copper sheet is an extremely malleable and flexible material, easy to bend and cut into shape. The copper sheet used in this sculpture was taken from old water tanks and joined using pop rivets – the most efficient way of joining sheet material.
1½ × 2½ × 44 inches

▶ LEO SEWELL • **Boxer**
As with any assemblage sculpture of this type, the strength and stability of the armature is all important. In this sculpture of a dog, the armature is a discarded piece of furniture, onto which the found objects have been screwed firmly into place. These have been selected not for their identity, but for their role in describing the form of the sculpture.
11 × 22 × 31 inches

◄ **HAMISH GILCHRIST ●**
Sparrowhawk
This naturalistic representation of a sparrowhawk has been constructed using mild steel rod and sheet, joined together using oxyacetylene and MIG welding techniques. The claws have been made from brass, and a texture has been applied to the bird using copper that has been melted and then dropped onto the surface. These techniques both take full advantage of the low melting point of copper and brass.
16 inches high

► **DAWN BERESFORD ● Vulture**
This bird assemblage is a powerful image of a bird and makes good use of common discarded objects. These have been cut, bent, and held in place using pop rivets, welding and wire.
36 × 36 × 72 inches

▲ ANTHONY STEVENS • **Kate's Bears**
Sited in a school, this sculpture cannot help but bring a smile to our faces. After being modeled in clay, a mold was made of each of the bears and then a resin cast made. The first coat of resin (the gel coat) had black pigment added. The sculpture was given a final coat of black epoxy marine paint.
7 feet high

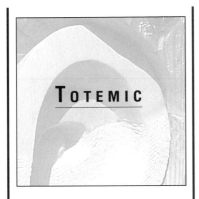

TOTEMIC

"Totemic" is a term used to group together sculptures which have a definite vertical configuration. Its origins are the standing figures within most sculptural traditions. A totemic sculpture may be abstract or contain abstract forms, but it will still refer to the figure. Most likely to be carved from a vertical block, it is a format that brings limitations to construction or assemblage where you have to be sensitive to the pull of gravity when joining disparate objects or forms together. The use of a base can greatly help this problem, however, providing stability and support for a sculpture that may otherwise fall over.

◀ ANTONY DENNING • **Woman from Wardour**
This elm wood carving makes good use of the original vertical format of its wooden block. It is an abstraction of the female figure, the base of which has been carved to give maximum stability. The surface has been rubbed down and polished to enhance the grain and emphasize the verticality of the sculpture.
35½ inches high

▶ LAURA WHITE • **Meditation**
Ancaster stone has been carved into a spiral form, which continues, as though unravelling, into the carving of the pitch pine wood. There is a clear demarcation line across stone and wood, one side rough, still showing traces of the tool marks, the other smooth. The stone is pinned to the wood, enabling it to stand vertically.
13 × 14 × 30 inches

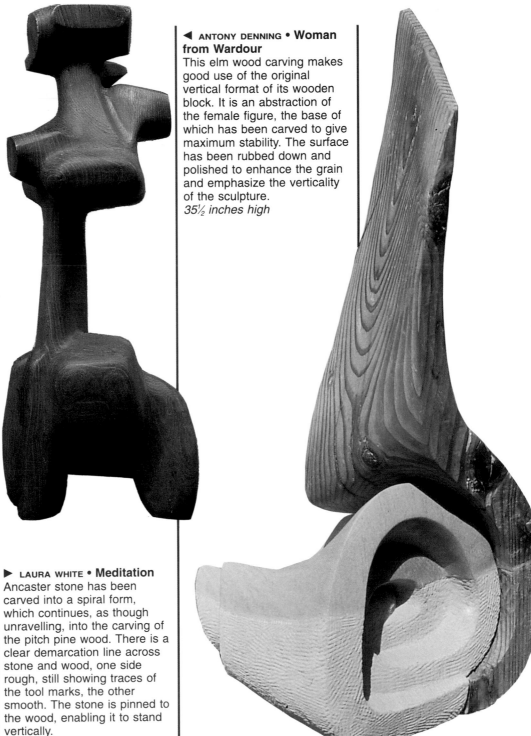

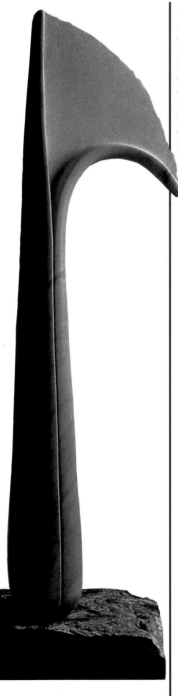

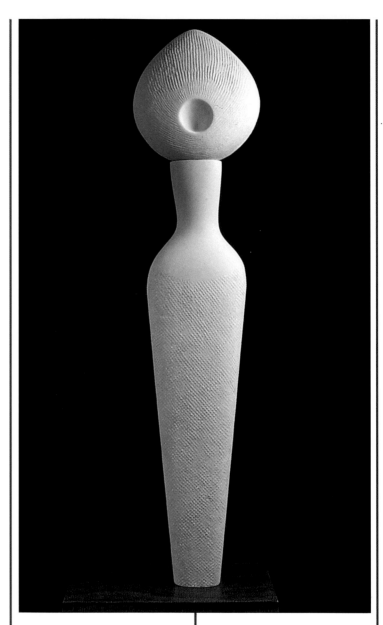

◀ JAYA SCHUERCH • IV
A wonderfully evocative carving of a flower form in Portuguese marble, it has been very delicately carved, especially around the top edge. The surface has been rubbed down and polished to highlight the coloring of the outside surface, providing an interesting contrast with the inside. The sculpture's vertical format is entirely dependent on the base on which it stands.

$9\frac{1}{2} \times 10\frac{1}{4} \times 38$ *inches*

▲ BARBARA HODGKINS •
Sentinelle 11
Two pieces of green marble have been carved to produce this vertical abstract form. The top section looks precariously balanced but is, in fact, attached to the main part. The tool marks have been left on the surface and provide a contrast with the polished interior surface of the top section.

12 × 18 × 44 inches

153

◀ FRIEDEL BUECKING • **Torch**
This assembled sculpture stacks plastic containers in such a way that their identity as functional objects is lost. Attention is drawn to the sculptural forms contained within the arrangement.
Life size

▶ RAPHAEL DADEN • **Inner Seed**
The base is an integral part of this sculpture, and in it you can see the geometry of the original block of wood. No attempt has been made to obscure the marks left by the carving gouge, so that the process by which the material was shaped is revealed. This rough surface contrasts beautifully with the interior lined with red fabric.
54 inches high

▶ BRIAN ORD • **Ikea, Ikea**
The main elements of this assemblage are items of wooden furniture, some of which have been cut up and reassembled within the sculpture. The table is used to provide support and stability to the sculpture, and the various parts have been joined together with screws and glue. With the minimum of effort, the sculptor has created a surrealistic figure reflecting his love/hate relationship with domesticity.
24 × 36 × 72 inches

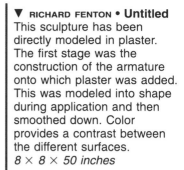

▼ RICHARD FENTON • **Untitled**
This sculpture has been directly modeled in plaster. The first stage was the construction of the armature onto which plaster was added. This was modeled into shape during application and then smoothed down. Color provides a contrast between the different surfaces.
8 × 8 × 50 inches

▲ JULIE WESTERMAN • **Bird/ Snake**
Great thought has gone into this carved wood sculpture to make sure that the bird and snake forms fit within the geometry of the original block of wood. The forms have been carved so that they lead the eye around the sculpture, and aniline dye has been applied to the wood to highlight them.
39½ inches high

155

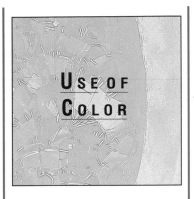

USE OF COLOR

Because only traces of color can be found on classical sculpture, we have no idea of their finished effects. For centuries after, the main materials of sculpture were bronze or stone, and color never played a part. It is only during this century that color has again become a part of the sculptor's vocabulary, due partly to the influence of colored sculptures from non-western cultures and partly to new materials and techniques. In sculpture, color can enhance a particular form. It can act as a compositional device, a single color uniting disparate elements. Color can also be used to heighten the drama inherent in a sculpture.

◄ **ROBERT KOENIG • Sacrifice**
Limewood is carved into an altar form, the base of which has stylized leaves and flames carved into and around the base. Color has been used here to differentiate between the leaves and flames because of their similarity of form. The stylization of the sculpture becomes complete with the addition of color to the trees on the altar itself.
14 × 25 × 49½ inches

◄ **A. TAIT • CUAF collageN**
This wallhanging sculpture
was inspired by a collage of
cut paper and paint and
developed into three
dimensions by adding papier-
mâché to a cardboard profile
of the original collage. The
sculpture was colored to
correspond to the colors in the
original collage.
2 × 8½ × 20 inches

▼ **V. COFFIN PRICE • The
Fishpond**
This sculpture started life as a
block of expanded styrofoam
carved into the shape of a
bowl, to which plaster was
added. The plaster on the
exterior of the bowl has been
smoothed into shape, while

the interior required more
detailed modeling and shaping
to define the forms of the
water and the fish. Color has
been used to highlight and
differentiate the various forms
contained within the sculpture.
16 × 47 × 47 inches

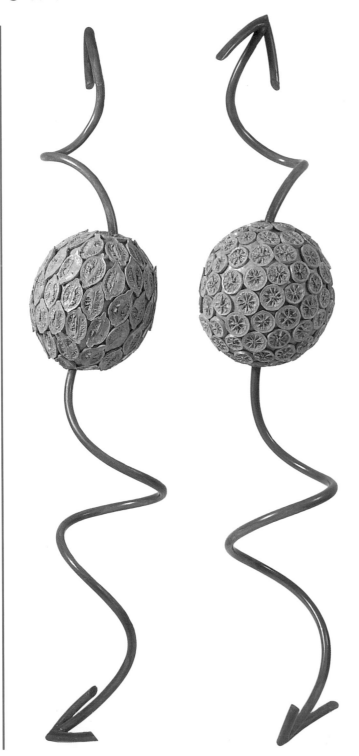

◀▲ AMANDA LORENS • **Skin and Flesh Lemon Zest**
You feel this sculpture has no chance of standing up – until you realize that it is supported by a line to the ceiling. The color combines with the form to produce a very dramatic sculpture indeed. The spiraling orange arrows are made from plastic tubing. The spherical resin and fiberglass shapes have been built up around a balloon. Resin casts of lemon slices have then been added to the shapes. Bright yellow pigment in the resin gives this very vivid coloring.
6 feet from floor

▶ AMANDA LORENS • **Fruits of Fire**
The steel chain used in this sculpture looks very improbable, a form that gives the impression of defying gravity. The small ball at the end of the chain is fiberglass resin. The large supporting spherical shape was made by first welding a mild steel framework together, onto which plaster has been applied.
6 feet

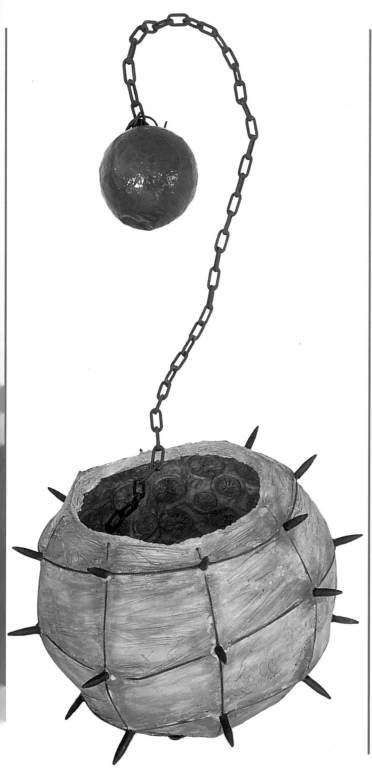

▲▼ JEZ NOOND • **The Natural History of Viruses**

In this comment on the ills of present-day society, the main part of each section is a found object, an aluminum hemisphere. One has been lined with plaster cast to the interior form, while the other has had a steel rim added. The artist has made very effective use of the color of the cut cable and vinyl which, when massed together inside each of the hemispheres, make for a dramatic visual experience.

13 × 26 inches

ORGANIC

Naturally occurring forms have long been a source of inspiration for sculptors. This is particularly true of abstract work. Organic sculptures have the feel and look of naturally occurring forms, rounded or soft-edged. There is a vast array of such forms which are sculptural in their essence, or have the potential to be developed into sculpture. By observing nature, we are able to understand the complexities of these forms and the relationships they have with one another. The sculptor's eye is able to discern those aspects of plant life, rock formations, seed pods, or vegetables that can be translated into sculpture.

▼ LAURA WHITE • **Untitled**
This piece, modeled in clay, is a maquette for a larger sculpture to be carved in stone. The forms make a direct reference to plant and animal life. The curled shape on top is reminiscent of a leaf, and the segmented form puts one in mind of a fossil.
6 × 7 × 10 inches

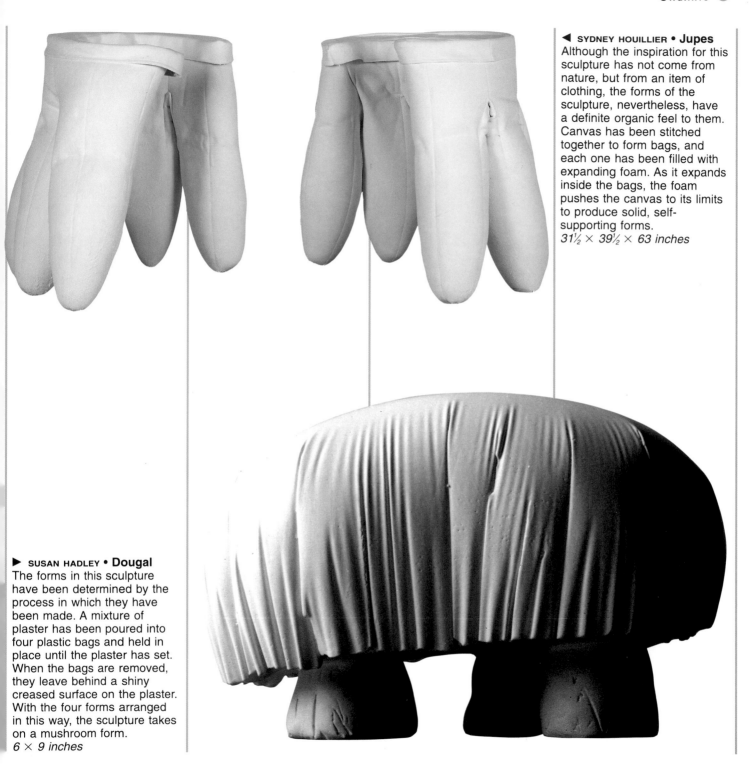

◀ SYDNEY HOUILLIER • **Jupes**
Although the inspiration for this sculpture has not come from nature, but from an item of clothing, the forms of the sculpture, nevertheless, have a definite organic feel to them. Canvas has been stitched together to form bags, and each one has been filled with expanding foam. As it expands inside the bags, the foam pushes the canvas to its limits to produce solid, self-supporting forms.
31½ × 39½ × 63 inches

▶ SUSAN HADLEY • **Dougal**
The forms in this sculpture have been determined by the process in which they have been made. A mixture of plaster has been poured into four plastic bags and held in place until the plaster has set. When the bags are removed, they leave behind a shiny creased surface on the plaster. With the four forms arranged in this way, the sculpture takes on a mushroom form.
6 × 9 inches

LANDSCAPE

In urban areas we are used to coming across a piece of sculpture sited in a shopping mall or a public square. But more and more sculpture is being made specifically to be sited within a landscape setting. In some cases, the setting itself will have been the source of inspiration for the sculpture. Sculpture can also be made which would interrupt or interfere with the natural order of the landscape to produce a new order. In both cases, there is no doubt that some sculpture benefits from being exhibited outdoors in a natural rather than an urban environment, where it enhances or complements the beauty that surrounds it.

▲ BRIAN YALE • **The Mrs T.**
The subject matter of a ship fits in well with this assemblage made on the seashore. The profile defined by the rope has been filled in with a variety of found objects, some of which were thrown up on the beach by the tide.
12 × 30 feet

▲ DEREK HOWARTH •
Mashonack Deep
The natural order of the landscape has been interrupted – cast concrete forms and a steel construction have been submerged in the ground to produce a sculpture that contrasts the natural with the human-made.
8 × 10 feet

▲ PETER RANDALL PAGE • Fruit of Mythological Trees
These three organic forms have been carved in Kilkenny limestone to form one piece of sculpture. Each carving refers to naturally occurring forms that you would expect to find in a landscape setting, without making a direct reference.
Tallest 46½ inches high

▼ PETER RANDALL PAGE • Secret Life III
The rough, naturally hewn exterior of each piece of this carved granite sculpture fits in well with the surrounding landscape. At the same time, it provides an interesting and dramatic contrast with the carved interior forms which have been smoothed to a high-polished finish.
45½ inches high

▶ IAN MIDDLETON • A Seat for the Princess
This sculpture uses a repeated form to great effect, producing an upward-moving sensation that complements the environment in which it is situated. The basic cushion form is a Portland cement cast reinforced with glass fiber. This was cast using a resin and fiberglass mold.
17 × 17 × 96 inches

CONSTRUCTION

A development in sculpture dating only from this century, construction sculpture is not tied to the use of a specific material, and it crosses the boundaries of all techniques and materials. It allows the sculptor great freedom of expression and has greatly added to the variety of sculpture that is now made. As its name implies, it basically involves joining materials together. Although usually associated with abstract sculpture, this technique often makes specific references to the world around us. Inevitably, constructed sculpture will contain forms that lean more toward the geometric than the organic.

◄ SUBIRACHS • **Mil Lenari**
A sculpture carved in Calatorao stone and travertine, its two pieces have been joined together to very dramatic effect. The sculpture has an architectural element, emphasized by the use of stone as a building material, the steps that have been carved on the top, and the crisp, sharp, geometric forms of the sculpture.
10 × 18½ × 21 inches

► JOSEPH WESNER • **Yoken**
This abstract constructed sculpture is made of reclaimed wood which has been screwed, nailed, and glued together. The sculpture forces you to focus on its purely physical sculptural qualities. This includes the nature of the material used, its rough-hewn quality, and the dynamic created by the ring of pieces holding the vertical stack together.
17 × 32 × 39 inches

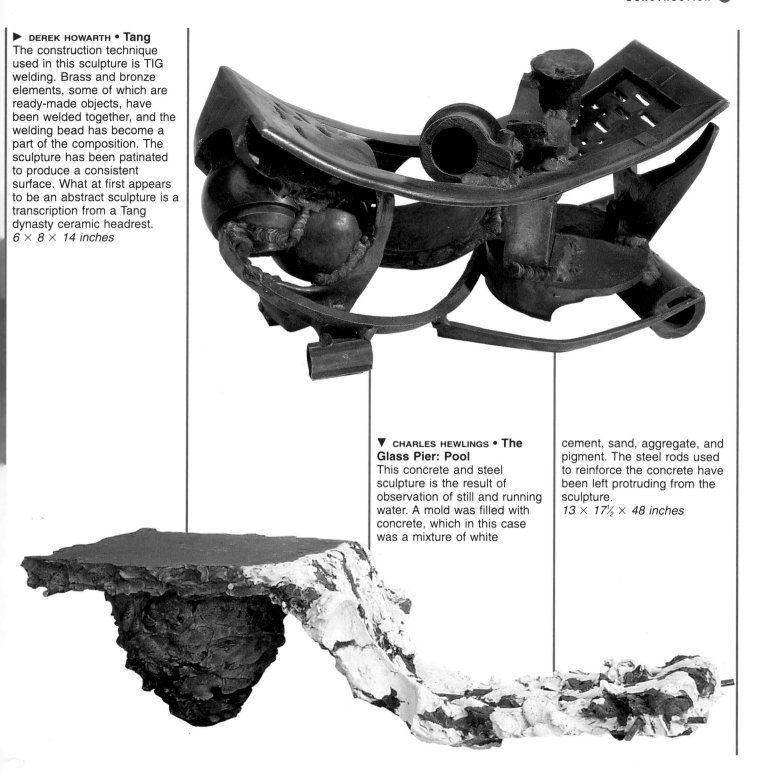

► DEREK HOWARTH • **Tang**
The construction technique used in this sculpture is TIG welding. Brass and bronze elements, some of which are ready-made objects, have been welded together, and the welding bead has become a part of the composition. The sculpture has been patinated to produce a consistent surface. What at first appears to be an abstract sculpture is a transcription from a Tang dynasty ceramic headrest.
6 × 8 × 14 inches

▼ CHARLES HEWLINGS • **The Glass Pier: Pool**
This concrete and steel sculpture is the result of observation of still and running water. A mold was filled with concrete, which in this case was a mixture of white cement, sand, aggregate, and pigment. The steel rods used to reinforce the concrete have been left protruding from the sculpture.
13 × 17½ × 48 inches

▶ GUY THOMAS • **The Mighty Stream**
Steel has been heated up, bent, and twisted using oxy-acetylene equipment. The shape and arrangement of the steel elements have been influenced by the rhythm and form of spaces in landscape. All the parts have been welded together, the steel was left to rust and then varnished.
10 × 20 × 35 inches

► SHAP McDONNELL ●
Streamline
At first glance, this sculpture looks like it might have had a specific function. It is constructed from steel plate that has been welded together, and the surface has been painted with a geometric design, erased in places to give the impression of wear and tear.

8 × 9½ × 31 inches

▼ GAVIN O'CURRY ● **Lost Souls**
An abstract sculpture, the construction of which is influenced by the urban environment, using a variety of techniques and materials – the steel has been welded, the wood cut, glued, and screwed together. Paint has also been used. The use of the glass and metal frame surround makes a specific reference to a window.

21 × 83 × 87 inches

◀ GORDON McINTOSH • **Keeping Your Balance**

Vivid coloring and a variety of forms have been used to produce a playful, enigmatic sculpture, constructed mostly of wood, which has been cut and carved to shape and joined using nails. The nails also have a part to play in the form of the sculpture, and it is interesting to see how the rope has been threaded through a piece of wood and then unspliced.

5⅓ feet

▼ MICHAEL MARRIOTT • **Span**

This arch which grows out of and returns to the earth uses two geometric elements which alternate with one another to produce a specifically abstract sculpture. Each has been cast in resin, then painted and attached to a central steel spine.

39¼ × 48 × 18 inches

► BRIAN ORD • **Defenestration of the Heart**

The familiar and the abstract are to be found in this sculpture constructed from wood and aluminum. The piece alludes to the workshop where the sculpture would have been made. The base takes the form of a saw bench, on top of which intersecting geometrical planes have been constructed. These have been interspersed with real tools such as hammers and dividers.

36 × 48 × 48 inches

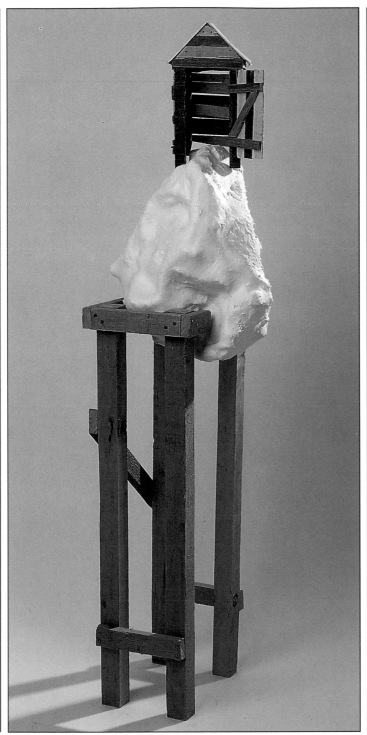

◄ WAYNE LLOYD • **Untitled (Journal)**
In this interesting combination of materials and techniques, the central mass is made from glass fiber, resin, and pigment laid over a chicken wire armature. The table-like structure has been cut from sawn timber nailed together. The hut form on top has been put together from strips of wood.
1 × 1 × 3 feet

▼ CHRIS LILLYWHITE • **Untitled**
This bringing together of found objects results in an enigmatic sculpture, which after prolonged study can be seen to allude to a figure, with the lightbulb and the vertical pole rising out of the roughly shaped tree trunk suggesting a body.
10 × 10 × 24 inches

▲ JOSEPH WESNER • Huanghe
A variety of media have been used in this construction including steel, steel mesh, and wicker basket. The objects and materials used have been cut, shaped, and manipulated to fit in with the composition. The emphasis on the textures and contrasts results in a tactile abstract sculpture.
24 × 28 × 42 inches

▼ HILARY BROWN • Thinking Woman (The Wheel)
Steel and recycled wood are used in this sculpture, whose point of reference is the traditional pose of *The Thinker.* Each piece of wood has been shaped, and then jointed and bolted together. Sheet steel has been bent and bolted onto the wood.
36 × 48 × 60 inches

OBJECTS

It is possible to make a sculpture of an object or derivation of an object, even though the sculpture itself is, of course, an object in its own right. Such a sculpture does not depend solely on traditional sculptural attributes, such as form, surface, proportion, or space for a successful reading of it. Nevertheless, very interesting sculptures are made where, for instance, a particular technique or process may lend itself to making a particular form, or we may be drawn to admire the technical virtuosity that went into making the sculpture.

◄ **ROBERT CALLENDER** • **The Wooden Rudders with Rust**
They may look like found objects, but they are not – the two huge rudder forms that make up this sculpture have been made from driftwood cut to shape. The pieces of wood are held together by strips of steel bolted on. The sculpture was left outside to allow the steel to rust and the wood to weather.
20 × 42 × 106 inches

▲ **DEAN WHATMUFF** • **Untitled**
Objects have been used to make an object which in turn becomes another object – the sculpture. Two cabinet doors have been reversed and joined together, to produce what appears to be an open book. A lectern has been made from wood for the book to rest on, and this has been colored with wood stain, while the pages of the book have been bleached.
28 × 38½ × 65½ inches

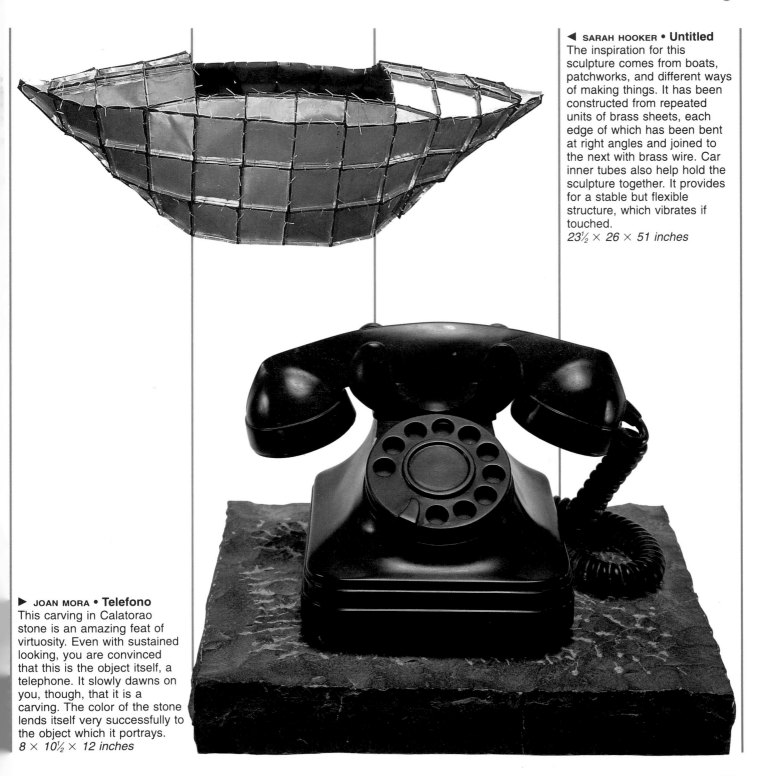

◀ SARAH HOOKER • **Untitled**
The inspiration for this sculpture comes from boats, patchworks, and different ways of making things. It has been constructed from repeated units of brass sheets, each edge of which has been bent at right angles and joined to the next with brass wire. Car inner tubes also help hold the sculpture together. It provides for a stable but flexible structure, which vibrates if touched.
23½ × 26 × 51 inches

▶ JOAN MORA • **Telefono**
This carving in Calatorao stone is an amazing feat of virtuosity. Even with sustained looking, you are convinced that this is the object itself, a telephone. It slowly dawns on you, though, that it is a carving. The color of the stone lends itself very successfully to the object which it portrays.
8 × 10½ × 12 inches

173

INDEX

A

abstract sculpture:
    assemblage 32–4
    construction 164–71
    plaster carving 50–2
adhesives 11
aluminum, construction in 169
aluminum wire 9
animals 146–51
arc-welding 119, 123
armature:
    design for 22
    for direct modeling 82
    for kiln firing 86
    technique 26–31
    uses 26
    welding 120–1
    wire 9, 23
assemblage 32–7
    of animals 147, 149, 150
    of figure 136
    of head 130
    of ship 162
    totemic sculptures 154, 155
    wallhanging 144
awl 18

B

Barrett, Max, *The Kiss* 129
Bartlett, Paul, *Janus variation from Metamorphosis Series* 128
bases 38–41
bed springs, sculpture made of 148
beeswax 11
Begbie, David, *Tight Truncus* 136
Beresford, Dawn:
    Elephant 147
    Vulture 150
bird:
    abstract assemblage 32–4
    direct modeling 82–3
        painting with glue 68
    figurative assemblage 35–7
    welding armature for 120–1

brass:
    construction using 165
    fencing 9
    sheets, sculpture using 173
brazing 42–5
    materials 10
bronze:
    cold cast 56
        portrait head in 126
    construction in 165
    mixing filler with resin 61–2
    portrait head cast in 127
Brown, Hilary, *Thinking Woman (The Wheel)* 171
Buck, Jon:
    Bird Embrace 139
    Looking to the Future 132
Buecking, Friedel, *Torch* 154
burlap 9

C

C-clamp 19
calipers 21
Callender, Robert, *The Wooden Rudders with Rust* 172
car body filler 10
carving:
    materials 8, 12–13
    plaster, repair 115
    profile drawing for 22
    techniques 46–55
        concrete 46–9
        plaster 50–2
        stone relief 110–11
        wood 53–5
carving gouges 21
casting:
    materials for 8, 12–13
    techniques 56–67
chipping hammer 20
chisels 21
ciment fondu 9, 12–13
    casting 56–60
    figures cast in 133, 135
clay:
    cutting tools for 21
    kiln firing 86–9
    maquettes of 23
    modeling 90–3
    types 8, 12
    uses 12–13
clay slip 8, 88
color:
    sculptures using 156–9
    uses for 68
coloring:
    materials 11
    techniques 68–75
concrete:
    aerated 12–13

carving technique 46–9
cast 137, 162
construction 165
Constable, Sasha, *Bath Piece* 141
construction 76–81
    examples 164–71
copper sheet, sculpture in 149
Cox, Patricia, *Family Traces* 141
Cox, Philip:
    Elephant and Calf 146–7
    The Green Children 135
craft knife 19

D

Daden, Raphael, *Inner Seed* 154
Denning, Antony, *Woman from Wardour* 152
DiMeo, Laura, *Remnants of Time* 137
direct modeling:
    painting with glue 68
    techniques 82–5
drawings 22–3
driftwood, sculpture using 144, 172
drill bits 18
Dunseath, Chris, *Veneer Skull* 128

E

elm wood, totemic sculpture 152
epoxy resin glue 11
equipment 14–21

F

Fenton, Richard, *Untitled* 155
ferric nitrate 11
fiberglass, safety precautions 61
figurative sculpture 132–9
    assemblage 35–7
    wooden construction:
        base 41
        coloring 68–9
        repair 113
figures 132–7
    life:
        armature design 22
        casting in resin 61–3
        coloring 75
        making armature for 26–8
        making mold of 100–3
        modeling 92–3
fillers 10
Finch, Patricia, *Sam Wanamaker* 126
fish:
    steel, wallhanging, brazing 44–5
    wood:
        base for 40–1
        carving 53–5
        coloring 72
fixing, materials for 8
foam, expanding, organic sculpture of 161

foot, constructed sculpture of 76–9
found objects:
    assemblage 32–7
        examples 144, 159
    construction 170

G

gas cutting 121–3
gas welding 10, 120–1
Gilchrist, Hamish, *Sparrowhawk* 150
gloves 15
glue gun 19
glues 11
goggles 14
granite, carved 163
Guiste De' Jersey, Cornelius, *Hands on Earth* 138

H

hacksaw 19
Hadley, Susan, *Dougal* 161
hammers 20
Hazzard, Charles, *Connections* 133
heads 126–31
    establishing proportions 90
    life-size, making armature for 29–31
    Oceanic:
        carving 46–9
        profile drawing 22
    portrait 126–7
        base 38–9
        casting 56–60
        coloring 74–5
        establishing proportions 90
        making mold for 96–9
        modeling 90–2
        repairs 112–13
Heathcote, David, *Tribhanga* 140
Hewlings, Charles, *The Glass Pier: Pool* 165
Hodgkins, Barbara, *Sentinelle II* 153
Hooker, Sarah, untitled sculpture 173
Houillier, Sydney, *Jupes* 161
Howarth, Derek:
    Mashonack Deep 162
    Tang 165
human form *see* figures
hydrochloric acid 11

J

Jakober, Ben, *Il Cavallo di Leonardo* 148
jelutong 8
joining, materials for 8

K

Kemp, David, *Fire Chariot* 147
kiln firing 86–9
knives 19
Koenig, Robert:
    Portal No. 5 142

Portal No. 7 142–3
Sacrifice 156

L

Laing, Gerald, *Portrait of Luciano Pavarotti* 127
laminating resin 8
landscape 162–3
leg, constructed sculpture 76–9
life figures *see* figures
Lillywhite, Chris, untitled construction 170
limestone:
  carvings in 138, 163, 173
  construction 164
limewood:
  carved and colored sculpture 156
  carved head 129
Lloyd, Wayne, untitled construction 170
Lorens, Amanda:
  Fruits of Fire 158–9
  Skin and Flesh Lemon Zest 158

M

McDonnell, Shap, *Streamline* 167
McGoldrick, Rosemarie, *In Memoriam: Kathleen* 145
McIntosh, Gordon, *Keeping Your Balance* 168
mallett 20
maquettes 23
marble, totemic carvings 153
Marriott, Michael, *Span* 168
masks, protective 14–15
materials 8–13
melting pot, electric 18
Middleton, Ian, *A Seat for the Princess* 163
mixed media:
  construction 171
  relief 141
mobile sculpture, riveting 116–18
modeling:
  see also direct modeling
  armature for 26–31
  materials for 8, 12–13
  repairing 112–13
  technique 90–3
  tools for 21
modeling stand 18
Mora, Joan, *Telefono* 173
moldmaking, techniques 94–107
molds:
  materials for 9, 12–13, 94
  release agents 9
  reusable rubber molds 104–7
  waste molds 94–103

N

Noond, Jez, *The Natural History of Viruses* 159

O

objects:
  see also found objects
  everyday:
    assemblage 32–7
    head made of 130
    as sculpture 172–3
Oceanic head:
  carving 46–9
  profile drawing 22
O'Curry, Gavin, *Lost Souls* 167
Ord, Brian:
  Defenestration of the Heart 169
  Ikea, Ikea 155
  Ikebena 144
organic sculptures 160–1
oxy-acetylene equipment 16–17
  bending and cutting with 121–3
  safety precautions 42, 119
  using 42–4

P

paper, laminated, animals modeled in 146–7
papier-mâché 8, 12–13
  coloring 72–3
  direct modeling 84–5
  figures modeled in 135
  head cast in 130
  wallhanging sculpture 157
photographs, modeling from 22
plaster 12–13
  abstract carving 50–2
    coloring 70–1
    repair 115
  for casting molds 94
  direct modeling 82–3
  making molds of 94–103
  mixing 94–5
  organic sculpture 161
  painting with glue 68
  relief:
    cast and carved 140
    coloring 71
    technique 108–9
plaster cast:
  base for 40–1
  carved 128, 139
  casting in rubber mold 64–7
  colored as bronze 131
  coloring 69
  of portrait head 127
  totemic sculpture 155
  using impregnated bandage 137
pliers 19
polyester resin *see* resin

polystyrene, sculpture in 157
pop rivets 11
Portland cement, sculpture cast in 163
Portland stone, figures carved in 134
portrait heads *see* heads, portrait
Price, V. Coffin:
  Egg Head 129
  The Fishpond 157
profile drawings 22
protective clothing 14–15

R

Randall-Page, Peter:
  Fruit of Mythological Trees 163
  Secret Life III 163
rasps 20
Rayner, Martin, *St Sebastian's Fish* 149
relief:
  examples 140–3
  mixed media 141
  plaster:
    cast and carved 140
    coloring 71
  stone carving 141
  techniques 108–11
    plaster 108–9
    stone carving 110–11
  wood carving 142–3
repairs 112–15
resin 12–13
  cast:
    colored 158–9
    construction 168
    examples 132, 133, 151
    repairing 114–15
  casting 56, 61–3
  coloring 75
  fillers for 56
  mixing 8
  safety precautions 61
rifflers 20
rivet gun 19
riveted sculpture, coloring 70–1
riveting 116–18
rivets 11
rubber 12–13
rubber molds 9
  casting with 64–7
  making 104–7
Ryder, Sophie, *Blue Horse* 148

S

safety precautions 5, 42, 61, 119
sandstone 8
  carved 129, 139
  saws 19
Scaldwell, Deborah, *Elephant Fossil* 131
Schuerch, Jaya, *IV* 153
scrim 9
sculpting, materials 8, 12–13

sealant gun 19
Sewell, Leo:
  Boxer 149
  Man 136
shellac, dissolving 9
ship, assemblage 162
silicone sealant 10
Skelton, John, *Winter Dreams* 134
spatial construction:
  coloring 69
  technique 79–81
steel:
  bending 121–3
  brazing 42–5
  constructions 162, 165, 166, 167, 171
  cutting 121–3
  mild 12–13
  plaster applied to 158–9
  riveting 116
  treating before coloring 11
  tubing, construction sculpture 148
  welded:
    coloring 74–5
    constructions 147, 150
    wallhanging (McGoldrick) 145
  welding 119–23
steel mesh, figure worked in 136
Stephens, Kate, *Strawberry Flesh* 137
Stevens, Anthony, *Kate's Bears* 151
stone 12–13
  combined with wood 152
  relief carvings 110–11, 141
Subirachs, *Mil Lenari* 164
surform 20

T

Tait, A.:
  CUAF collageN 157
  Head 130
Taplin, Guy, *Flying Sanderlings* 144
tenon saw 19
Thomas, Guy, *The Mighty Stream* 166
tin, riveting 116–18
tin snips 19
torso, stylized:
  coloring 72–3
  kiln firing 86–9
  repair 114–15
totemic sculptures 152–5

V

varnishes 11
veneer, skull sculpted in 128

W

wallhangings 144–5, 157
  brazing 44–45
Watson, Elizabeth, *Figures at a Table* 135
welding:
  materials 10

protective clothing for 14, 119
safety precautions 119
technique 119–23
Wesner, Joseph:
Huanghe 171
Yoken 164
Westerman, Julie:
Bird/Snake 155
Bringing Home the Bacon 133
Whatmuff, Dean:
30 Years in the Bathroom 145
untitled object sculpture 172
White, Laura:
Meditation 152
untitled organic sculpture 160
Williamson, Shaun, *Medieval Knight* 139
wire:
armatures of 23
maquettes of 23
sculpture made of 148
wood 12–13
carving 53–5
combined with stone 152
constructions 164, 167, 168, 169, 171
relief carvings 142–3
staining 11, 68
totemic sculptures 152, 154, 155
wood filler 10

Y
Yale, Brian:
head assemblage 130
The Mrs T 162
Yeoman, Martin, *Sir Brinsley Ford* 127

Note: *Ciment fondu* can be ordered direct from Lefarge, phone: 804-543-8832

CREDITS

The author would like to thank the following individuals whose sculpture has been shown in some of the step-by-step techniques:

Katherine Fanthorpe 44–5 (brazing), 86–89 (stylized torso); Cornelius Guiste de' Jersey 110–1 (stone carving); Derek Howarth 122–3 (electric arc-welding); Nick Kubicki 92–3 (life figure); Alice Ramm 104–6 (hot pour rubber); Liz Watson 90–1 (portrait head)

Greg Harrington for modeling

and Nicola Streeten for her help and encouragement during the preparation of this book.

Quarto Publishing would like to thank all the sculptors who kindly submitted work for inclusion in this book.

We are also indebted to the following agents and galleries: Clive Adams, Ashwell, Herts; Differentiate Ltd, London; Bridget Fraser, Henley-on-Thames, Oxon; Sala d'Art Artur Ramon, Barcelona, Spain; Andrew Usiskin Contemporary Art, London; Rainyday Gallery, Penzance, Cornwall and Wolf at the Door, Penzance, Cornwall.

The following photographers have work reproduced in the book: Warwick Baggaley *135* above; Stefano Baroni *153* left; Bob Berry *168* above; Jerry Hardman-Jones (shot at Wenlock Priory) *163* below; Jerry Hardman-Jones (shot at Yorkshire Sculpture Park) *163* above and Lu Jeffrey *146*.

Quarto would also like to thank Morley College, London for allowing us to use their facilities during photography shoots; The Royal Society of British Sculptors, 108 Brompton Road, London SW7 3RA for their invaluable assistance; Professor Glynn Williams, Royal College of Art, London; and Dorothy Frame for the index.

Finally Quarto would like to thank the following suppliers who kindly provided materials and equipment for photography:

Alec Tiranti Ltd, 27 Warren St, London W1P 5DG
BOC Gases, Hackney Cylinder Centre, Eastway, Hackney, London E9 5NS
Carlos, 131 Cloudesley Rd, London N1 0EN
The Colour Centre, Church Works, Offord Rd, London N1 1EA
Eltham Welding Supplies Ltd, 2–12 Parry Place, London SE18 6AN
Franchi Locks & Tools, 278 Holloway Rd, London N7 6NE
John Bell & Croyden, Dispensing Chemists, 50 Wigmore St, London W1H 9DG
Southern Site Services Ltd, 87–90 Victoria Dock Rd, Silvertown, London E16 1DA